MASTERWORKS
OF
CHILDREN'S
LITERATURE

MASTERWORKS

OF

CHILDREN'S

LITERATURE

Volume Eight
The
Twentieth
Century

EDITED BY

William T. Moynihan
Mary E. Shaner
GENERAL EDITOR: *Jonathan Cott*

THE STONEHILL PUBLISHING COMPANY
IN ASSOCIATION WITH
CHELSEA HOUSE PUBLISHERS
NEW YORK

Cover illustration by Trina Schart Hyman from *Peter Pan*. Used by permission of the illustrator.

PROJECT EDITOR: Joy Johannessen
EDITORIAL COORDINATOR: Karyn Gullen Browne
PRODUCTION: Susan Lusk, Carol McDougall

Index compiled by Joy Johannessen, Jay Livernois, and Richard Rotert

First Printing
Printed and Bound in the United States of America

Library of Congress Cataloging-in-Publication Data
Masterworks of children's literature.
  Bibliography: v. 8, p.
  Includes index.
  Contents: —v. 8. The twentieth century /
edited by William T. Moynihan, Mary E. Shaner.
  1. Children's literature. [1. Literature—Collec-
tions] I. Cott, Jonathan. II. Moynihan, William T.
III. Shaner, Mary E.
PZ5.M38   1986   820'.8'9282   86-11727
ISBN 0-87754-459-X (v. 8)

Chelsea House Publishers

*Dedicated to the Memory of
Jeffrey Joshua Steinberg
Founder and President of
Stonehill Communications, Inc.*

Contents

Illustrations

Introduction

William T. Moynihan

O this is the creature that does not exist.
They did not know that and in any case
—its motion, and its bearing, and its neck,
even to the light of its still gaze—they loved it.
"The Unicorn," RAINER MARIA RILKE[1]

THE FIRST SEVEN VOLUMES OF MASTERWORKS OF CHILDREN'S LITERA-
TURE present authoritative texts of poems, plays, fiction, picturebooks, and educational works published between 1550 and 1900 and
central to the study of literature for children. Volume 8 has a different format. There is no comparable need for an anthology of such
works in this century; they are already available, often in many editions. This volume, therefore, brings the series to a conclusion by
surveying the major developments in twentieth-century English and
American children's literature. It also provides a comprehensive index to the earlier volumes.

The present essay places modern children's books within a critical
and historical context and surveys the gradual shift from the middle-
class subject matter of nursery and nanny to stories about broken
homes, hostile adults, and a mass-media society in crisis. This intro-
ductory overview is followed by six essays that examine the volume's
six main topics: realistic fiction; new fiction, or, as it is sometimes
called, the "problem novel"; the portrayal of black Americans in
children's books; children's fantasy; science fiction for young readers;
and illustrated children's books.

I

To judge from what we have been able to learn about the earliest
modes of cultural transmission, human beings have always used sto-

1

ries, poems, games, and rituals to pass central elements of a particular culture along to their children. Many of these stories were told by older people, many of these poems were sung, many of these games involved plots and chants, and many of these rituals acted out social, religious, and psychological relationships. Already our subject is becoming complicated, and when we look at written methods of transmitting stories and rituals from generation to generation or culture to culture, their connections with children become more attenuated. As we move from cave paintings and oral narratives to self-conscious literary forms like romance, fantasy, and the novel down to our own multimedia electronic century, complications multiply. What Og could tell or sing only to a small group, Ogsford Press can disseminate effectively throughout the entire world. A story that once lasted no longer than its narration or performance now lasts for centuries.

Thus, in the twentieth century, "children's literature" is a label for more kinds of books than reason, taste, or common sense can explain. Included under that label are thousands of titles marketed each year for children, and an even larger number of books—some written for children, some not—stored in libraries. Very few can claim to be enduring literature. A simple list of the broadest categories into which they fall will tell us a great deal about the present confused and ill-defined state of the field.

    1. Books for preschoolers and toddlers. These include everything from highly regarded masterpieces like Maurice Sendak's *Where the Wild Things Are* to water-resistant vinyl-covered books that a child can safely chew when tired of turning the pages.

    2. Thousands and thousands of books for children from seven to seventeen. Their common characteristic is that they are lively, skillfully turned-out products directed towards specific age groups. This category includes topical books (on race, sex, sports, single-parent homes, etc.), fantasies, novels, historical novels, and science fiction.

    3. Those few books that seem to have been written for both adults and children: nineteenth-century works like *Pinocchio* and *Alice*, more recent works like Tolkien's *Lord of the Rings* and Alan Garner's *The Owl Service*.

    4. Reprints of ancient folk tales, fairy tales, myths of various peoples, and older classics originally composed for adults

but now understood to be in the province of children's literature. These include, for example, Greek and Roman myths, King Arthur stories, *Robinson Crusoe, Around the World in Eighty Days,* and *Huckleberry Finn.*

5. Modern adult books by such writers as Jack London, Ernest Hemingway, J. D. Salinger, and William Golding, not to mention a score of science fiction writers. Although they are not marketed to children by any publisher, there is always a small number of adult books that children adopt as part of their reading.

This is a collection of oranges, apples, landscape paintings, and garbage pails. No one has been able to offer a generally acceptable description of this sprawling mass of texts. There have been three general responses: forget about definitions—leave the problem of what is a children's book up to the publishers; let adults exercise adult taste and books will soon enough be divided into the only division that counts—the good and the bad; or, a refinement of the good-and-bad approach, let scholars and literary historians be the arbiters—they have always been the ones to describe and distinguish works of art, and they are the ones to do it for children's books.

Writer and critic John Townsend takes the first view. He holds that "the only practical definition of a children's book today . . . is 'a book which appears on the children's list of a publisher.' "[2] There is, of course, some sense to what he says. Publishers separate their offerings according to the age of the intended reader. Illustrated books for preschoolers and toddlers are not works of literature and cannot be judged by literary standards. They are a separate art form and have to be considered accordingly, as Ann Devereaux Jordan does in her "Small Wonders: Baby Books and Picturebooks," below. To separate these books from works of literature does not mean that they lack aesthetic merit. Just the opposite: the best ones often exhibit the same qualities of mind and imagination as all enduring art.

Publishers, however, give little indication that they are greatly concerned with literary quality when it comes to children's books. If they were, they would not publish so many. "Modern books for children are rather horrible things when you see them in the mass," said George Orwell while working in a London bookshop in the 1930s.[3] Seen en masse, this century's books for kids would total billions. Individual books by Baum, Potter, Grahame, Gág, Seuss, Sendak, have sold millions of copies. The Golden Book series alone sold thirty-nine million copies in one year, 1947. With minor fluctuations, the number of new titles published each year increased annually until 1979. In 1900 there were about five hundred new books published each year; the number peaked in the late 1970s at about three thousand new titles annually.[4] During the 1980s the figure has fluctuated, ranging from twenty-five hundred to three thousand new books each year.[5] What does this publishers' bonanza have to do with literature? In art, quantity does not automatically produce quality. And if we define literature as a verbal art that reveals concretely and movingly what it means to be a human being, the answer is even clearer: almost nothing.

Of the three hundred thousand or so titles that have been published in England and the United States during this century, probably a fraction of one percent have sufficient literary merit to outlast the century—to pass Dr. Johnson's absolute test of worth (as set forth in his *Preface to Shakespeare*): "length of duration and continuance of esteem." There are a few other books in this mass that will survive because of historical importance, and a few more that will very likely earn a kind of immortality because of their illustrations. These few will constitute the children's literature of this century; these are the books with which this final volume of MASTERWORKS is primarily concerned. We cannot learn from publishers which of their books are likely to survive any more than we can trust a hen to grade her own eggs. A fraction of one percent is not an encouraging survival rate.

C. S. Lewis, appealing for adult standards, pronounced "almost as a canon" that "a children's story which is enjoyed only by children is a bad children's story."[6] This would seem a perfectly sensible approach—if we had the right standards to apply. The greatest works of literature, such as the *Odyssey*, the *Bhagavad-Gita*, and Dante's *Divine Comedy*, have always been the subject of moral, historical, and aesthetic criticism. Moral criticism alone, however, has been largely reserved for any work of art that might affect a wider and less cultured audience. Naturally, then, criticism of lesser works has been primarily moral, praising them for their influence in making good citizens or condemning them when they seem to undermine the civil order. Since children are considered especially vulnerable, moral critics usually take them into account. The questions first asked by Plato in *The Republic* have been repeated every generation ever since.

> And shall we just carelessly allow children to listen to any pointless tales which may be devised by any casual persons, and to receive in their minds ideas for the most part just the opposite of those we would wish them to have when they are grown up?[7]

As the introductions and headnotes to the earlier volumes of this series suggest, most of the criticism of individual texts for children in earlier centuries consisted of the warnings of this or that religious or ethical sect against the subversive effects of this or that text. Renaissance educators and preachers fulminated against *Robin Hood* as a tale of "bold bawdry and open manslaughter,"[8] full of filth that would corrupt the young. In the eighteenth century, journals like the prestigious *Critical Review* rejected children's books as "scarcely objects of criticism."[9] A typical nineteenth-century reaction to the quality of children's books was that of one of the most renowned clergymen of his time, Henry Ward Beecher: they could be "compared to little else than the locusts, the lice, and the frogs, often, of Egypt." Children, he felt, were in danger of being carried away by "wishy-washy" stuff that he could describe only as "the swill of the house of God."[10] Such moral criticism is an inevitable part of society, though today it is more often directed against pornography and television than children's books.

At the beginning of this century, an enlightened social critic and feminist, Ellen Key, had seen enough of the locusts, the lice, and the frogs to move her to an eloquent complaint.

> There is no greater fault in modern education than the care spent in selecting books for different ages. . . . A general crusade against all children's books, and freedom for the young to read great literature, is essential to the sound development of the modern child. What is too old for him may be set aside according to the taste of the child himself. Suppose at the age of ten years, the child is absorbed in *Faust* (I know such cases); the child then gets at this age an impression for life that does not prevent him receiving from the same poem another impression at twenty years, or again another at thirty or forty years.[11]

The intensity of Ellen Key's complaint is that of a moral critic, but the complaint has an aesthetic end in mind; it calls for raising, or at least not lowering, standards of taste. But the standards of education have sunk lower since she urged the claims of *Faust* for children, moving for decades in the opposite direction from the one she recommended. We would do well to consider her position for a moment.

Key was not contrasting "children's books" to a dull, stodgy, establishment-approved bit of tedium; her example was more provocative. She was opposing dull, stodgy, establishment-approved "children's books" in favor of a morally, religiously, and psychologically complex story about the devil, temptation, sin, adultery, death, out-of-body experiences, and nightmarish plunges into the depths of the psyche, a story that ends in the exaltation of the chief sinner by the forgiving principle of the Eternal Feminine. It took nearly sixty years for other twentieth-century critics to be as bold as Ellen Key. In terms of subject matter, she took a position voiced by few even today, and she stated that position with more concern for aesthetic values than almost anyone now writing.

But because she wrote for an intellectual audience and was concerned to make a startling proposition, Key ignored the heavily populated middle ground so familiar to us. Robert Louis Stevenson, Louisa May Alcott, Mark Twain, H. Rider Haggard, Rudyard Kipling, and L. M. Montgomery come easily to mind, as well as genres such as fairy tales, fantasy, and science fiction. (Actually *Faust* has plenty of all three.) There is no reason, however, to believe that she would have rejected these works—she could not have if she followed her own implied aesthetic values.

It was Clifton Fadiman who emphasized the role of scholars and historians in helping to distinguish between children's books and children's literature. Writing in 1976, Fadiman said, "We are trying at the moment to establish [the] topography and boundaries for a children's literature. Now the specific identity of any art becomes more firmly established as it develops self-consciousness. Of that self-consciousness, scholars and historians are the expression."[12] Fadiman's sense of the field's lack of identity was well founded. He had searched through literary histories and handbooks—English, American, Russian, German, French—and found no mention of the subject.

If Fadiman is right about critics, historians, and scholars, then the last half of the twentieth century should see children's literature attain a new sense of itself. More so than at any other time in history, children and their literature have become the focus of serious study. Children's literature is now recognized as a field worthy of scholarly attention. Its legitimacy and breadth have been established by such compendious tomes as *The Oxford Companion to Children's Literature* (1984); scores of books and hundreds of essays have explored its origins, development, and quality; learned journals have treated problems of influence, definition, and interpretation.

This critical effort has been generally of two kinds: it has ordered and reconstructed the history of children's literature since the seventeenth century; and it has delved into the dim past to piece together the pre-Gutenberg literature available to children. Let us quickly work our way backwards in time, looking first at "modern" children's books—those published from the seventeenth through the nineteenth centuries—then turning to some recent examples of research on children's stories from the Middle Ages and earlier. We will conclude by considering what new identity these and other findings of contemporary criticism may possibly provide to children's literature.

The seven previous volumes in this MASTERWORKS series are part of the post-Gutenberg reconstruction. Thanks to MASTERWORKS we have representative English texts from the period of John Amos Comenius's 1658 illustrated geography book for children, *Orbis Sensualium Pictus,* to the end of the nineteenth century. We have forgotten texts, rare texts, and creative imitations and adaptations of adult books. They indicate a development that is easily summarized. First are the chapbooks of the seventeenth and eighteenth centuries, then entertaining and edifying books like the Newbery firm's four hundred-odd titles for tots that appeared from 1744 to 1815. The nineteenth century saw a continuation of such stories—what in America might be called the McGuffey Reader syndrome—texts filled with earnestness, high ideals, clear moral teachings, and a basic vocabulary.[13] The nineteenth century also saw accomplished writers like Charles and Mary Lamb, Hawthorne, Thackeray, and Ruskin adapt the classics or compose original works for children as alternatives to the age's heavy-handed moralizing. By the last decades of the century, a number of distinguished children's books had appeared on the literary landscape.

Among the first of these works was Lewis Carroll's *Alice's Adventures in Wonderland* (1865), which created a new kind of fairy tale for English and American readers. There followed Louisa May Alcott's *Little Women* (1868), Mark Twain's *Adventures of Tom Sawyer* (1876) and *Adventures of Huckleberry Finn* (1884), and, between Twain's volumes, Robert Louis Stevenson's *Treasure Island* (1881). Children's books were asserting their claim to a place in literature, and they were doing so by making it increasingly difficult to distinguish between children's and adults' books, children's and adults' authors. Some authors, like Mark Twain, wrote for an audience that might just as easily include adults as children. Some, like Kipling, wrote for a mixed audience *(Kim)* but also for each half separately.

Apart from retrieving the printed legacy of children's books, the other thrust of contemporary scholarship, to return to Fadiman's geographic metaphor, has been to explore the topography of children's literature in earlier times. Scholars have provided much specific evidence to confirm what was long assumed; namely, that adults and children shared the same literature in ancient cultures, and that tales we now consider "children's stories" were in the common possession of all long before anyone thought of the printing press and long before anyone began to publish books especially for children.

Even nursery rhymes appear to have been the property of adults before they were inherited by children.[14] And Robert Darnton's *The Great Cat Massacre*[15] is among the latest of many books to demonstrate the persistence of fairy tales among adults. There is, however, early evidence of a few works written explicitly for children. We have Chaucer's *Astrolabe* for his son, and St. Augustine's *Adeodatus* for his, and we have learned that advice to children was artfully developed into a common literary trope among the Egyptians.[16] But the important thing to keep in mind is that most ancient works of literature were shared by both adults and children. Precisely how they were presented to the young is lost in the obscurities of history, but the stories available to children in earlier centuries were the same *kinds* available in print or on television today.

This is no place better exemplified than in the literary remains from Sumer—some five thousand clay tablets dug out of the ruins of a school for young scribes.[17] From these we learn that Sumerian boys, probably between the ages of seven and seventeen, were introduced to their profession and to the values of their culture through proverbs, animal fables, topical moralistic tales, and myths. The proverbs were brief precepts, maxims, and adages. They told the young how to behave and how to cope with their teenage responsibilities. The fables were proverbs made more vivid; like those of Aesop, La Fontaine, and Joel Chandler Harris, they depicted animals as humans. Even in Sumer there was a fox-and-crow fable to teach the young not to believe every piece of flattery. And there was a lion-and-wren fable to remind the forgetful that prudence and intelligence were worth cultivating—as Grahame's Mr. Toad was to demonstrate anew several millennia later.

Scholarly investigations of the literary experiences of children in the Middle Ages further indicate how and what young and old shared. In brief, they apparently shared just about everything from fairy tales and popular romances to holy writ.[18] The crisscrossing lines of descent from myth and fairy tale down to *Robin Hood* and then to adventure stories, or from myth and epic through medieval romance to modern fantasies, are tangled but everywhere to be seen.

The close association between adult literature and children's literature perhaps appears most clearly in the romance genre, or what Northrop Frye calls "the myth of romance." Frye's discussion not only suggests the near-identity of much of children's literature with such romance but also underlines the point that Key and Lewis and other modern critics have repeatedly made: children's books have to be judged in the same aesthetic terms as adult books. Frye's description of romance (much abbreviated) is this:

> The romance is nearest of all literary forms to the wish-fulfilment dream. . . . In every age the ruling social or intellectual class tends to project its ideals in some form of romance, where the virtuous heroes and beautiful heroines represent the ideals and the villains the threats to their ascendance. . . . The perennially child-like quality of romance is marked by its extraordinarily persistent nostalgia, its search for some kind of imaginative golden age in time or space. . . . The essential element of plot in romance is adventure, which means that romance is naturally a sequential and processional form, hence we know it better from fiction than drama. . . . The complete form of the romance is clearly the successful quest, and such a complete form has three main stages: the stage of the perilous journey and the preliminary minor adventures; the crucial struggle; . . . and the exaltation of the hero.[19]

Children and adults alike seem to agree that among the finest works of romance literature written in this century are those by J. R. R.

Tolkien and Ursula Le Guin. Theirs are books for all ages. Obviously modern animal fables are also in the line of direct descent from the remote past. They had a shared audience then; they have a shared audience now. They are stories that adults have found appropriate for children and that children have found accessible. Mary Shaner's "Twentieth-Century Children's Fantasy," below, provides this volume's analysis of the genres of romance and fable in modern children's books. In "Children's Science Fiction," Thomas J. Weber demonstrates the large area of overlap between adults' and children's books in this century's most recent literary genre.

The didactic novel has supposedly fallen out of favor these days, but the ancients assumed that all literature has as its purpose to teach and to delight. Didactic fiction is an essential part of literary history, and most fiction written for the young draws upon that tradition. A good many novels discussed in Rosanne Donahue's "New Realism in Children's Fiction" and Mary Shaner's "Realism in Twentieth-Century Children's Literature," below, are clearly didactic works and are treated as such. Although recent children's novelists have yet to produce works comparable to those of Bunyan, Swift, D. H. Lawrence, Huxley, or Orwell, they have written novels that can be judged by the same standards.

If we are to make distinctions and judgments among the thousands of books represented in our original five categories, we must begin by seeing them as generically connected with adult books. Children do not start reading adult books simply because they have larger vocabularies. Seventeenth-century children adopted a book like *Pilgrim's Progress* because its didacticism was aesthetically more appealing than that of the tract texts written expressly for them. Conversely, twentieth-century adults read Tolkien because he wrote great fantasy.

Perhaps the litmus test of the field's sense of its own identity lies in the fact that many critics today are looking at children's literature in the way Ellen Key suggested but from new critical perspectives. These perspectives call for reexamining the adult role in the creation of children's books. Jacqueline Rose, for example, says of Barrie's *Peter Pan,* one of the most noted stories of the century,

> *Peter Pan* stands in our culture as a monument to the impossibility of its own claims—that it represents the child, speaks to and for children, addresses them as a group which is knowable and exists for the book, much as the book (so the

Peter Pan, J. M. Barrie, illustrated by Trina Schart Hyman

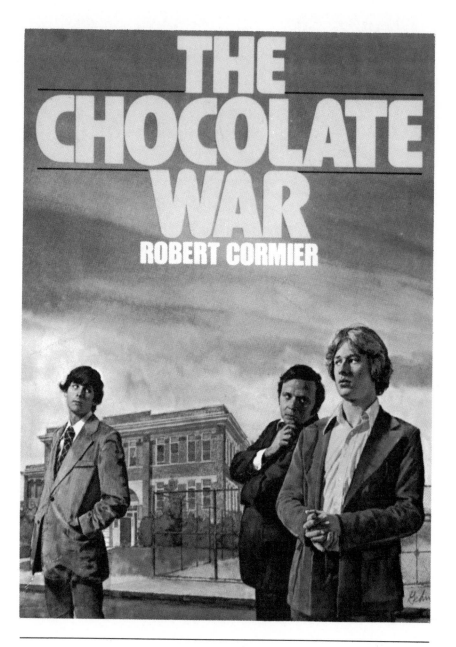

The Chocolate War, Robert Cormier

claim runs) exists for them. . . . *Peter Pan* is the text for children which has made that claim most boldly, and which most clearly reveals it as a fraud. *Peter Pan* has never, in any easy way, been a book for children at all, but the question this throws back to us is whether there can be any such thing.[20]

It is, of course, too simple to say that the publication of Newbery's *Little Pretty Pocket-Book* in 1744 was what turned a cottage industry into a factory whose production grotesquely expanded over the next two centuries. But something like that did happen. A product that in ancient societies had been handmade from the finest stories by bards, parents, pedagogues, and priests suddenly started being mass-produced—a good deal of it by hack writers and hungry publishers. It has taken time for the work of genuine craftsmanship to emerge above the flood of tracts, "wishy-washy swill," and pulp thrillers for the young. The legitimacy of the field of children's literature is still often obscured by the mass of second-rate books.

But literary historians and critics are now offering new ways of sorting this mass of mediocrity—the historian by allowing us to see the present in terms of the past, the critic by paying attention to art rather than the marketplace. Critics and historians, not publishers, are invoking the standards called for by both Lewis and Key, and are beginning to create the literary identity that Fadiman found wanting in children's books. The publisher asks, "Will it sell? Will parents buy it?" The critic asks, "Is it literature? Is it as good a fable as Aesop's, as good a fairy tale as the Grimms', as good a romance as Malory's, as good an adventure story as *Robin Hood?*" There is no way of avoiding the self-evident: the only permanent works of children's literature are those that appeal to adults as well as to children. Where children's books are concerned, the adult is so present at every level of judgment that we would do well, as Rose suggests, to rethink the whole question of what the phrase "children's literature" really means.

II

As one looks back on this century in terms of attitudes towards children and childhood, a single irony stands out: the difference between the way the century began and the way it is ending. It opened on a note of high optimism. Reformers were campaigning for child labor laws to improve the lot of children. Children, they said, should be valued not for their economic role in the kitchen, in the mines, in the mills, or on the farm but simply because they were, in Viviana Zeliger's term, "priceless."[21] The child was innocent, untainted by adults, semidivine. To cite Ellen Key once again, it was to be "the century of the child." She felt that in 1901 the Western world had reached a point where new mothers could bring forth new children to create a new world. The new child would be a "superman who will be bathed in that sunshine whose distant rays but colour the horizon of today."[22]

By the 1980s, an increasing number of social commentators had reached the conclusion that both children and the concept of childhood itself were endangered. The child's life, his mind, his psyche, were all "at risk," according to Vance Packard, because of an "anti-child culture."[23] The twentieth century had slowly and shortsightedly created, as Yale child psychiatrist William Kessen put it, "modern forms of damnation that confront our children."[24] These new forms of damnation would not be treated extensively in children's books until the 1960s, but when they did appear, they underlined the view that the world had indeed become a hazardous place for the young.

Children's stories in the early decades of the century were filled with danger but no damnation. The afterglow of Victorian genius was still very strongly felt, and the dangers were of the "Perils of Pauline" variety. The young and innocent, bungling and naive, somehow always managed to escape because they were well intentioned, not wicked, and they also had parents or surrogate parents who warned them or helped them. This sense of childhood as a time guarded by adults, a period in which the child learns through experience to become as wise as, or more often even wiser than, the adults, has never completely disappeared from children's stories.

But such children and such families became fewer and fewer as the century grew older. Different children, different families, and finally very different subjects appeared. It was a gradual process. The well-heeled middle-class youngsters in the earlier children's stories began to be replaced by immigrant children, children of various ethnic and racial backgrounds, children facing poverty in the 1920s and 1930s. In 1945 appeared a pioneering children's book by a black author, Jesse Jackson's *Call Me Charley* (see James Miller's "Black Images in American Children's Literature," below). Then came a whole tide of novels in the sixties and seventies portraying children and childhood in light of the social upheavals of those decades. Story after story described minority and ethnic difficulties and aspirations, the "now" generation and its sexual mores, the culture of rock and drugs, the battle against sexual stereotypes, urban warfare and tensions, the broken family, the threats of pollution and nuclear weapons.

Obviously, the different kinds of children's books—picturebooks, fables, fantasies, fiction—have mirrored these changes differently, and the commendable new diversity in characters, settings, and themes has been handled with varying degrees of skill. Let us examine a few significant examples of each type in terms of their artistry and their reflection of the period in which they were written.

The skills of fabulists have produced fine books throughout the century, but still among the best is the earliest, Beatrix Potter's *The Tale of Peter Rabbit* (1902). An Aesop for her time, Potter taught and delighted young and old alike. She wrote with economical genius, intelligence, and humor. At the opening of *Peter Rabbit* the reader is immediately introduced to one of the harshest facts of life: the hero has already seen death. We are told that Peter's father was, famously, "put in a pie by Mrs. MacGregor." Thus the tone is set for Potter's work. Her bunnies, cats, squirrels, all live in a world where they must be on guard. They are saved by luck and good sense. All the charm of Potter's language and illustrations cannot obscure the fact that hers is a cautionary art—witty, touching, ingeniously understated, and brilliantly worked into a mosaic of lines and colors.

Potter was still producing her little masterpieces when Kenneth Grahame's Messrs. Rat, Mole, Badger, and the Odyssean Mr. Toad paraded onto the stage of literary history and secured for themselves and their author a share of that immortality reserved for the timeless works of literature. Numerous critics have pointed to the rich texture of the story, which conveys a sense of English social history along with a profound sense of humanity. *The Wind in the Willows* (1908) is a gentle and penetrating work of genius. It is animal fable, fairy tale, mock epic, fantasy, comedy, and social comedy. There is danger in Grahame's world, but the nursery is not far away. The real menaces can be held off, the child-animal can "bungle through." It is an innocent and happy world.

A great admirer of Grahame's, A. A. Milne, published his own version of the "other world," the world of nursery rhymes, talking toys, meaningful inflections, upper-middle-class pathos, and animals, in *Winnie-the-Pooh* (1926) and *The House at Pooh Corner* (1928). Milne, like Grahame, created a lost paradise, an innocent world of childhood, a place peaceful and inviting enough for us, the readers, to enter into, there to relive some of our own past. " 'Pooh' is still a big culture hero," said Alison Lurie nearly half a century after *Winnie-the-Pooh*'s publication. "He means as much to the Now Generation as he did to us back when."[25] *Winnie-the-Pooh* is an elegy to childhood as Eden:

> So they went off together. But wherever they go, and whatever happens to them on their way, in that enchanted place on the top of the Forest, a little boy and his Bear will always be playing.[26]

The other notable fable of the century is far different. It is E. B. White's *Charlotte's Web* (1952). This book is very American, having nothing of the nanny or the leisure class about it. Here nature is not a well-kept garden or park, and the animals are not from the nursery; they are barnyard animals. The people are just plain country folk. *Charlotte's Web* does not deal with spirits or protect the child (and adult) from death by placing the action in a world of eternal play or art. But it does render nature's cyclic inevitability so surely that it softens the death of its spider heroine and ends with as fine a sense of closure as art can fashion. Death comes as naturally as a season. The story does not, however, create a world that is entirely a fable; there is a strange mixture of the real farm family and the country fair with the fabulous world of talking barnyard creatures. Common sense mixes unobtrusively with the imagined otherness of spider and pig. It is America's most impressive animal fable of recent decades.

The most fully developed genre in children's literature of this century is fantasy. America's first example, in 1900, was L. Frank Baum's *The Wonderful Wizard of Oz*. There were fourteen Oz books in the next twenty years, and Americans had a story that, in spite of its wooden writing, said something memorable about both America and childhood. *The Wizard of Oz*, thanks especially to the movies and television, has become part of the imagination of almost every American.

Like all lasting literature, *Oz* works on more than one level. As Russell Nye pointed out some years ago, "There is a strain of moralism in Baum's work, a strain of satire—gentle, implicit, but persistently there—a strain of thoughtful humor that lends his narratives of Oz a third dimension unusual in American juvenile literature."[27] Oz not only fulfills Baum's stated intention of refurbishing the fairy tale with a New World "wonder tale"; it likewise manages to convey a sense of childhood in populist America at the turn of the century.

A comparison with *Winnie-the-Pooh* is instructive. The Pooh books describe an English upper-class childhood

> ... where one lone child might live on a huge green estate with a dozen stuffed animals for playmates, in a fantasy world where he himself was in complete control. Baum's book ... reveals a world full of conflict and danger where the heroine lives in a harsh grey world with only a little dog for a playmate (but a live dog, not a stuffed one). ... Dorothy and her friends must deal with events as they occur, while Milne's [characters] ... generally frame or manipulate events according to their own expectations.[28]

It should be added that death is also not unknown to Dorothy. Her mother has died, and another woman dies in the tornado. In a way Dorothy is the epitome of the resilient child—the new woman for the new century. Yet the lesson she learns, over and over, is simple: there is no place like home. Turn-of-the-century America wanted its women and children safe at home, and that's where its favorite fantasy leaves Dorothy.

Dorothy's English counterpart flew across a London stage in 1904, and he has been flying ever since. Peter Pan carries with him on that flight something very much of the time as well as something ageless, something sentimentally cloying and slightly inexplicable. He seems to be part nature deity and part Edwardian child. Speaking of his Edwardian qualities, Martin Green tells us that Peter was

> the child of charm. ... Before then, as far as I know, it was not a quality anyone had attributed to John Bull. But suddenly we had Lewis Carroll and Edward Lear and Puck of Pook's Hill [by Rudyard Kipling], and Christopher Robin was Saying his Prayers. ... Stories of adventure and action were replaced by stories of fairies and flowers. Men were replaced—in children's minds—by women.[29]

Green's concern with Peter's transvestism cannot be passed over without comment, for Peter's asexuality, or bisexuality, or presexuality if you wish, must have something to do with his phenomenal permanence in the popular imagination. He is a divinity of childhood, and his shrines are not only in the West End of London and Disney World. His reappearance every year in dozens of theaters in England and America during the winter solstice (like some infant sun god) is more important than the fact that women play the role of Peter and Wendy cleans his lodgings. Peter Pan may be embarrassing in his charm. Many would prefer that he have hooves and prance on wild Attic mountainsides. But Peter Pan, for all his saccharine stylization, has become one of the most powerful expressions of childhood's mythic sacredness. Simlar portrayals of the child as sacred and a special source of knowledge are to be seen in Antoine de Saint Exupéry's *Le Petit Prince* (1943) and Steven Spielberg's movie *E.T.*

There are differences between fairy tales and fantasy, but these are not as important as the likenesses. Fantasy is best seen as the fairy tale writ large. The fairy tale is to fantasy roughly what the one-act play is to a full-length drama. The metamorphosis of myths or fairy and folk tales into medieval romances and then into nineteenth- and twentieth-century fantasies is, as stated earlier, the main line of development in children's literature. This development (paralleled in a different way in realistic fiction) expresses some of society's changing attitudes toward childhood.

Most of the children in this century's fantasies are more like Dorothy than like Peter Pan. They are not beings caught in an eternal stage of boyhood or girlhood. They are normal children who have much to learn in a world where the natural and supernatural merge as they never do in ordinary experience. This does not mean the fantasies are protective; almost the opposite is true. Dorothy's homeward journey through Oz, like the journeys of many children in fairy tales, is in one sense a struggle for survival in the face of incredible dangers.

There is, however, a difference between children in fantasy and children in realistic fiction; the fantasy child is more often fortune's child. Although the child of fantasy may be a type of favored innocent, the world through which that child passes is threatening, and the things to be learned are hard truths. As the twentieth century grew older, fantasies dealt with harder and more complex truths, and the children in them came closer to resembling their brothers and sisters in realistic fiction.

The Tale of Peter Rabbit, written and illustrated by Beatrix Potter
Winnie-the-Pooh, A. A. Milne, illustrated by Ernest H. Shepard

Five Children and It, E. Nesbit, illustrated by J. S. Goodall

The fantasy writings of E. Nesbit, who was almost an entire children's book industry in herself, are among the best from the early decades of the century. *Five Children and It* (1902) is typical. The children are normal, healthy, active, curious, and usually well mannered. They discover the Psammead, who, genielike, has the power to make wishes come true. What the children in Nesbit's story must learn is what centuries of children—and adults—learned from fairy tales like "The Fisherman's Wife" and "Three Wishes": sometimes the worst thing for human beings is to get what they wish for.

In 1917 J. R. R. Tolkien began writing a tale that would initiate a minor renaissance of fantasy in later decades of the century. He did not publish *The Hobbit* until 1937. But that book, together with its sequel, *The Lord of the Rings* (1955), signaled a new kind of romance fiction that would create a new audience.

The Hobbit might well be subtitled "The Small Dwarf as Child." For how can the young reader help but identify with the hobbits, who are smaller than the dwarfs of Middle Earth? If the hobbits embody Tolkien's idea of children, then his notion of childhood is clearly medieval, perhaps even Augustinian. The child is neither good nor evil but capable of being either—or both. This child exists in a world of danger, hardship, and temptation, of myth and symbol and magic, but is not vested by nature with any sacred or magic power simply because he is small or naive. Tolkien's hobbit-child dwells in a post-1917 world, and its learning must be total. Hobbits must become aware of myth, geography, language, codes, customs, spells, traditions, character types, classes, and hidden mysteries. Above all, they must know courage and cowardice, loyalty and betrayal, sincerity and pretence, hope and despair. Theirs is a world where moral responsibility is never easy, defeat is always possible, and victories come at a great price.

This is not a new subject matter for literature, of course. Its sources are in religion, folk tales and fairy tales, and myths—especially in that quintessential English myth, the story of King Arthur. Ever since Mary MacLeod's *The Book of King Arthur and His Noble Knights* in 1900, numerous twentieth-century authors have mined this and other legends to produce fantasies and historical novels. There seems to have been no generation that has not produced a retelling of the Arthurian legends. The most masterful recent examples are T. H. White's *The Sword in the Stone* (1938) and subsequent tetralogy, *The Once and Future King* (1958). Superbly written, these novels are humorous, allusive, moving, and powerfully imaginative. White's books themselves inspired retelling in a different art form—the musical *Camelot*. Other notable re-creations stemming from Arthurian myths, or at least echoing their tone, are Susan Cooper's *The Grey King* (1975) and *Silver on the Tree* (1977).

The steady stream of fantasy writing in England and America since the 1950s includes several other important sequences. C. S. Lewis's remarkable seven-volume Narnia series appeared between 1950 and 1956. It presents the chief events of Christianity as happenings in the mythical world of Narnia, a world of strange animals, witches, and magic. Between 1952 and 1982 Mary Norton wrote five stories about tiny beings who live in ordinary houses and exist by borrowing all their necessities. The Borrowers series is a meticulous and eerie exploration of smallness, helplessness, dependency, and coming to grips with the harshness of life.

In America there were three outstanding writers of fantasy in the 1960s and 1970s. Madeleine L'Engle's work combines the preternatural and the futuristic, religion and science. In *A Wrinkle in Time* (1962), for example, the child Charles Wallace possesses extrasensory perception, and this he must use to resist evil in a science fiction world not governed by the laws of Newtonian physics, a realm where only love can triumph over evil. Ursula Le Guin's children must learn their own strength, their own limits, and the strength of the limitless world about them. Her Earthsea trilogy, which appeared between 1967 and 1972, presented children as apprentice Magi mastering the total wisdom of an ancient society. In her books, as David Rees says, "there is a wealth of minute detail about birds and plants and fish; of concern with simple craftsmanship like boat-building. . . . Man in harmony with nature; man destroying it: Ursula Le Guin's philosophy is not only conservative but deeply conservationist."[30] The reader of Le Guin must be an intelligent learner, for she has much to teach. Lastly, for sheer moral imagination, there's Natalie Babbitt's fantasy *Tuck Everlasting* (1975), which has at its center a young girl's choice between stagnant immortality and a normal lifespan of the allotted three score and ten.

Alan Garner's novels have elements of fantasy and elements of realistic fiction. Typically, he presents average, hard-pressed young people whose lives are caught up in mythic events. *The Owl Service* (1967), perhaps his most acclaimed work, shows youngsters unwittingly and helplessly reliving the events of an ancient Welsh myth.

Garner's conception of childhood is dominated by two concerns: the presentness of the past and the alienating effect of modern schooling. He says he discovered while a student that being familiar with a Greek myth helped him "to come to terms with the way my girl-friend's mother was behaving." And he feels that working-class children are separated from their origins and families by education. Communication between the past and the present, the broken connections between parents and children—these themes preoccupy many of the characters in his fiction. His writing, he hopes, will help the young understand their problems and lead to a healing of the many breaches.[31]

The route from Victorian to modern that we have traced in twentieth-century fantasy is even better marked in realistic fiction for children. The beginning and ending points, at least, are as distinct as the Victorian gingerbread cottage and the Philip Johnson house of glass. Robert Lee Wolff defines "the real core of Victorian children's fiction" as follows:

> . . . the life of the nursery, the lessons in the schoolroom, the domestic fireside, religious observance, the holiday by the seaside, the picnic on a grand excursion to see a ruined abbey, the changing of the seasons, the delights of Christmas, the contact with the poor in the rural cottage or the city slum, . . . the dramatic changes of fortune, . . . the terrors and tragedy of a death in the family—and, above all, the *meaning* of all these experiences for growing up, for acceptance of what seemed like cruel blows, for due recognition of a child's relationship to God and God's universe.[32]

What is one likely to find in juvenile fiction since the 1960s? Painful experiences of being a child, harassment and brutality in school, the flight from home into an even more grim world, single parents, abusive elders, early and often harmful sexual experiences, the almost total absence of significant religious experience in a family context, the mistreatment of the poor, aged, and weak, the drug culture, and, above all, the inexplicable character of life's cruelties and the necessity for a stoical stance in the face of what seems to be an incomprehensible universe.

The characters of the earlier children's fiction—E. Nesbit's boys and girls, Anne of Green Gables, Arthur Ransome's vacationing children, even Rudyard Kipling's Kim—all shared common values about their respective countries and human nature. They all looked back to *Robinson Crusoe, Treasure Island,* and *Little Women* as fictional precursors. But in the last half of the century writers of fiction for children seem to share fewer values. Their characters exist in a world where parents are wrong, schools are wrong, the government is wrong. The precursors of many of the later works are J. D. Salinger's *Catcher in the Rye* (1951), with its detached, cool, pretense-proof critic of adult phoniness, Holden Caulfield, and William Golding's *Lord of the Flies* (1954), in which the young have to build their own society or survive as animals.

Children's fiction in this century has unfolded between these two polar attitudes, the Victorian and the modern. The best of the early novels are by Frances Hodgson Burnett, Kate Douglas Wiggins, and L. M. Montgomery, while the most notable later fiction—important mainly because of the new range of subject matter—appeared after 1960. In between some fine ethnic fiction and some even better historical fiction saw print.

Burnett's minor classic, *The Secret Garden* (1910), exemplifies the best features of fiction for the young in all eras: a combination of adventure, rites of passage, and a *Bildungsroman* quality—the growth of a young mind or the attainment of a wiser and more mature perception of life. It begins with young Mary Lennox being "the most disagreeable child ever seen" and ends with her as one of the wisest children ever seen. Sickly, orphaned, humanly selfish Mary is reshaped into a kind, considerate child by the healing powers of nature. And she, in turn, passes on this miracle of healing by helping an even more disturbed younger child.

In Kate Douglas Wiggins's idealistic *Rebecca of Sunnybrook Farm* (1903) bright, pleasant, fatherless Rebecca comes to live with her maiden aunts and gradually softens and changes them. L. M. Montgomery's *Anne of Green Gables* (1908) also concerns an orphan. Anne is bookishly and comically precocious, spirited, friendly, plagued by minor troubles, but, finally, kind and self-sacrificing. She gives up a scholarship to help her elderly benefactor and save the farm. It is a story now felt by some to be too sentimental. (The same charge might also be made against some of Dickens's work.) But Montgomery's novel was a triumph in its time and still has the power to move its readers. Dated or not, it is a piece of fiction that has lasted. It has now been made into an excellent TV production that will very likely further prolong its life and reputation.

In 1924 new immigration laws virtually excluded certain ethnic and racial groups from the United States by setting extremely low quotas. These laws sprang from prejudices that were soon challenged in children's books about various ethnic groups, their countries, and their histories. From this time on, social concerns appeared in children's fiction more and more frequently until they became familiar themes. Among the best ethnic books, all Newbery Medal winners, are Elizabeth Foreman Lewis's *Young Fu of the Upper Yangtze* (1933); Monica Shannon's *Dobry* (1934), which deals with boyhood in Bulgaria; and Kate Seredy's *The Good Master* (1935) and *The White Stag* (1937), about life in Hungary.

The problems of minority groups were a frequent subject for Florence Crannell Means. During the forties she wrote *Whispering Girl* (1941) about the Hopi, *Great Day in the Morning* (1946) about a talented black girl, and *The Moved-Outers* (1945) about displaced Japanese-Americans during World War II. While recognizing prejudice and inequity, Means sometimes appeared to encourage unquestioning conformity to the dominant white culture, but she was nevertheless a strong and convincing voice on a long-neglected subject.

Perhaps the best American fiction for children between the wars was historical. Surely the most memorable publication of the thirties was Laura Ingalls Wilder's Little House series. The seven novels in this series, which appeared between 1932 and 1943, drew heavily on Wilder's own childhood experiences. Clifton Fadiman saw them as a single work and commented,

> While no absolutely first-rate history or biography has been written for children, I would claim that the field has produced at least one masterly autobiography, on its own level as worthy of study as the *Confessions* of Rousseau or St. Augustine: Laura Ingalls Wilder's *Little House* series.[33]

A more conventional historical novel, Esther Forbes's *Johnny Tremain* (1943), is an energetic and powerful treatment of the beginning of the American Revolution.

In the fifties in England appeared Rosemary Sutcliff's historical novels *The Eagle of the Ninth* (1954), *The Silver Branch* (1957), and *The Lantern Bearers* (1959). Also noteworthy are Cynthia Harnett's *The Wool-Pack* (1951) and *The Load of Unicorn* (1959) and Henry Treece's *Viking's Dawn* (1955), but Sutcliff is the premiere English historical novelist for children.

Louise Fitzhugh's *Harriet the Spy* (1964) typifies the innovative sixties novel. Harriet is precocious, brash, curious, and painfully honest. In an earlier era she would have been a prime candidate for reform or a change of heart. But Harriet in this book does not change. As a fictional type, she is the forerunner of Judy Blume's and numerous other new-style heroines. Blume's characters have Harriet's toughness and precocity without her intelligence. Blume's main claim to literary fame is that she introduced taboo subjects into books for children; menstruation is a topic in *Are You There God? It's Me, Margaret* (1970), and sexual intercourse takes place in her novel *Forever* (1977).

Many of the new realists are traditional in style and theme while dealing with subjects and attitudes that were previously considered unsuitable for children. Betsy Byars, Katherine Paterson, Lois Lowry, Sue Ellen Bridgers, and Cynthia Voigt deal with death, alienation, suicide, emotional illness, and poor home relationships but generally do not use obscene language and are not explicit about sexual acts.

In England, Josephine Kamm's *Young Mother* (1965) caused a stir with its depiction of a pregnant unwed teenager. K. M. Peyton's Pennington in *Pennington's Seventeenth Summer* (1970) and *The Beethoven Medal* (1971) is sexually active and finally marries Ruth when she gets pregnant. Aidan Chambers deals with homosexual love in *Dance on My Grave,* Jill Paton Walsh presents the moral complexities of mercy killing, and John Rowe Townsend treats child neglect, anti-Semitism, and street life.

It is American innovators who have been more controversial because of their protagonists, subject matter, and style. In Paul Zindel's *The Pigman* (1968), the teenage narrators are totally alienated from their parents. They become as irresponsible as their parents by betraying elderly Mr. Pignati, "the Pigman," who has kindly given them the freedom of his home. In Ouida Sebestyen's *On Fire* (1985) there is a sexual act between two brothers. S. E. Hinton's novels depict a world of violence and pessimism. But it is Robert Cormier's often praised *The Chocolate War* (1974) that has become the focus of objections to the New Realism. The novel has been criticized because of its frank language and because its pessimism is too insistent, too undiluted. Still, Cormier is a powerful writer, and *The Chocolate War* is a distinguished "school novel" in the tradition of such books as *Tom Brown.*

But it is not so much a case of a particular novel as it is of the

A portrait gallery from *Harriet the Spy,* by Louise Fitzhugh

On Fire, Ouida Sebestyen, cover art by Richard Williams

whole new direction in juvenile fiction. Parents in these novels are overwhelmed, indifferent, cruel, crippled, neurotic, or stupidly self-ish. Almost always the young must fend for themselves; they are in the hands of the Lord of the Flies. They must cope with brutality, disease, drugs, their own weaknesses and inexperience, rape, viola-tion, and death. This is a wisdom literature of a new kind. These are the cautionary tales for the "century of the child."

We have argued for the literary-ness of children's books on the grounds of their generic similarity to works of acknowledged literary value. We have emphasized the general correspondence between romance literature and children's literature, and claimed that the best romance literature written in this century can be found in books that appeal to children. Theoretically we might be able to make the same case for the new fiction. It is certainly adult in subject matter and style—but not in excellence. It may be that irony and tragedy are inherently unworkable as modes for children's books, and these are the modes of the new fiction. Only a writer of genius can resolve this question.

What does not have to await the appearance of genius is evidence that the new fiction is another expression of the disappearance of childhood. Everywhere, as noted earlier, the analysts of society have seen signs of the destruction of childhood. "Since the 1960's children have come to resemble adults more closely than they have done for centuries. In the clothes they wear, the language they use, and the things they know, in all aspects of their daily behavior, children seem less childlike."[34] To that we might add: the books they read are less childlike too.

Television has played a major role in making children more adult, and adults more childish. Thus we have come full circle, from chil-dren sitting with adults before priest and poet to children sitting with adults before the television screen. Not since the pre-Gutenberg cen-turies have children and adults been so dependent on the same art forms. Books, music, films, television—they are all shared. The 1980 Nielsen Report on television affirms what we all can provide examples of: children and adults watch the same TV shows. The Nielson Report listed the top fifteen shows for adults (those over eighteen) and for children (ages twelve to seventeen). Eight of the shows appeared on both lists. These same eight "also made the favored list of those between the age of two and eleven."[35] One cannot escape the feeling that the new fiction is following television rather than extending the possibilities for a new kind of significant children's literature.

Two stories will serve as exemplars of twentieth-century changes in childhood and children's books. Montgomery's *Anne of Green Gables,* published in 1908, ends with Anne quoting Browning: "God's in His heaven, all's right with the world." Robert C. O'Brien's *Z for Zachariah* (1974) is the story of another orphan named Ann, a survivor of an atomic war that has wiped out her family. Ann is alone on the family's sheltered farm when another survivor appears, an adult male. A suspicious, tense collaboration begins. The man's behavior becomes more and more threatening until finally he demands sex. On the novel's last page, Ann flees into the radioactive unknown. All is not right with her world.

Notes

1. *Sonnets to Orpheus,* trans. M. D. Herter Norton (New York: W. W. Norton, 1942), p. 77.

2. John Rowe Townsend, *A Sounding of Storytellers* (New York: J. B. Lippincott, 1971), p. 10.

3. George Orwell, *The Collected Essays, Journalism and Letters,* vol. 1 (London: Secker & Warburg, 1968), p. 244.

4. John Tebbel, *A History of Book Publishing in the United States,* 4 vols. (New York and London: R. R. Bowker, 1975–81), vol. 2, pp. 692–710; vol. 4, pp. 467–88.

5. National Children's Book Council, New York, N.Y.

6. C. S. Lewis, "Three Ways of Writing for Children," in *Only Connect: Readings on Children's Literature,* eds. Sheila Egoff et al. (New York: Oxford University Press, 1980), p. 70.

7. *Republic* 377b–c. See also Nicholas Tucker, *Suitable for Children? Controversies in Children's Literature* (Berkeley and Los Angeles: University of California Press, 1976).

8. Quoted in Bennett A. Brockman, "Children and the Audiences of Robin Hood," *South Atlantic Review* 48 (May 1983): 74.

9. Quoted in Robert Bator, "Eighteenth-Century Prefigurements," *Children's Literature* 11 (1983): 175.

10. Quoted in Tebbel, *A History of Book Publishing,* vol. 2 (1975), p. 596.

11. Ellen Key, *The Century of the Child* (New York: G. P. Putnam's Sons, 1909), pp. 266–67. Cf. Anton Chekhov's similar sentiments, quoted in MASTERWORKS, vol. 1, p. xviii: "I don't like what is known as children's literature; I don't recognize its validity. Children should be given only what is suitable for adults as well. . . . One shouldn't write for children; one should learn to choose works suitable for children from among those already written for adults—in other words, from genuine works of art."

12. Clifton Fadiman, "The Case for Children's Literature," *Children's Literature* 5 (1976): 19.

13. Tebbel, *A History of Book Publishing,* vol. 2, p. 600, comments: "One does not think of 'McGuffey's Readers' as 'children's books' . . . although they were read by generations of children, but as one critic has said, they were 'instinct with drama' and it would be difficult to identify them with their straightfaced rivals in educational publishing."

14. See Iona and Peter Opie, comps., *The Oxford Nursery Rhyme Book* (Oxford: Oxford University Press, 1955), pp. 1–5.

15. Robert Darnton, *The Great Cat Massacre and Other Episodes in French Cultural History* (New York: Random House, Vintage Books, 1984), pp. 9–72.

16. See Martin L. West, *Hesodius: Work and Days* (Oxford: Oxford University Press, 1978); and Thomas and Karen Jambeck, "Chaucer's *Treatise*

on an Astrolabe: A Handbook for the Medieval Child," Children's Literature 3 (1974): 117–23.

17. For a thorough discussion of the Sumerian material, see G. Adams, "The First Children's Literature," forthcoming in Children's Literature. See also Werner Jaeger, Paideia: The Ideals of Greek Culture (Oxford: Oxford University Press, 1939), and Early Christianity and Greek Paideia (Cambridge: Cambridge University Press, 1961); Henri I. Marrou, A History of Education in Antiquity, trans. George Lamp (New York: Sheed & Ward, 1956); Elva S. Smith and Margaret Hodges, The History of Children's Literature (Chicago: ALA, 1980); Bennett A. Brockman, "Robin Hood and the Invention of Children's Literature," Children's Literature 11 (1982): 1–17; and William and Meradith McMunn, "Children's Literature in the Middle Ages," Children's Literature 4 (1975): 21–29. Leonard R. Mendelsohn's "Sophisticated Reading for Children: The Experience of the Classical Jewish Academy," Children's Literature 2 (1973): 35–39, outlines literature available to young Jewish children in their schools "from Babylon to Brooklyn."

18. Brockman, "Children and the Audiences of Robin Hood." See also his "Medieval Sons of Innocence and Experience," Children's Literature 2 (1973): 40–49. Also useful is Children's Literature Association Quarterly 10 (Spring 1985), which has a special section dedicated to Warren W. Wooden, dealing with literature for children from the Middle Ages to the eighteenth century.

19. Northrop Frye, Anatomy of Criticism (Princeton: Princeton University Press, 1957), pp. 186–87.

20. Jacqueline Rose, The Case of Peter Pan; or, The Impossibility of Children's Fiction (London: Macmillan, 1984), p. 1.

21. Viviana Zeliger, Pricing the Priceless Child: The Changing Social Value of Children (New York: Basic Books, 1985). For a more detailed discussion of the "child redeemer" in late nineteenth-century literature, see Bernard Wishy, The Child and the Republic (Philadelphia: University of Pennsylvania Press, 1968), pp. 81–181.

22. Key, The Century of the Child, p. 107.

23. Vance Packard, Our Endangered Children: Growing Up in a Changing World (New York: Little, Brown, 1983). The number of experts warning about the suffering of children and the indifference of adult society is very large, and their essential message is clear: we, especially in the United States, are harming our children. Robert Coles's Children of Crisis: A Study of Courage and Fear (New York: Delta, 1962) was the first of five volumes of interviews with American children. These volumes provide basic evidence concerning the plight of America's young in the 1960s and 1970s. Other recent studies of the demise of childhood are Valerie Pulakow Suransky, The Erosion of Childhood (Chicago: University of Chicago Press, 1982); Marie Winn, Children Without Childhood (New York: Random House, 1981); Letty Cottin Pogrebin,

Family Politics (New York: McGraw-Hill, 1983); and Neil Postman, *The Disappearance of Childhood* (New York: Delacorte, 1982).

24. Quoted in Packard, *Our Endangered Children,* p. xx.

25. Alison Lurie, "Back to Pooh Corner," *Children's Literature* 2 (1973): 11.

26. A. A. Milne, *The House at Pooh Corner* (New York: Dutton, 1961), pp. 179–80.

27. Russell Nye, "The Wizardess of Oz—and Who She Is," *Children's Literature* 2 (1973): 120.

28. Ruth B. Moynihan, "Ideologies in Children's Literature: Some Preliminary Notes," *Children's Literature* 2 (1973): 166–67.

29. Martin Green, "The Charm of Peter Pan," *Children's Literature* 9 (1981): 20–21; see also Rose, *The Case of Peter Pan.*

30. David Rees, *The Marble in the Water* (Boston: Horn Book, 1980), p. 88.

31. Interview with Alan Garner, quoted in Townsend, *A Sounding of Storytellers,* pp. 95–96.

32. *Masterworks of Children's Literature,* vol. 5 (New York: Chelsea House/ Stonehill, 1985), pp. xiii–xiv.

33. Fadiman, "The Case for Children's Literature," p. 18.

34. Winn, *Children Without Childhood,* p. 205.

35. Postman, *The Disappearance of Childhood,* p. 131.

Realism in Twentieth-Century Children's Literature

Mary E. Shaner

In writing of fiction for children, the term "realism" requires some explanation, since there are certain aspects of the real that even today are modified, softened, or altogether eschewed in books written for children. For the purposes of this essay a realistic novel is one that takes place in this world, in the present or in the historical past, and in which events and characters conform to the known laws of physical nature. The category of realism is necessarily broad, and includes the daily-life, "family" story, the story of the solitary child, and the historical/period novel. It is a category in which we can see very clearly many of the changes in children's literature that have transpired from the beginning of the century to the end. Since our knowledge of the psychological effects of and responses to experience has increased in the course of the century, we will sometimes find characters and motivations in the works of earlier decades somewhat unrealistic psychologically. The realistic works of the past twenty-five years for the most part comprise New Realism, whose characteristics are strikingly different from those of the traditional realism for children that precedes it (see Rosanne Donahue's "New Realism in Children's Fiction," below).

The Family Story and the School Story

The family story for children was popular during the nineteenth century, and some of the most memorable books of that era *(Little*

Women, The Daisy Chain) can be grouped in this subgenre. Many such works were, however, characteristically didactic and sentimental. The English writer E. Nesbit was greatly responsible for transforming this type of story into something new. Although she was not the first to use the child as a first-person narrator, she was perhaps the first to do so with a minimum of condescension and to depict with amazing accuracy the workings of the child's mind and imagination. *The Story of the Treasure Seekers* (1899) was initially thought to be for adults; and indeed many of the episodes first appeared in *Windsor* and *Pall Mall,* adult magazines.[1] However, while this picture of children's daily-life adventures narrated by Oswald Bastable was and is enjoyed by many adults, its most consistent audience has been children. The immediate sequel, *The Wouldbegoods* (1901), is probably the best of the three Bastable books, comic, energetic, and true to life, without overt didacticism or sentimentality (except for, as R. L. Green points out, "one monumental lapse over the supposed dead Boer War hero"[2]). *The New Treasure Seekers* (1904) is somehow less convincing, less original. *The Railway Children* (1906), about another family of true-to-life children, employs a third-person narrator who is occasionally obtrusive. This book has many charms typical of Nesbit: a good story line, attractive characters (especially Bobby, the responsible and sensitive oldest girl), and a realistic depiction of children's adventures and interactions with one another. However, Nesbit does lapse into sentimentality, especially in the denouement, and the fact that it is a very seductive sentimentality makes its indulgence, if anything, rather worse.

The American daily-life family story in the early twentieth century had few successors to Alcott. Lucy Fitch Perkins's "twins" stories did treat of ordinary homelife but were set in other lands. *The Dutch Twins* (1911), *The Japanese Twins* (1912), *The Irish Twins* (1913), and so forth have attractive youngsters enjoying the small adventures of everyday life, but the exotic settings are responsible for a good deal of these books' charm. Eliza Orne White's *A Borrowed Sister* (1906) and *The Blue Aunt* (1918) are notable for their realistic domestic settings and believable characterization. *The Blue Aunt* is unusual in having a strong awareness of World War I in the background. The social attitudes of these books, however, especially toward women, are considerably outdated and sometimes grate upon modern sensibilities.

Although one might have expected the subgenre to flourish earlier, it was not until the 1940s that the American family story in the twentieth century came into its own. A single year, 1941, saw both Elizabeth Enright's Melendy family (in *The Saturdays*) and Eleanor Estes's Moffat family (in *The Moffats*) come into existence. Because of the coincidental initials, these authors and their fictional families are frequently confused, and indeed they have their similarities. However, Estes's chronicles of the Moffats, especially *Rufus M.* (1943), are more outstanding for their humor and warmth. Estes demonstrates a deep understanding of childhood's passionate desires (Rufus's longing for a library card, for example) and deep anxieties.

In England, the thirties saw the appearance of Arthur Ransome's excellent *Swallows and Amazons* (1930) about the Walker children and the Blackett sisters. Twelve books appeared in this series, ending in 1947 with *Great Northern?* These works deal with the vacation-time adventures of a likable and competent group of youngsters who are particularly at home in boats. Their parents are very far in the background. One adult, Captain Flint, uncle to the Blacketts, joins the children in their play adventures. The books are not profound; problems, if any, are rarely shown having significant mental or emotional effects. But the imaginative children are a pleasure, and when, in *We Didn't Mean to Go to Sea* (1937), the kind of adventure they have imagined really happens, they are able to cope with it.

The Family from One End Street (1937) by Eve Garnett may be the first British children's book to focus on an urban working-class family. As such, it was much praised for innovativeness and insight in its own time, probably too much so, for we now can see the condescension, the outsider's approach to the Ruggles's life as quaint and colorful, with which the author unconsciously imbued the story. The family is far from unattractive: unified, mutually supportive, good-humored, and loving. But in their contacts with people from other, higher classes of society, they are perhaps too respectful, grateful, and admiring, and certainly unbelievably unresentful.

When *Henry Huggins* appeared in 1950, it represented the beginning of over thirty years of fine family stories by Beverly Cleary. Henry's adventures with his dog Ribsy, his friend Beezus, and her sister Ramona have provided American children with mild domestic comedy, and sometimes grief, in clear, unpretentious prose. Recently, *Dear Mr. Henshaw* (1983), a book outside the series, won the Newbery award. It reflects some of the changes that have taken place in the domestic novel for children, for the young protagonist's parents are divorced, and the truck-driving father whom he longs to see is neglectful and careless, forgetful of promises. Leigh corresponds with his favorite writer, the Mr. Henshaw of the title, and Henshaw replies, providing an objective audience for Leigh's troubles.

Another author who has brought the family novel into modern times is Lois Lowry. Her books about Anastasia Krupnik and her family (*Anastasia Krupnik*, 1979; *Anastasia Again*, 1981; *Anastasia at Your Service*, 1982; *Anastasia, Ask Your Analyst*, 1984; and *Anastasia on Her Own*, 1985) have the traditional two-parent family, but the parents are more strongly drawn individuals than in, say, Enright's novels. Both are warm, intelligent, and humorous. Anastasia herself is brighter and more confident (but also older) than most of the children in the above novels. The events of daily life are the primary material of the books, but serious problems occasionally arise and are dealt with in some depth. In the first novel Anastasia's feelings about the death of a beloved grandparent and the birth of a baby brother are presented realistically. In the second, the move to a new neighborhood and the adaptations it entails provide the basic plot. Lowry shows her characters going through the ordinary crises of life with human resentments and uncertainties, but also with love and even, sometimes, wisdom.

Some of the works of Judy Blume are family stories, although most are limited to the status of "problem novels" by a narrow focus on a single topic. *Tales of a Fourth Grade Nothing* (1972) does present us with a modern family, apartment dwellers in an urban environment, who make an interesting contrast to the families portrayed in earlier works. Peter, the narrator, is wiser than his parents, especially his frantic mother. He feels resentful of his overindulged baby brother, Fudge, over whom neither parent has any control. When Fudge eats Peter's pet turtle, he is rushed to the hospital but of course suffers no harm. The parents give Peter a puppy to make up for the loss of the turtle, and thus all problems are resolved. Blume's works enjoy great popularity among children, but to the mature eye they seem very superficial and flimsy. The humor is childish, which may account for much of the books' appeal. In the traditional family story, the parents represent security and comfort; they are wiser than the children and can help put trouble into perspective when anxiety overwhelms the child. In *Tales of a Fourth Grade Nothing*, Peter must provide stability and support for his mother; *she* is the one who is anxious and sees things out of proportion to their real importance. No one really consoles or comforts Peter but himself.

Anastasia on Her Own, Lois Lowry, cover art by Diane de Groat

Tales of a Fourth Grade Nothing, Judy Blume, cover art by Roy Doty

Helen Cresswell's Bagthorpe Saga, which started in 1977 with *Ordinary Jack*, is highly entertaining. The Bagthorpes, apart from Jack, are all nearly mad with self-conceit and competitiveness. Their adventures usually turn upon schemes to win fame or fortune, or merely to be one up on each other. Five-year-old Cousin Daisy, who has a touch of pyromania, might be able to give even Fudge competition for the title of Most Maddening Child in Fiction. But Daisy is inventive in her mischief and often devastatingly logical. She is never merely undisciplined and destructive. The outrageous adventures of the Bagthorpes are an exaggeration of reality and so do not properly fit the tradition of the family story. However, their surreal lives are built out of very real and ordinary human tendencies drawn very large, as in good caricature. (For more examples of modern treatment of the family story, see Donahue, "New Realism," below.)

A type of daily-life story that has enjoyed greater success in Britain than in America is the school story. The difference doubtless stems from the fact that most American children attend day schools, usually public, rather than private boarding schools. Although school and teachers do figure to some extent in the plots of most realistic novels about the daily life of American children, they do not usually replace the ambience of home and family as they do in British school stories. A few American series are set in prep schools (Merritt Parmelee Allen's Mudhen series, for example), but in general the closest American equivalent to the atmosphere of the British school story is to be found in Young Adult books set in colleges, like Cynthia Voigt's *Tell Me If the Lovers Are Losers*.

The British school story, especially in the nineteenth century, includes some works of considerable merit, such as Hughes's *Tom Brown's School-Days* or Kipling's *Stalky & Co*. During the twentieth century, the literary quality of the school stories has not generally been high, although the books have been no less popular for that. Charles Hamilton's Billy Bunter and his friends have never lacked readers, nor have Angela Brazil's healthy schoolgirls.

There are, however, at least two authors whose contributions to the school story are well above the common run of such tales. William Mayne's stories of a cathedral choir school are gently humorous and affectionate in tone, and frequently have the same sense of history and continuity of human endeavor that enriches Mayne's other works. *A Swarm in May* (1955), in which a young boy's discovery of a medieval bee-ball leads to the resurrection of an ancient custom, is the best of these books. Antonia Forest's series about the Marlow family (beginning in 1948 with *Autumn Term*) is not always set in a girls' school, but with one exception (*Peter's Room*, 1961), the at-home books are the weakest of the series. The books set at the school, Kingscote, show the girls making and losing friends, trying to resolve their dilemmas honorably (some involve significant moral issues), learning to cope with hostility, and developing, slowly but definitely, the distinctive characteristics, not all of them good, that make each of them an individual. Ginny's moral cowardice, Lawrie's self-centeredness, Ann's priggishness, and Nicola's courage and fortitude emerge with greater clarity as the series proceeds. *End of Term* (1959) may be the best of the at-school books in the series, although *Cricket Term* (1974) has an equally interesting and complex plot.

The Child as Isolate

The first edition of *A Critical History of Children's Literature* (1953) observes, "There is a noticeable tendency in American realistic stories to emphasize a single child. The child may or may not be the member of a large family but the interest of the story centers in a special person," in contrast to the "group activities of English children."[3] This distinction was even at the time somewhat arbitrary: Elizabeth Goudge's *The Little White Horse* (1946), Richmal Crompton Lamburn's William books, Monica Edwards's career novels in the fifties, and Enid Bagnold's *National Velvet* (1935) are evidence that the novel centered upon a single child is not the property or the product of "American individualism." More useful than speculation about aspects of national character revealed by such books is study of the changing image of the isolate child, the solitary child, whether orphaned, an only child, or merely a "loner" within a family or group, who must shape his or her own identity, for whatever reasons, outside the context of the traditional family.

The most obvious instance of the child as isolate is the orphan, and in children's books we have what might be called "the orphan phenomenon," a surprising number of child protagonists, most of them female, who have no parents. They are, of course, lineal descendants of the many orphans of pietistic nineteenth-century fiction, and also of the plucky climbers of Horatio Alger's creation. One of the earliest and best loved of these orphan books is *Anne of Green Gables* (1908).

L. M. Montgomery's spirited red-haired orphan has survived the test of time well. In the first book, at any rate, Anne is as brave, bright, sensible, and competitive as any feminist could wish; if, in later books, marriage and motherhood somehow diminish her, that is regrettable, and a sad comment upon "happy marriages" in the early part of this century. But in the first book, Anne competes with Gilbert and often wins. If there is one feature of *Anne of Green Gables* that does not quite ring true, it is something we as readers would be unwilling to have changed. That is Anne's own character, which is passionately affectionate (although hot-tempered), imaginative (sometimes excessively so), reliable (if occasionally absentminded), gregarious, and profoundly optimistic. Yet she is a child who, we are told, never knew her parents, has been passed from family to family, has seen brutality, and has never known love. We are told that she has been scarred by this desolate childhood, but we never see her scars; it seems unrealistic that so wonderful a character could have come untainted through those dark years, yet we as readers are heartily glad that it should be so. So full of life is Anne that she can revivify the elderly brother and sister Matthew and Marilla Cuthbert, with whom she comes to live. Her triumph is the winning of Marilla's love and Marilla's admission of that love. This is typical of orphan books: the child desires love and a secure home and usually acquires them by the end of the story. Anne's situation is atypical, however, in that she acquires the home early in the book but the love between her and Marilla grows slowly; by the conclusion, it is one of the most convincingly real depictions of familial love in children's literature.

Another memorable orphan of the period is Mary of Frances Hodgson Burnett's *The Secret Garden* (1911). She is a cold, unloving child when first we meet her, but she changes as she begins to take an interest in gardening and then in the prospect of helping Colin learn to walk. The boy Dickon is a kind of nature deity, and Mrs. Sowerby a sort of Magna Mater through whose beneficent influence Burnett's simple pantheism is filtered. Mary's character may be more true to psychological reality than Anne's, for her initial self-centeredness and unaffectionate behavior seem congruent with what we know of her past. The transformations of both Mary and Colin are perhaps unrealistically rapid, but the therapy—positive, creative activities that take the youngsters' minds off themselves—seems sound enough. There is some sentimentality, especially having to do with Colin's dead mother, but the bulk of the novel is down-to-earth and engagingly real, and the primary emotional response of the reader, which is joy, is fully earned.

Although most of the orphans of this era's fiction were female, there is a male: the hero of Gene Stratton Porter's *Freckles* (1904). This book about a young orphan who is hired by a lumber company to guard a section of swamp from tree thieves has many thoroughly unbelievable and sentimental elements (Freckles is a lost scion of the Irish aristocracy; he speaks with an Irish brogue although he was placed in an orphanage in Chicago before he learned to talk). But Porter is a good naturalist and, when writing of what she knows, an absorbing storyteller.

Jean Webster's *Daddy-Long-Legs* (1912) is an epistolary novel in which a bright young orphan girl corresponds with her unknown male benefactor, whom she nicknames "Daddy-Long-Legs." When she matures, she marries him. There is a good deal of humor in the story, but the romantic plot seems highly improbable. Eleanor H. Porter's *Pollyanna* (1913) enjoyed enormous popularity in its time but is excessively sentimental and clichéd. Pollyanna's "Glad Girl" optimism is enough to make a hardened cynic of the most kindly and cheerful of readers. Lacking Anne of Green Gables' ability to laugh at herself, Pollyanna seems insubstantial and one-dimensional.

In Dorothy Canfield's *Understood Betsy* (1917), an orphan is exposed to two different sets of devoted relatives and their opposed ideas on child-rearing. The urban maiden aunts with whom Betsy first lives smother her with love and their notions of child psychology. They infect her with their own neuroses and hypochondria. When she goes to live on a farm with her "Vermont relatives," she learns to do chores, act independently and responsibly, face her fears with courage, and appreciate a love that is secure without being overprotective, warm without being overdemonstrative. The book is sensible (as is Betsy by the end) and warm, although the modern reader cannot but note that the expectations of the Vermonters, which Betsy indeed meets, are perhaps a bit high for a nine-year-old, and one can scarcely call their love "undemanding."

The years between the wars also produced books about orphans, many of them refugees. Since many talented writers and artists emigrated to America following World War I, it is not surprising that "orphan novels" set in Europe should appear at this time. Typical of these are Kate Seredy's *The Good Master* (1935) and *The Singing Tree* (1939), in which Cousin Kate from Budapest, upon the death

The Secret Garden, Frances Hodgson Burnett.
illustrated by Tasha Tudor

The Moffats, Eleanor Estes, illustrated by Louis Slobodkin

of her mother, comes to live on a farm in rural Hungary with Jancsi's family. She is spoiled and wild but evolves into a brave and affectionate child.

The heroine of Doris Gates's *Sensible Kate* (1943) is a child who conforms to the adult vision of the good and sensible girl. Like Anne of Green Gables, she is a plain little red-haired thing. Anne yearned to be beautiful, not so much because of what beauty might bring her, as simply because she loved beauty in all things; however, Anne did not therefore devalue either wisdom or virtue that came in plain packages. Kate is less wise. She "longed above all things to be pretty and cute. If you were pretty, everyone was crazy about you, even your relatives. If you were cute, nothing was expected of you except cuteness. . . . Kate had taken good sense as her portion and had tried to make of it what she could. Still, down in her heart she knew or thought she knew, that good sense wasn't really important."[4] Kate is a nice child who eventually wins love and a good home despite her plainness. But the central conflict over the value of cuteness versus sensibleness seems trivial to the modern reader, although it was undoubtedly timely enough when Shirley Temple was a superstar. In Helen F. Daringer's *Adopted Jane* (1947), the heroine is similarly reliable and hardworking but not outstandingly pretty. She goes "visiting" to two households one summer, and the people in both learn to love her and want to adopt her. In the end, she chooses to go to the widow whom she does indeed love but who also needs her more.

Both *Sensible Kate* and *Adopted Jane* are realistic in showing the children as somewhat insecure and doubtful of their ability to win love. However, unrealistically, neither girl shows much hostility or rebellion (at least Anne of Green Gables had a shocking temper), both trust strange adults with astonishing speed, and both, although not babies, are not only adopted, they have some choice between adoptive parents. Yet children above the age of three or four are notoriously hard to place for adoption. These are pleasant books with likable heroines, but the happy endings are as unrealistic as *The Wizard of Oz*.

Similarly, in the fifties, Natalie Savage Carlson's Orphelines are so happy in their orphanage (Jane, above, also feels affection for the matron of her orphanage) that they do not really want to be adopted. Although there are undoubtedly many orphanage employees who love and understand their charges, most such institutions are too crowded and the staffs too harried to give a great deal of personal attention to each orphan. Few children in such institutions, one suspects, would say that life there was an adequate substitute for life with a family of their own. Of course, books like *The Happy Orpheline* (1957) and *A Pet for the Orphelines* (1962) do not aspire to be truly realistic novels. They are in a nonsexual sense romantic comedies, and their habitat is more air than earth.

In the last twenty years or so, the orphan's condition has been less romanticized in children's fiction. Vera and Bill Cleaver's Mary Call Luther in *Where the Lilies Bloom* (1969) shoulders the responsibility of looking after herself and her orphaned siblings in an attempt to avoid being placed in an orphanage. The life is hard, and the burden eventually too heavy for Mary Call, but she is quite clear in her mind, as is Edith in Rosa Guy's *The Friends* (1973), that it is worth any effort to stay out of an institution and to keep her brother and sisters together. Foster homes, both good and bad, are depicted realistically in such books as Betsy Byars's *The Pinballs* (1977), Katherine Paterson's *The Great Gilly Hopkins* (1978), and Marion Bauer's *Foster Child* (1977). Some of the children in these stories, as in real life, are not literally orphans but have been abandoned by parents either unable or unwilling to cope further with a child. The children react to their being unwanted in ways ranging from brash aggressiveness to quiet despair (see also Donahue, "New Realism," below).

The romantic traditional treatment of orphans in the earlier fiction of this century is for the most part not truly realistic. However, psychologically and emotionally it is often more satisfying than an exact and realistic depiction of the orphaned state might be. These early books show the orphans seeking two things: personal identity (Anne becomes Anne of Green Gables instead of "Anne of nowhere-in-particular") and a true home with all it entails—love, family, security, and a sense of belonging. These are the goals of mythic quest, goals sought hopefully by every human being, child or adult. Seen on this level, the orphan is that parentless, placeless element in all of us that yearns for a sure knowledge of who we are and where we belong, and that sometimes inspires children in a perfectly happy two-parent family to fantasize about being orphans, about establishing an identity independent of parents, and about living another life free of the limiting expectations imposed by their excellent and much-loved families. In light of this aspect of the "orphan phenomenon," it may be truer and more appropriate to show the orphan's quest as an essentially hopeful endeavor having a happy conclusion than to confuse truth with fact and show orphans unloved, unwanted, and forever displaced. Of course, many of the new realistic books on the subject also offer hopeful endings. In Byars's *The Pinballs*, the children know they must leave the foster home where they have felt some security; but they have learned to care about one another, and they have also learned that they can take some independent action to help shape their own lives: they do not have to let themselves be pushed around like pinballs.

The book depicting the solitary child who is not an orphan but either an only child or a child temporarily separated from its parents has some thematic similarities to the book about orphans. The child often uses its isolation as a means of strengthening personal identity and acquiring resources, whether friendship or new inner strengths, that support advancing maturity. A striking example of this kind of book is Ruth Sawyer's *Roller Skates* (1936), in which Lucinda is left in the care of two easygoing maiden ladies when her parents go abroad. Free to ramble about New York City in the 1890s on her skates, she makes friends with people from class and ethnic backgrounds very different from her own, becoming "inoculated," as her Uncle Earle tells her, against snobbery, the creeping disease of her class.

In Gene Stratton Porter's *A Girl of the Limberlost* (1909), a book intended for an adult audience that has become the property of teens and subteens, Elnora Comstock, an only child, lives in the Limberlost swamp with her somewhat unbalanced mother, who blames her for her father's death. Elnora turns to nature for comfort, becoming a skilled observer of the swamp. There is, of course, a good deal of sentimentality in the plot, but there is also an interesting subplot about the adoption of a wild orphan boy by the Comstocks' neighbors. Characterization is vivid, especially of Elnora's mother, and if Elnora is sometimes just too good to be true, she is also courageous, intelligent, and self-reliant.

L. M. Montgomery's *The Blue Castle* (1926) was similarly intended for an adult audience. Valancy, its cowed heroine, is in her late twenties, an "old maid" and only child living with her domineering mother and colorless spinster cousin. Due to a mix-up of names, she receives from her doctor a diagnosis of fatal heart disease. Believing she has only a year to live, she breaks away from her family, becomes housekeeper to a drunkard and his dying daughter, asks a suspected outlaw to marry her, and generally becomes another woman. Despite the sentimentality of the story, it effectively demonstrates the need of the child (at whatever age) to find some distance from family in order to become an individual in her own right.

This theme is addressed much more directly in modern realism (see Donahue, "New Realism," below). The child is often shown fighting the family in order to break free into a space of its own, as in Emily Neville's *It's Like This, Cat* (1963) or Barbara Wersba's *The Dream Watcher* (1968), or sometimes exploring and evaluating the adult world like an anthropologist taking notes on an unknown tribe, as in Louise Fitzhugh's *Harriet the Spy* (1964). Modern realism also addresses the darkest side of the solitary child's condition, that of the child who is driven into isolation by abusive, neglectful, or indifferent parents. Some of these children are "loners," discussed below; others are driven so far into themselves as to lose all touch with reality, as in Kin Platt's *The Boy Who Could Make Himself Disappear* (1968).

"Loners" are children who have chosen isolation, not necessarily for its own sake but because companionship or "fitting into" a larger group entails giving up or compromising some essential part of themselves. Such stories are usually about personal integrity, and the most clear-cut examples of this theme appear only in the last twenty years or so. This may be because of the value Western society placed on conformity in the first half of the century, or it may be because an implicit critique of the norm and the status quo underlies every loner's determination to maintain his or her difference and solitude. The fact that loners have been frequent protagonists of adult novels throughout the century suggests forcibly that the harshness of the loner's vision and experience was considered "unsuitable for children" until the breakthroughs of recent realism made the child as loner more acceptable.

Ivan Southall's *Josh* (1971) has as its hero a boy who is set apart from a small rural Australian community because he is city-bred and because he writes poetry. He refuses to pretend to be like the local louts, although that would make his life easier; he eventually rejects the community that has rejected him and leaves to walk the hundred miles back to the city. This is a bitter book, and Josh's independence is expensive: it costs any trust and respect he might have felt for the locals and, more generally, any natural urge toward community.

Similarly, the cost of personal integrity is too high in Robert Cormier's *The Chocolate War* (1974; see also Donahue, "New Realism," below). Jerry is not a typical loner, since in the early stages of the book he shows some desire to merge with the school community, be on the football team, have a few friends. Indeed, his initial cooperation launches the events that snowball into a calamity: he goes along with a prank ordered by the Vigils (a secret society) and refuses to sell chocolates. When the Vigils rescind the order, *that* is the sticking point. Now Jerry finds—and perhaps surprises even himself—that he has the essential qualities of the loner. He was willing to join in a prank, but he is not willing to be a mere cat's-paw of the Vigils. He persists in his refusal to sell the candy even in the face of threats. Finally, he is brutally beaten, and as he is carried to the ambulance he tells his loyal friend that it wasn't worth it.

In *The Runner* (1985), Cynthia Voigt's fourth book about the Tillerman family, "Bullet" Tillerman is in almost constant conflict with his cold, domineering father, a man who has driven away Bullet's brother and sister before him. Bullet and his mother are much alike and understand one another almost wordlessly. But the mother has her own peculiar integrity, which means she never enters into open conflict with the father. Bullet is also isolated at school. There are students whom he likes, but he has no close friends, and he studies other people in some wonderment, marveling at how little they understand themselves, and wondering whether they wholly believe the lies they tell about their motives. The setting is Maryland in the sixties, and Bullet is racially prejudiced. A champion cross-country runner, he is dropped from the team when he refuses to help train a black student. However, when he learns that the fisherman whom he has helped for years, and who is the closest thing to a real friend he has, is in fact black, Bullet revises his thinking and begins to coach the black runner. They become friendly, and the black, Tamer, realizes what few people perceive about Bullet: he always tells the exact truth as he sees it, but he never says more than that. Bullet does not care if he is misunderstood, so he does not explain or clarify. After Bullet and Tamer have won their respective events at the state field and track competition, Bullet asks Tamer to promise that he will not fight in the war in Vietnam but rather finish school and raise his family. Tamer promises. But Bullet quits school, goes into the army, and dies in Vietnam.

Despite the death of its hero, *The Runner* is the most optimistic of the three "loner" novels discussed here. It shows the loner maintaining what is admittedly an odd integrity to the end, without bitterness. Bullet insists upon being himself, but he does not resent the price of his selfhood. He goes into the army to defeat his father, for he knows that if he were to stay on the farm, which he loves, his father would eventually wear away even Bullet's intransigence. Bullet rejoices in doing things well, whether running or farming. But his father is not a good farmer, nor would he ever permit Bullet to run the farm. Bullet does not stay to be forced to act against his principles.

All these books about the child as isolate explore themes as old as fairy tales, which are full of children who are solitary either in nature or condition. But where the "loner" books are realistic about the price the community demands of those who refuse to conform to it, in fairy tales the nonconformist is often vindicated in the end. His foolishness is wisdom, his differentness is necessary to the kingdom. The community needs the isolate. The fairy tales are true, but the realistic novels demonstrate the fact that society resents both the need and the necessity. The price of being solitary is exacted by the community. Yet such books as *The Runner* suggest also that community is an illusion; that the loner is the one who recognizes that we are each separate and shivering in the dark.

Historical and Period Novels

Like John Rowe Townsend,[5] we have found useful Jill Paton Walsh's distinction between the historical novel, written "wholly or partly about the public events and social conditions which are the material of history, regardless of the time at which it is written," and what she calls the "costume novel," which is set in the past but not concerned with historical events.[6] We have chosen to call the latter type the period novel, since "costume novel" sounds somewhat pejorative.

There is a third type of novel that is much more difficult to place: the novel that takes place at an earlier period in time, often during the author's childhood, but is perceived as contemporary rather than historical. Some of these have already been treated, for example, Ruth Sawyer's *Roller Skates,* set in the 1890s, and Eleanor Estes's Moffat series, set in pre-1914 America. Others, such as the Little House books of Laura Ingalls Wilder, are treated as historical novels here because they portray details of daily life and interests that add up to a picture of "social conditions which are the material of history," even though they do not deal with events of historical importance and did not take place in the distant past at the time of writing. Such

Viking's Dawn, Henry Treece, illustrated by Christine Price

Smith, Leon Garfield, illustrated by Antony Maitland

distinctions are to some extent subjective, and doubtless many readers would move a particular book from this section to another.

In Britain, the nineteenth century ended with Emma Marshall writing the last of her rather charming but now little-known historical novels, *Penshurst Castle* (1894), about Sir Philip Sidney. Stanley Weyman was producing his romantic historical adventures set in France (*The Man in Black,* 1894; *Under the Red Robe,* 1896), which have survived the changing tastes of the twentieth-century audience rather better than Marshall's work. But the historical adventure novel, indeed, the historical novel generally, entered something of a dry spell in the early twentieth century. There were few historical novels of note until the years between the wars, when Geoffrey Trease wrote *Bows Against the Barons* (1934). This book about Robin Hood as a leader of the peasantry against oppression differs from previous historical novels in taking a "radical" or revolutionary political position. Trease's early novels are sometimes naive and overly simple in their politics, but they are also refreshing, exciting, and energetically written.

Historical novelists had always, consciously or unconsciously, used their books as a medium to assert a political or religious (and they are sometimes the same) position. Consider Charles Kingsley's rabid anti-Catholicism in *Westward Ho!* (1855) or the good nineteenth-century Anglicanism of Charlotte Yonge's novels.[7] But prior to Trease, most of the historical novels for children were somewhat conservative in thrust, nationalistic, patriotic, and establishmentarian. Trease began, mildly enough, a trend toward more realistic portrayals of the darker side of life in "Merrie England," toward awareness of cross-century relationships with modern social and political problems, and toward questioning of "official" views of history and positions on historical events. Trease's further historical novels for children (he has also written school stories, mysteries, and adult novels) include *Comrades for the Charter* (also 1934), about the Chartist movement, *Cue for Treason* (1940), about the English Civil War, and two novels about Garibaldi's campaigns, *Follow My Black Plume* (1963) and *A Thousand for Sicily* (1964).

The 1950s in England saw the emergence of Rosemary Sutcliff, possibly the best historical novelist for children in the twentieth century, certainly the most consistently good. Her interests are more philosophical than political, and in this respect she runs counter to the trend noted in Trease. Her earliest books seem intended for the younger audience. The plots are simple, the protagonists preadolescent, the adventures ultimately safe in *The Queen Elizabeth Story* (1950), *The Armourer's House* (1951), and *Brother Dusty-Feet* (1952). She takes up her most successful themes in her novels for adolescents, especially those set in Roman Britain. *The Eagle of the Ninth* (1954), *The Silver Branch* (1957), and *The Lantern Bearers* (1959) trace a single Romano-British family from the battles with the Picts in the north through the withdrawal of the legions from Britain. *Outcast* (1955) is an almost Hardyesque account of the harsh life of a slave who finally finds love and a place to belong in the home of a Roman engineer in Sussex. *Dawn Wind* (1961) sees the beginning of a unified Saxon Britain. *The Shield Ring* (1956) is about the Norse resistance to Norman oppression in the Lake District. *Knight's Fee* (1960) and *The Witch's Brat* (1970) take place in early Norman Britain under Henry I. *The Mark of the Horse Lord* (1965) returns to Roman Britain, but from the point of view of the tribes conquered or pushed back by Rome. *Warrior Scarlet* (1958) is about a Bronze Age tribe on the Sussex Downs.

Greatly influenced by Kipling's work, especially by the Roman stories in *Puck of Pook's Hill,* Sutcliff delineates a vision of English history as a constant pushing of the "Light," the civilized virtues of knowledge, sensitivity, creativity, community, and human caring, against the "Dark" of brutality, destructiveness, lawlessness, and cruelty. The villains are not all on one side, nor are the heroes. In her best book, *The Mark of the Horse Lord,* a former Roman gladiator kills himself rather than give the Gaelic tribe whose kingship he has usurped into the power of the Romans. Sutcliff's protagonists are often damaged people, crippled in spirit or body, who through endurance, courage, creativity, or integrity win a place in the community of their fellows.

Henry Treece (often confused with Geoffrey Trease, above) was a prolific novelist whose works for children are often stereotypical and formulaic. His best books are his two Viking trilogies: *Viking's Dawn* (1956), *The Road to Miklagard* (1957), and *Viking's Sunset* (1960), about the adventures of a Viking from youth to middle age; and *Hounds of the King* (1955), *Man with a Sword* (1962), and *The Last of the Vikings* (1964), about the medieval Norwegian king Harald Hardrada. These books remain popular because they are fast-paced adventures; Treece attempts no social comment or philosophical theme. His posthumous novel *The Dream-Time* (1967), about a Stone Age boy who wants to be an artist, not a warrior, is much admired.

But John Rowe Townsend is rightly critical of its anachronistic attitudes.[8]

The novels of Hester Burton show a strong consciousness of social and political problems as well as historical events. *Castors Away!* (1962) is set in England at the time of the Battle of Trafalgar. Her best books are *Time of Trial* (1963), in which Mr. Pargeter, charming, wise, kind, but also politically naïve, is jailed for the publication and sale of "seditious" materials detailing the appalling social conditions of early nineteenth-century England; and *No Beat of Drum* (1966), about the working classes of the same period.

Jill Paton Walsh, who is perhaps best known for her realistic novels *Goldengrove* (1972) and *Unleaving* (1976), began her career as an author with *Hengest's Tale* (1966), a historical novel about the northern European tribes after the fall of Rome. *The Emperor's Winding-Sheet* (1974), about a slave boy at the court of the Eastern emperor during the fall of Constantinople, is a powerful book and beautifully written. *The Huffler* (1975), a short book about a well-bred Victorian girl who briefly escapes her stodgy family and its middle-class restrictions to travel to London with a working-class boy on a barge, demonstrates Walsh's interest in the subject of class conflict, which she also explored in her realistic novel *Fireweed* (1969). *A Chance Child* (1978) is in part a time-travel fantasy in which Creep, an abused, unwanted modern child, makes his way into the nineteenth century and remains there. But it is the realism of the life of the working child in the mines, the potteries, and the factories that dominates this novel, the bleak years of the Industrial Revolution in which children paid for society's technological advancement with their freedom, their youth, and, all too often, their lives.

A Parcel of Patterns (1984) is one of Walsh's best novels. This story of a Derbyshire village that shuts itself off from the outside world when the Great Plague of 1665 strikes is simply narrated by Mall, a village girl. Through her eyes we see the growing horror as the Plague flourishes and the villagers die; we see also the conflict between the faith of the Puritans and the reality of the Plague, for they believe the Plague is a punishment sent from God, but the good and the wicked alike are dying. Mall's own loss of family and lover brings her to the end of her simple faith. But she endures and comes to a kind of truce with God, an admission that she does not understand His ways, but a hope that perhaps He loves and understands His creatures.

The Stone Book (1976), *Granny Reardun* (1977), *The Aimer Gate* (1978), and *Tom Fobble's Day* (1977): this remarkable quartet of books by Alan Garner tracing a Cheshire family of artisans and craftsmen from the late Victorian era to World War II really defies classification. Each book focuses on a child in the family, and the changing exterior world is merely a backdrop for the continuity of family, work, and community. Garner's style in these works has been refined to a stunning poetic simplicity, and the dialogue captures effectively the dialect of both period and place.

The remarkable eighteenth-century novels of Leon Garfield are so robust and extravagant as to be almost fantastic. Hogarthian in vision, Dickensian in character, and occasionally Rabelaisian in language, one might call them, except that to do so implies that Garfield's work is derivative. But he is very much an original and rarely suffers from lack of control. His first book, *Jack Holborn* (1964), is an adventure story after the fashion of *Treasure Island. Smith* (1967) takes place on the scruffy edges of London's underworld and has the vivid atmosphere of the period that is now so strongly associated with Garfield's writing. His books also include *The Drummer Boy* (1970) and *The Strange Affair of Adelaide Harris* (1971).

Garfield's best work to date may be *The Apprentices* (1982), a group of twelve stories, each about a different eighteenth-century apprentice. Originally published between 1976 and 1978, the stories are linked by a strange, saintly boy whose torch casts light on things people prefer not to see. *The Apprentices* contains some of Garfield's most characteristic material. In "The Valentine," for instance, Hawkins, an apprentice undertaker, is in love with Miss Jessop, the daughter of a rival undertaker. She, in turn, is in love with a dead boy whose grave she decorates every St. Valentine's Day. The feud between two apprentices to a maker of plaster figurines is resolved in "The Enemy" when one makes a portrait figurine of the other, believing that if he smashes it, his enemy will die. And the making of the figurine does destroy his enemy, by turning him into a friend. These characters lead lives that are sometimes brutal, but they are also full of hope—hope of success, hope of wealth, and hope of love. Although Garfield's period pieces are often comic, he makes serious social comments that have relevance to the lives of the poor and exploited today.

Sid Fleischman's period novels, most of them set in the American West of frontier times, share the boisterous exuberance of Leon

Garfield's books but lack Garfield's range of both emotion and language. Fleischman works on the realistic edge of the "tall tale" tradition and occasionally slips across it into the farcical. Typical works are *By the Great Horn Spoon!* (1963) and *Humbug Mountain* (1978).

American historical fiction for children was well served in the early decades of the century by Cornelia Meigs, who wrote historical novels that were neither superficially researched nor shallow in theme. Of her many books, however, few survive today, and her best-known work is *Invincible Louisa* (1933), a biography of Louisa May Alcott. Of the historical novels, her best are *Master Simon's Garden* (1916), about how a beautiful garden made by Master Simon over the objections of his Puritan neighbors becomes a source of pleasure to succeeding generations; and *The Two Arrows* (1949), an exciting story of two brothers exiled from England to Maryland in the late eighteenth century.

Charles B. Hawes's seafaring adventures are thrilling period novels, particularly *The Dark Frigate* (1923), about a young seventeenth-century seaman who makes his rite of passage from innocence to experience upon a voyage on which neither people nor ships always fly their true colors. Caroline Dale Snedeker's *Downright Dencey* (1927) is a period novel about a nineteenth-century Quaker girl on Nantucket. It emphasizes the importance of the Quaker faith in the local community and provides a good picture of island life in the nineteenth century.

Laura Ingalls Wilder's Little House series, based on her own childhood, began in 1932 with *Little House in the Big Woods. Farmer Boy* (1933) tells of the boyhood of Almanzo Wilder, whom Laura married. The other seven books in the series deal in meticulous detail with the daily life of the Ingalls family as they homestead in various locations throughout the Midwest. Wilder's clear, simple prose is well matched by her subject, the nature of the pioneer life and family. The toil of every member of the family is treated not as drudgery but as the necessary stuff of which life is made, and often its results are beauty or even fun.

Survival is not always a certainty in these books. In *The Long Winter* (1940), which most critics agree is the best of the series, the family comes very close to starvation. Their fuel is gone, and they must twist hay into sticks for the fire. They eventually have nothing to eat but bread made from coarse-ground wheat. Still the blizzards come. The howling wind is a personal enemy, its constant noise nearly driving them mad. But Pa tells Laura, "It [the blizzard] has to quit sometime. We don't." So Laura feels a spark of hope. Spring comes late, but it comes.

All of Wilder's books present a picture of the family as a loving, mutually dependent, and mutually supportive unit. The community is similarly interdependent and supportive. When Almanzo and Cap risk their lives to bring wheat to the starving town, the storekeeper tries to make an exorbitant profit on the sale of the wheat. The angry men of the town confront him, and he backs down when Pa points out that if he wants to do business when times are good again, he had better treat people right when times are bad. He needs the townspeople as much as they need him. For an accurate and moving picture of frontier life, Wilder's series is incomparable. Even the mother's deplorable attitude toward the Indians is probably a true reflection of a prejudice common at the time.

Elizabeth Coatsworth's numerous historical novels are well written, with lively plots and likable characters. Many are no longer in print, which seems a pity, for they are good books by any standard. *Away Goes Sally* (1934) is the story of a family moving from Massachusetts to Maine in a house on runners, drawn through the winter landscape by oxen. Four books about Sally follow this one, all vivid and mildly humorous. Even when writing about medieval Scandinavians, as Coatsworth does in *Door to the North* (1950), she is a gripping story-teller. In this novel of exploration, an atmosphere of brooding misfortune hangs over the travelers, and when, in what is now northern Minnesota, three of them are lost on the plains, the tension and fear are palpable.

An outstanding American historical novel appeared in 1943: *Johnny Tremain*. Esther Forbes's novel about a Boston silversmith's apprentice who loses the use of his right hand and thus his vocation is beautifully researched, and Boston in the eighteenth century comes vividly alive. Paul Revere, Sam Adams, James Otis, and other heroes of the American Revolution figure as characters, of whom the most unforgettable is Otis, that strange, brilliant, brain-damaged man. Johnny himself is a very human character with many flaws; he is proud, hot-tempered, and sometimes foolish, as in his failure to see Cilla's worth for so long. But he is also a basically decent and idealistic boy whom the reader comes to care about very much.

Recent years have seen the influence of contemporary realism on the historical novel in the form of less glorification of war and vio-

Little House in the Big Woods, Laura Ingalls Wilder,
illustrated by Garth Williams

Johnny Tremain, Esther Forbes, illustrated by Lynd Ward

lence, more realistic presentation of historical events, and more realistic depictions of characters from minority groups. Irene Hunt's *Across Five Aprils* (1964) focuses on the impact of the American Civil War upon a soldier's family back home, the economic hardship, the conflicts with neighbors, the waiting for news. Ann Petry's *Tituba of Salem Village* (1964) presents the Salem witch trials from the perspective of an accused slave. Elizabeth Borton de Treviño's *I, Juan de Pareja* (1965) is an excellent account of the life of a slave (a historical figure) belonging to the artist Velázquez. *Thunder at Gettysburg* (1975) by Patricia Gauch tells the story of the battle from the viewpoint of a girl living in Gettysburg. *Zoar Blue* (1978) by Janet Hickman describes the impact of the Civil War on the German Separatist settlement of Zoar, Ohio. *My Brother Sam Is Dead* (1974) by James Lincoln Collier and Christopher Collier makes a striking contrast to *Johnny Tremain*. Based on fact, it tells how the patriotic Sam, a soldier in the American army, is shot by the Americans "as an example" for a crime he did not commit. The book gives detailed and repelling accounts of skirmishes and includes crimes and unjust actions committed by both sides.

The development of the realistic novel in the twentieth century has been consistently away from romanticism and sentimentality toward a blunter, more "naturalistic" realism. The culmination has been the New Realism, in which character, language, and situation are all more frankly (and often darkly) drawn from the real world. Even in the more recent historical novels, the comfortable distancing from suffering afforded by elegant costumes or established attitudes about past events has given way to the immediacy of human pain, as in Walsh's *A Chance Child* or the Colliers' *My Brother Sam Is Dead*. The secure, protected world of the family and the previously sacrosanct image of good parents have both been forced to admit the realities of divorce, division, and parental fallibility. Yet when one surveys the realism of the century, the authors and titles that stand out are often pre–New Realism, like *The Secret Garden* or *Little House on the Prairie*. Although it is early yet to judge, the new lamps of realistic children's fiction do not as yet outshine the old. We may not be entering a "Golden Age" of children's books, but we seem to be seeking an alloy tough and true as steel. Ours is a doubting age, distrustful of the too hopeful gleam.

Notes

1. Roger Lancelyn Green, "The Golden Age of Children's Books," in *Only Connect: Readings on Children's Literature,* eds. Sheila Egoff et al. (Toronto and New York: Oxford University Press, 1980), pp. 13–14.

2. Ibid., p. 14.

3. Cornelia Meigs et al., *A Critical History of Children's Literature* (New York: Macmillan, 1953), pp. 545–46.

4. Doris Gates, *Sensible Kate* (1943; reprint ed., New York: Viking, 1971), pp. 15–16.

5. John Rowe Townsend, *Written for Children: An Outline of English-Language Children's Literature,* new ed. (New York: J. B. Lippincott, 1983) p. 226.

6. Jill Paton Walsh, "History Is Fiction," *Horn Book,* February 1972, pp. 17–23.

7. See Marion Lochhead, "Clio Junior," in *Only Connect,* eds. Egoff et al., pp. 17–27.

8. Townsend, *Written for Children,* p. 222.

New Realism in Children's Fiction

Rosanne Donahue

THE 1960s BROUGHT A NEW APPROACH to the treatment of social problems in children's books. The attitudes that had forbidden the discussion of certain topics were weakening, and society was becoming generally more tolerant of open discussion of what had previously been taboo. This enlightenment produced "New Realism." Because the field of children's literature is ever-changing, particularly in response to shifts in the social climate, authors are now writing realistically about such themes as death, sex, drugs, alcoholism, homosexuality, bigotry, and similar issues that were once considered unsuitable (or at least unsuitable if too candidly portrayed) for children's books. New Realism recognizes few restrictions; it attempts to portray children not just as individuals, but as individuals who must make independent choices in situations for which there are no clear-cut rules. The external world looms large in the background, but the focus is on the child who is searching for his or her own self in a world filled with problems.

New Realistic novels are very popular with the young because they deal openly with issues that were once hidden; children see all around them, in everyday life, the problems of drugs, alcohol, sex, etc. A general feeling among authors seems to be that reading about protagonists who face similar problems may help children cope with their own anxieties. Whether one believes that these novels can be therapeutic or not, there does seem to be a consensus that at least the concerns the New Realism addresses are not difficult for the child to imagine. The child of the 1960s, 1970s, and 1980s, who becomes street-wise at an early age, sees through the unrealistic, the sentimental, and the merely cute. For example, many books of the first half of the century presented a romantic view of the orphaned condition that gave little consideration to the probable reality of the orphaned or abandoned child's state. Now there are books about foster homes that show the bitterness of feeling rejected as well as the fear sometimes associated with foster homes.

Problem Novels

A subcategory of the New Realistic genre is the problem novel, which concentrates on a narrow examination of a specific problem or affliction. The great flaw of the problem novel is that it tends to be strictly content-oriented; themes and characters are not fully developed; there is little effort to go beyond the specific problem and see it in the larger context of the characters' total lives and the culture's total ambience. The adult, if not the enemy or creator of the problem, is never strong enough or smart enough to be of any help. The child has to solve his or her own problem if there is to be a solution. Because the majority of the problem novels pay little attention to character or thematic development, they lack universality.

The problem novel probably originated in the nineteenth century with the Sunday school tract. Books like *Bessie Bleak and the Lost Purse* and *Little Maggie's Trials and Triumphs* were popular with both parents and children; such literature often dealt with problems that were fairly specific, but always there was a religious and moral solution. Purity and piety solved everything. In the thirties and forties authors such as Florence Crannell Means wrote books about racial and social prejudices. The problem novel as we know it today has broadened in content since the late sixties and early seventies because of the relaxation of previous limitations on books for the young and also because of the increased emphasis on open discussion of social problems with children. The problem novels tend to be very popular. Children do not seem bothered by flimsy characterization or formulaic plot. Instead, they often feel that the authors of today are "right on target."

Although most problem novels are not produced by mainstream

children's novelists, occasionally an author with some claim to distinction in the broader area of the realistic novel writes a problem novel (for example, M. E. Kerr's *Little Little,* about the trials of two young people suffering from dwarfism). Many problem novelists write one book and are not heard from again; a few, like Robin Brancato, are steady and reliable writers of readable problem novels.

Problem novels have become trendy and predictable: the sixties problem novel saw children suffering anxieties about the Vietnam War, gang wars, racism, and pressure to have sex; the seventies novels featured alcoholism, drug use, and various sexual experiences; in the eighties child abuse, kidnapping, and teenage abortion have emerged as issues. Once the problems have become "old," they lose interest for both children and authors. The popularity of these novels may lie in the fact that they focus on whatever is current; instead of vanishing as a subgenre, the problem novel moves forward and focuses on the latest social concern.

Central to most of the recent problem novels is a sense of the failure of adults to help children; in fact, in many of the novels the children's problems are caused by adults. This disjunction between child and adult is sometimes manifested by the child's flight from the adult world. For example, in *Street Smarts* (1981) by Bruce Reeves, twelve-year-old Teresa Carlotta (T. C.) takes Caper—a terribly abused neighbor boy—and runs away because no adult will "get involved" with Caper's situation. Even though T. C.'s family lives in a commune and supposedly rejects the established values of society in favor of a more loving and open self-determined community, none of them consider Caper's suffering their business. Nor do they see that what is community to them is invasion of privacy to T. C., who longs for a bit of personal space, something she would not have to share with everyone. Were T. C. a more attractive character, our sympathy for her would make *Street Smarts* a stinging indictment not merely of adult selfishness but also of the failed idealism of the dropouts of the sixties. However, the characters lack substance, so the issues cannot move the reader strongly.

In David Roth's *A World for Joey Carr* (1981), fourteen-year-old Joey leaves home because his father won't let him keep Butch, a little stray dog who is all Joey has to love since his mother's death. Joey takes Butch and runs away to his grandparents' house; on the way, Butch dies protecting Joey from a pack of wild dogs. Joey's father comes to take him home, and they resolve their differences when the father realizes how lucky he is to have Joey back. *A World for Joey Carr* has closure, unlike *Street Smarts,* in which the reader does not know what will happen to T. C. or Caper. However, the conclusion is unsatisfactory because it takes a near-tragedy to bring it about; the reader is left to assume that love can only be attained after a catastrophe.

The New Realistic portrait of a child surviving on his or her own in society is very different from that of the Horatio Alger stories. In addition to hunger and cold, which Alger characters know, the modern child must fear human predators. Some books even present children to whom the world has been so harsh that they know their only safety lies in finding a place to be totally alone.

In Felice Holman's *Slake's Limbo* (1974), Slake's solution to the threats with which his life is filled is to make a room for himself in the wall of a subway tunnel. He prefers this solitary existence to a life of constant fear and insecurity. It is a remedy for his condition and in the book is presented as the best, perhaps the only one. Slake's ingenious maneuvers to obtain food and money have all the fascination of the survivalist methods of *Swiss Family Robinson.* Eventually he gets very sick, stumbles out onto the track, and is found by the driver of a subway train. In the hospital, he realizes that his subway hideaway is now gone. But he is not discouraged: thoughtfully, he contemplates the city's roofs. His upward gaze seems heroic, that of a young Alexander seeking new worlds. We feel a certain elation: Slake will be free again. But was he ever free? Has he in fact, for all his ingenuity, started down the long, homeless road that leads to sleeping on gratings at forty-five, dying under an overpass at sixty?

It is easy to romanticize the hard-core street life, but not necessarily realistic. Nonetheless, Slake is the modern Alger hero. Like Alger's characters, he takes advantage of every opportunity to achieve his goal; but his goal is not riches, only solitude and survival. Like an Alger boy, he sells newspapers, but his are secondhand, the discarded papers left by travelers on the platform or cars. His is not a "rags-to-riches" story (more like "rags-to-shreds"), but he has precisely the kind of initiative, the almost monomaniacal drive, that pushes Alger's heroes to riches and will push Slake into a series of limbos.

Other problem novels illustrate the ways in which children internalize parental and societal pressures. In Deborah Hautzig's *Second Star to the Right* (1981), Leslie Hiller is starving herself to death, apparently striving for a perfect body. *Anorexia nervosa* is a current

Silas Snobden's Office Boy, Horatio Alger, Jr.,

Queenie Peavy, Robert Burch, illustrated by Jerry Lazare

problem among teenagers, especially girls; our culture stresses the beauty of thinness. Anorexia is also a way for a child to punish the parents she does not dare to hate openly. Leslie's mother is, to the outside's eye, a very loving mother, but her love is far from unde-manding. Leslie struggles with anorexia as she struggles with the smothering love of her mother. Leslie's battle could be the subject of a poignant book for teenagers if the characters were developed. A love-hate relationship between mother and daughter, if developed, would be believable and thought-provoking for both child and adult. Instead, because of weak characterization, Leslie appears to be a spoiled and selfish child.

Children confused, disappointed, or otherwise alienated by their parents are also protagonists of the problem novel. In *Taking Terri Mueller* (1981) by Norman Fox Mazer, Terri lives with her father and has been told that her mother is dead. She eventually learns that her father kidnapped her at such an early age that she has no memories of her mother. At the age of thirteen she is reunited with her mother but does not fit in with her mother's new family. She eventually leaves and goes back to her father, where she feels secure and comfortable. This conclusion may be true to life, but it leaves the ethics of the father's action unresolved, and the issue of how Terri and he will reestablish their relationship of trust is left open. Many children today are kidnapped by one of their parents following a divorce, so it is not surprising to see this issue the subject of a modern problem novel.

Another book centered on the child's confusion about his or her relationship with a parent is *Queenie Peavy* (1966) by Robert Burch. Queenie cannot wait for her father to get home from prison, because then he can help her solve all of her problems. When her father finally does come home, Queenie is surprised and hurt that he neither can nor wants to help her. This theme is attractive to preadolescents and adolescents because it illuminates a reality in their lives, the fact that parents can be hard to understand and do not themselves always try to understand their children's needs.

Changes in the child's family structure and the disruptions they cause have also become popular subjects for the New Realistic writers. Norma Klein's protagonists in both *Confessions of an Only Child* (1974) and *Mom, the Wolf Man, and Me* (1972) need answers to the same question: will there still be time for anyone to care about me? One protagonist has to accept the arrival of a new baby, while the other has to learn how to face her mother's new marriage. Both books resolve the insecurities of the child to the point where the child is looking forward to the new arrival.

Divorce is even more disruptive, especially when a prospective or actual remarriage ends the child's hope that the parents might get back together again. In John Neufeld's *Sunday Father* (1976) Tessa turns against her father and refuses to be civil to his fiancée, Zandra, and her daughter, Fran. Tessa does not want her father to get married; if he would just live with Zandra, he might still come home at some point. Such novels illustrate the desire of the child for stability and security within the family. Whether they are therapeutic reading for children in similar circumstances (the books seem to be so intended) cannot be said for certain. It may be that they at least alleviate the child's fear of being the only person to have a particular problem.

A major concern of society today is child abuse; this concern is mirrored in the large number of children's books about the abused child, among them Kin Platt's *The Boy Who Could Make Himself Disappear* (1968), Irene Hunt's *The Lottery Rose* (1976), Willo Davis Roberts's *Don't Hurt Laurie* (1977), and Joanna Lee and T. S. Cook's *Mary Jane Harper Cried Last Night* (1978). In *Mary Jane Harper Cried Last Night,* the authorities take too long to prove that Rowena is abusing Mary Jane; Rowena's wealthy parents hinder the investigation, and before the case ever gets attention, Rowena smothers Mary Jane with a pillow. In the other three novels, the child is taken away from the parent in time to save his or her life, but not before the child has been permanently scarred. The somber tone of these books reflects the seriousness of the problem.

Novels set in the foster home deal with the same theme of the unprotected and vulnerable child. In Marion D. Bauer's *Foster Child* (1977), the foster parent is a frightening figure. This is one of the few books that deal with sexual abuse, but it evades the full implications of the abusive situation. Renny is frightened, angry, and defenseless when her foster parent, Mr. Beck, fondles her. She and another foster child, Karen, run away and return to Karen's real parents, where they find a loving home. But the social worker wants them to go back to Mr. Beck, even though he has been reported before, because Karen's mother has a history of mental illness. This picture of the bureaucratic mind may be accurate, but the illogic of the standards for acceptable foster homes boggles the mind. Through her own determination and drive, Renny finds another foster home that the social worker reluctantly considers acceptable; but no one does anything about Mr. Beck, who, the reader assumes, is left to molest his other foster children in peace.

Alcoholism is a social disease that has invaded all classes in our society and all age groups. A child cannot be protected from the effects of a parent's alcoholism any more than a parent can be protected from the effects of a child's alcoholism. The seventies and eighties have seen alcoholism become the number one sickness among teenagers. It is not surprising that it is a very popular subject for the problem novels. Most modern writers who focus on alcoholism do not try to soften its impact. Both the emotional and the psychological problems associated with alcoholism are dealt with frankly and realistically.

The teenaged Niki in *High and Outside* (1980) by Linnea Due is an alcoholic; she has shared the cocktail hour and dinner wine with her parents since she was fourteen years old. Now, at seventeen, she is hiding fifths of gin in her closet to get her through the night. She tries to get support from her parents, but they will not accept what she knows to be true because it is too painful: "You've been on the honor roll since junior high. You're a star athlete. And you have lots of good friends. How could you possibly imagine you're an alcoholic?"[1] Niki hits rock bottom, tries to kill herself, and then gets help. In Isabelle Holland's *Now Is Not Too Late* (1980) a daughter is reunited with her alcoholic mother, who she thought was dead. Many terrible memories that had been repressed surface. In *A Stranger in the Family* (1980) by Judie Wolkoff, Marcie tries to endure both her father's drunken rages and her friends' merciless taunts about his alcoholism. In *The Boy Who Drank Too Much* (1979) by Shep Greene, Buff Saunders drinks beer, wine, spirits, anything he can get his hands on to try to forget that he hates his drunken father for killing his mother in a car accident and for beating him up constantly. All of these novels end realistically in implying that there is a long road ahead for the alcoholic and the family.

The hackneyed subject of young love has become both in reality and in the realistic teenage novel the startling subject of young sex. The fact that teenagers have sexual desires and needs is addressed openly and freely in a number of books. This new atmosphere of frankness is in many ways refreshing. However, Judy Blume's *Forever* (1977) illustrates that a wealth of explicit sexual detail does not make a novel but a manual. There is no romance to Katherine and Michael's "relationship." The first time they are prepared to make love, Kath-

erine gets her period; later, when Michael's parents go out for an
evening, Katherine and he meet again for the long-awaited joy. They
have three glorious hours together, which Katherine spends worrying
about where and how to do it. Not on the bed, because she might
bleed; the floor is too hard. The tone does not seem to be comic,
which is a pity; conscious humor is the only thing that might save
the scene. They finally settle for a towel folded over on the floor;
now they are ready, but Katherine remembers that one of them
should do something to prevent pregnancy, so Michael gets a "rub-
ber" he happens to have in his wallet. Again they are ready, but
Michael ejaculates too soon. He explains that it was probably because
of all the talking. After many thwarted attempts, they finally manage
to have sex. Blume describes the act itself in considerable detail. This
reduction of the physical expression of love to mere mechanics may
be a realistic description of the modern teenager's approach to sex;
but one is reluctant to assume that an entire generation has reduced
humanity's best emotion to a four-letter obscenity. However, this
book is important, if only because after *Forever* there are few taboos
left to be violated in the realistic teenage novel.

One of the few "forbidden subjects" still treated very cautiously
even after *Forever* is homosexuality. Few teenage novels deal with it
at all; fewer still deal with it well. In the earlier part of the twentieth
century, gay people do not figure in any obvious way in most children's novels at all. Boys are discouraged from being "sissies" or
"muffs," and girls are discouraged from being "tomboys" (at least
beyond a very strict age limit); these terms are obviously slurs attached
to any departure from the norms of sex-role behavior. But whatever
buried fears society may be concealing beneath its alarm at these
deviations in behavior, such behavior is not, in the early books, explicitly linked to homosexuality (quite rightly, as it happens—depar-
tures from society's notions of correct sex-role behavior are not
indices of sexual choice). Only in stories of "passionate friendships"
between members of the same sex, as in some of the British "school
stories," does one find relationships that emotionally, if not physically,
can be called homosexual. No doubt the authors of such works would
be astounded, perhaps even horrified, to find that they could be
taken so. A good example is H. A. Vachell's *The Hill* (1905), the story
of a David-Jonathan friendship between two schoolboys that only
ends when, in manhood, one is killed in the Boer War.

In recent years, the realistic teenage novel has at least acknowledged that there is such a thing as homosexuality. In John Donovan's *I'll Get There. It Better Be Worth the Trip* (1969), the narrator, Davy Ross, and his friend Doug Altschuler have some sexual feelings for each other; Donovan shows them kissing.

> I guess I kiss Altschuler and he kisses me. . . . It just happens.
> And when it stops we sit up and turn away from each other.

Davy reassures himself that he and Altschuler are too tough to be "queers." When Altschuler spends the night with him, they evidently go further, but the only hint of this is in Davy's account of the morning after.

> . . . but I have a new way of looking at Altschuler because of what we did together last night. Don't get me wrong. I'm not ashamed. There was nothing wrong about it, I keep telling myself.[2]

By the end of the book, Davy and Altschuler have decided they should make out with some girls and forget about "the other." They have also decided they "can respect each other." Their one night together may have been just ordinary sexual experimentation; indeed, there is little evidence to the contrary except Davy's too fierce insistence that they're not "queer." Compared to the heterosexual action in some of the new realistic novels, the action of Donovan's novel is hardly sexual at all.

Isabelle Holland's *The Man Without a Face* (1972) recounts the development of friendship and affection between a teenage boy and the middle-aged former teacher who tutors him for his entrance examination into a private school. The man, Justin, is gay, but the reader does not learn this as a certainty until quite late in the book, and Justin never makes any attempt to seduce the boy, Charles. Charles, on the other hand, is a lonely boy, unhappy at home with his often-married mother and two stepsisters, the oldest of whom is cruel and difficult to the point of psychosis. His father died long ago, so Charles doesn't really remember him, but because his father was a heroic pilot during World War II, Charles has turned him into an ideal father and a great man in his mind. Justin becomes a focus for all the boy's pent-up love and admiration; in fact, although Justin behaves impeccably, Charles behaves somewhat seductively toward him, not altogether unconsciously. When Charles finds out about his hero-father's death from alcoholism, he is shattered. He flees to Justin, and while Justin is holding him and comforting him, Charles has an ejaculation. The next morning Justin tries to ressure Charles that what happened was a normal reaction to strain and shock. But Charles is frightened and therefore cruel. He says enough to indicate scorn and contempt for Justin. After his new stepfather comes to collect him, he never sees Justin again. Justin dies of a heart attack a few months later, leaving his house and books to Charles.

Holland is a good storyteller, and her characters have depth. Justin, in particular, with his scarred face, his stern pedagogy, his affection for stray and injured animals, and his devout Catholicism, is a complex and attractive character. But the conclusion of this story is disturbing because it seems part of a pattern in novels in which a male admits being gay. In Sandra Scoppettone's *Trying Hard to Hear You* (1974) one of the male lovers dies in an auto accident. In Aidan Chambers's *Dance on My Grave* (1982) one of the male lovers has died in a motorcycle accident. It would appear that characters like Davy and Altschuler in *I'll Get There. It Better Be Worth the Trip,* who date girls and don't really think they're gay, can live, if not happily after homosexual contact. But when a male is avowedly homosexual, the conclusion of the book is almost An Awful Warning: be a gay male and die. There may be exceptions, but certainly this odd phenomenon is the rule.

Lesbian relationships, on the other hand, are permitted happy endings, as in Nancy Garden's *Annie on My Mind* (1982) or Scoppettone's *Happy Endings Are All Alike* (1978). Although Liza in *Annie on My Mind* has to face a trustees' hearing at her school over her relationship with Annie, and Jaret in *Happy Endings* is brutally beaten and raped by a boy who thinks he can blackmail her with his knowledge of her affair with Peggy, at the end of both books, the lovers are facing the future together.

Of the few teenage novels depicting gay inclinations, those about males are both discreet about sexual contact and discouraging about long-term gay companionship. The lesbian novels are both more open and more optimistic. The realism of these novels is somewhat deadened by formulas: gay sexual contact will produce fear and withdrawal in a character; one partner will fear exposure; one set of parents (or one parent) will be understanding and supportive, the other won't. These and other formulaic situations are very predict-

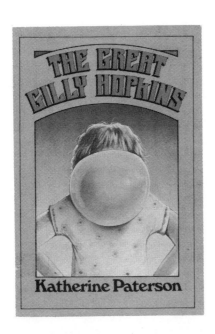

The Great Gilly Hopkins, Katherine Paterson, cover by Fred Marcellino
The Boy Who Drank Too Much, Shep Greene, cover by Gloria Singer

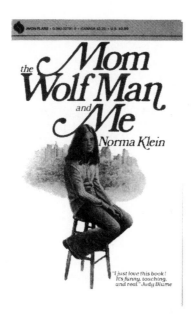

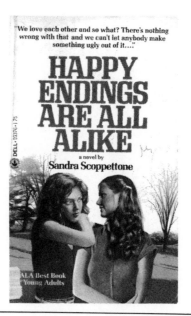

Mom, the Wolf Man, and Me, Norma Klein,
Happy Endings Are All Alike, Sandra Scoppettone

able in the books. Only Holland's and Chambers's novels rise above the formulas by virtue of superior characterization.

By far the most common topic of the New Realistic problem novel is death. The death of a loved one is usually shown as a turning point in the life of the protagonist, and, realistically, the deaths are indiscriminate: there are deaths of grandparents, fathers, mothers, brothers, sisters, and friends. Death comes in the form of sickness, accident, and even murder. Then there are novels about suicide, in which some characters actually succeed, some try but fail, and some simply contemplate it throughout the book.

Vicky Austin has a difficult time dealing with the fact that her beloved grandfather is dying in the third book of the Austin family series by Madeline L'Engle, *A Ring of Endless Light* (1980). A number of novels deal with the death of a parent. In *Grover* (1970) by Vera and Bill Cleaver, Grover has to deal with the fact that his mother shot herself because she could not stand the pain and fear of cancer. Grover's father feels that his wife had a responsibility to endure. Grover not only has to face life without his mother, he has to cope with his father's feelings and try to understand what happened. In *I'll Live* (1982) by Stephen Manes, Dylan accepts the fact that his father is dying of cancer, but he cannot accept his father's decision to commit suicide. Irene Hunt's *William* (1977) shows William and his sisters, suddenly orphaned by the death of their mother, moving in with Sarah, an unwed mother who is willing to assume responsibility for the family.

Certain of the problem novels focus only on the guilt felt by the protagonist who is left behind. In *River Runaways* (1981) by David Roth, two teenage boys from unstable homes run away; one drowns and the other is left to wonder why. In *Facing Up* (1984) by Robin Brancto, Jep has to try to live with the knowledge that he was driving the car in the accident that killed his friend Dave.

The death of a loved one is always extremely difficult, but especially when the death is lingering and the loved one is a child. In Mary Pope Osborne's *Run, Run, As Fast As You Can* (1982), Hallie finds herself an outsider when her family moves to Virginia. She is forced to play with her little brother Mickey; their relationship grows until Mickey is hospitalized with stomach pains. Hallie is unaware how sick Mickey is until the night he dies. Once she understands she accepts it quickly. "I felt very peaceful. I knew Mickey was okay somewhere without me. Now I just had to be okay without him."[3] The speed with which Hallie arrives at this calm and sensible adjustment to death is surely psychologically and emotionally unrealistic. Osborne's novel illustrates the too easy coping that often occurs in the problem novel. A different, realistic look at a child's confusion about death is offered in Katherine Paterson's *Bridge to Terabithia,* discussed below.

Murder seems a surprising subject for a children's book, but in modern realism, perhaps, its appearance was inevitable. There is, of course, a murder in Ruth Sawyer's *Roller Skates* (1936), but it is an incident, not central to the plot. In *The Truth Trap* (1980) by Frances Miller, nine-year-old Katie McKendrick is found murdered in the old Palace Theater, an abandoned moviehouse. Her fifteen-year-old brother, Matt, is accused of the murder. Lieutenant Ryder, disgusted by the crime, is out for vengeance and has no mercy on Matt; he takes Matt down to the morgue and forces him to look at Katie.

> Matt looked. At the small naked body, cut and badly bruised. At the battered head, blond hair damp across the forehead, freckles running up and over the small straight nose, dark lashes on chalky skin.[4]

The Truth Trap is both sensational and sentimental. Katie's murder is grim enough, simply as the murder of a child. But this description of the naked corpse of a child the reader has known for only sixteen pages is deliberate emotional manipulation. To evoke even deeper emotion, the author adds in the first fifteen pages that Matt and Katie's parents died in an automobile accident three weeks earlier, that Katie is completely deaf, that a home could be found for Matt but that Katie would have been sent to the state school for the deaf and mute, and that Katie carries a stuffed Snoopy Dog. In order to be together Katie and Matt ran away. The story does not get better. Matt has been lying about his age so that people will not get suspicious about the two of them traveling alone, and also so he can find work. Because he is thought to be eighteen, he is put in jail rather than in a juvenile facility and is beaten up and raped. The murder of a child is shocking in itself and does not need any device other than straightforwardness in order to have an impact. Lois Lowry demonstrates that simplicity is much better than overelaboration in these matters, as is seen later in the discussion of *Autumn Street.*

Another novel that uses murder as a sensational plot device is *When No One Was Looking* (1980) by Rosemary Wells. The motive for murder here is quite unbelievable. Kathy is a tennis star pressured by her overbearing mother to be the champion. To save Kathy from her mother's rage if Kathy should lose, her friend Julia kills her leading opponent. This would be a realistic plot only if Julia were depicted as psychopathic, psychotic, or otherwise deranged, since there are many much more sensible and moral solutions to Kathy's problem. But Julia is depicted as a fairly normal teenager (apart from the murder, of course).

Suicide among teenagers is on the rise, and therefore it is not surprising that a large number of realistic teenage novels show the protagonists contemplating suicide at a time of conflict, or that death by suicide has become a popular topic in the teenage novel. Susan Beth Pfeffer's *About David* (1980) and Gail Radley's *The World Turned Inside Out* (1982) both focus on the effect a suicide has on the people left behind. Gloria D. Miklowitz's *Close to the Edge* (1983) and Sue Ellen Bridgers's *Notes for Another Life* (1981) both deal with an attempted suicide and the rebuilding of a life.

In *About David*, Lynn attempts to understand why her best friend, David, shot his parents and then himself. In *The World Turned Inside Out,* Jeremy takes a job at the mental hospital where his brother Tyler had been a patient because he wants to understand why Tyler drowned himself. Both Lynn and Jeremy need to know if they could have prevented the suicides; did either miss a clue, a signal, a plea for help? All of these questions are asked in both books but only answered in *About David.* David was eighteen and had known since early childhood that he was adopted by his critical, perfectionist parents, Bob and Lorraine. His suicide note reads, "Forgive me, but this is the only way to prevent further tragedy. I take full responsibility for the death of both my parents and myself." Lynn finds David's journals; his last entry was "Lorraine is pregnant." Perhaps David could not face the possibility of a "real" baby pushing him further away, or he may have wanted to save the baby from the grief he had had with Bob and Lorraine as parents. David's turmoil was well hidden. No one suspected how far he had moved away from sanity, and Lynn could not have foreseen his actions. In *The World Turned Inside Out,* Jeremy struggles with his emotions throughout the novel, only to come to the not very illuminating conclusion "Tyler's mind wasn't right."

In *Notes for Another Life,* sixteen-year-old Kevin attempts suicide because he is scared that he might have inherited his father's mental instability. He takes an overdose of pills because "it seemed like the best thing to do." When Kevin comes home from the hospital, he is ashamed and embarrassed about what he tried to do. The doctor tells the family that his body is healing quickly but his spirit will take time. The whole family wants to help, but Kevin begins to feel watched; everybody wants to know where he is going and what he is doing. After his initial anger, Kevin feels secure in the knowledge that his family is trying to protect him, even from himself. This novel is written in beautifully understated prose. Its tone is quiet and sad. The strong, matriarchal grandmother provides the stable setting in which Kevin can come back into contact with the world.

Jenny Hartley of *Close to the Edge* often feels that something is missing from her life and thinks about suicide, yet it is her friend Cindy who attempts suicide. Jenny feels so close to giving up herself that she starts reaching out to others in an attempt to understand why she wakes each morning feeling lost and scared, and what the connection is between what she feels and what Cindy did. Jenny starts working with "the Sunshine Seniors," a group of senior citizens who are very outspoken; it is from these survivors that she learns about faith, love, and the joys of living. Jenny tries to persuade Cindy to come and meet these people, but Cindy refuses. Cindy is making up all the schoolwork she has missed; she has given herself a deadline and finally seems to be at peace with herself. Cindy gives Jenny a necklace that Jenny has always admired. The next night she kills herself. Jenny is devastated and realizes that Cindy's behavior was symptomatic of suicide. Her new friends, the senior citizens, help her realize that living takes humor, ingenuity, and guts. They have never given up, in spite of all their aches and pains, so why should she? Although the philosophy is a bit facile, the depiction of a depressed teenager comforted by feisty old people is pleasing.

There are many other books about teenage suicide: *Wait Until Tomorrow* (1981) by Harriet May Savitz, the story of a troubled teenager looking for a reason to live; *The Girl Who Wanted Out* (1981) by Bianca Bradbury, the story of a girl who does not want to face living after the car accident that crippled her and killed her boyfriend; and *Switching Tracks* (1982) by Dean Hughes, in which a teenager must live with the guilt of his father's suicide.

The New Realism is by nature topical: it often deals with problems of only current and temporary interest. For instance, the novels of S. E. Hinton about gang warfare, *The Outsiders* (1967) and *Rumble*

Homecoming, Cynthia Voigt, cover art by Ted Lewin

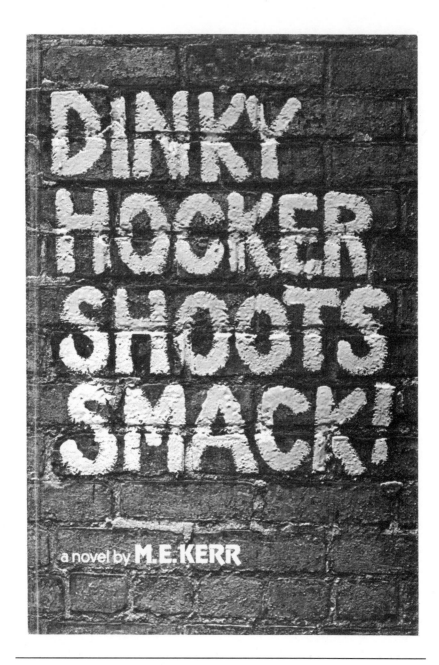

Dinky Hocker Shoots Smack!, M. E. Kerr, cover art by Jay J. Smith

Fish (1975), seem passé now, although there are still gangs and they still fight, mostly (if the newspapers are to be believed) about drug sales territories. The mid-sixties and seventies adolescent novels in which girls want to have sex but are frightened and must be talked into it are badly dated. Problem novels fade from the scene as the problems they deal with vanish or are displaced by other social concerns. Most such books are not well written, and their formulaic formats provide little of original worth to be preserved by the reading public. The characters can be very one-dimensional ("Troubled Teenager," "Alcoholic Mother," "Pregnant Girl," "Independent Liberated Girl," and so forth), and the style of the writing flat and uninteresting, full of clichés. Very few of these books transcend the formulas for their particular topics.

Beyond the Problem Novel

Despite the limitations of the problem novel, the more honest, less sentimental approach to subjects such as sex is probably a good thing. When all is said and done, in the hands of the better writers, like M. E. Kerr, Paul Zindel, Robert Cormier, Katherine Paterson, Betsy Byars, Cynthia Voigt, Lois Lowry, the English authors Jill Paton Walsh and John Rowe Townsend, or the Australian author Ivan Southall, the New Realism becomes a genre that crackles with energy and tension. Undidactic, deeply understanding, highly original, these writers and their ilk have made unique contributions to literature for the older child.

New Realism not only does not ask children to believe in a perfect world, it highlights the imperfections. The protagonist is commonly in conflict with and alienated from the adult world. The alienation is faced but not always resolved, as is illustrated by Robert Cormier's *The Chocolate War* (1974). Jerry learns that when he does not conform to adult expectations, he may have to endure the anger of an adult. In *The Chocolate War*, the adult is Brother Leon, the headmaster of Jerry's school, who has pushed Jerry unmercifully to break his resistance to selling chocolates. The book does not end on a happy note: Jerry is put into an ambulance after a thorough beating by a member of the school gang who has acted with Brother Leon's approval. Whether Jerry was right to cling to his position (as conventional realistic novels of previous decades assert) and thereby become a better, braver human being is not stated; certainly the suffering Jerry doesn't think it was worth it. This conclusion is typical of the genre, which tends to be open-ended, like the real world, where there are not happy endings to all problems and life just goes on. Commonly, no full closure is achieved. The protagonist is left at a point in his or her own life where other facets of the same problem will need facing or new problems can be seen creeping in.

Much of early children's literature focused on middle-to-upper-class happy families in rural settings. New Realism, like the modern populace, has moved away from the rural setting into the urban and suburban environment. Changes in family structure are also shown: the New Realistic family usually consists of children with divorced parents, single parents, or about-to-be-divorced or dying parents. Some even show the children surviving on their own, as in Bruce Reeves's *Street Smarts* and David Roth's *A World for Joey Carr.*

Cynthia Voigt also depicts a family of children surviving on their own, in *Homecoming* (1981). Dicey leads her brothers and sister the length of the Connecticut coastline, a trip that takes many days, in order to reach Great-Aunt Cilla. The children have been abandoned in a Connecticut shopping center by their mother, and thirteen-year-old Dicey wants to keep them together. When they make it to Great-Aunt Cilla's house, they find that she has died. Cousin Eunice, who is living in the house, tries to keep them, but the arrangement does not work and the children may have to be separated. Dicey raises money and takes to the road again in an attempt to reach their grandmother in Maryland, whom they have never met. The sequel, *Dicey's Song* (1983), develops the growing relationship between the Tillerman children and their eccentric grandmother. *Homecoming* was Cynthia Voigt's first novel, but there is nothing amateurish about this well-written, artfully constructed book.

In *A Solitary Blue* (1984), Voigt develops the story of Jeff Greene, whom we first met in *Dicey's Song* as an unhappy, quiet teenager. *A Solitary Blue* is Jeff's story. Whereas we first saw Jeff through Dicey's eyes, we now see Dicey through Jeff's eyes. Jeff was also abandoned by his mother as a child; unlike the Tillerman children, he is an only child and has a father. Jeff wants his mother, or at least he wants the mother that he has created out of memory and longing. In many ways Jeff is worse off than Dicey; her parents are now dead, but she has younger brothers and a sister who need her, and a grandmother who, while strange, is not unlovable. Jeff has no one; his father has withdrawn from everyone. He has built a mental wall for protection, and there is no room for Jeff behind that wall. Jeff feels that he had better be good or his father will leave too. Jeff's mother reenters his life, years after she left him, and ultimately the meeting is worse than Jeff could ever have imagined. The first summer Jeff spends with his mother, her charm and beauty are everything he remembered. The following summer she has no time for him. The novelty of being worshipped by her son has worn off for this shallow, materialistic woman. She betrays Jeff's trust and affection. Jeff has to live through the desertion all over again. But this time his father is strong enough to be his friend. All three of the Voigt books discussed are realistic and show moving journeys to mature relationships among families and between child and adult, which Reeves's and Roth's novels ignore.

The situation of the child at odds with a parent, which we saw in Deborah Hautzig's *Second Star to the Right,* is handled very differently when both parent and child are fully developed characters. In M. E. Kerr's *Dinky Hocker Shoots Smack!* (1972), Dinky's mother is so involved in the rehabilitation of drug addicts that she has no time for overweight Dinky. Mrs. Hocker, like Dickens's Mrs. Jellaby, finds strangers' problems more interesting than those of her family. On the night of the banquet honoring Mrs. Hocker for all her community work, Dinky writes "Dinky Hocker Shoots Smack" in bright Day-Glo paint on the sidewalks, the sides of the buildings, and car doors so that the whole community will be sure to see it. Not surprisingly, Mrs. Hocker realizes that Dinky needs her attention, and Mr. and Mrs. Hocker take Dinky to Europe to help her try and lose weight. In *The Cartoonist* (1978) by Betsy Byars, Alfie locks himself in his attic bedroom and refuses to come down because he can't bear the thought of his brother Bubba and Bubba's wife taking over his only sanctuary as their room. Bubba is Alfie's mother's favorite child, for whom she has neglected Alfie and his sister. Alfie gets to keep his room, but not because his mother cares about him; Bubba and wife move in with her parents. Alfie realizes that he did not really win; winning would mean persuading his mother to change.

Dinky's and Alfie's mothers are very real characters. The reader sees firsthand their insensitivity to and neglect of their children; therefore, the actions of Dinky and Alfie are understandable, and welcome. Dinky's defacing of public property is not the act of a malicious, spoiled teenager, nor is Alfie's locking himself in his bedroom the act of a selfish child. Both children are crying out for help and attention. Dinky's mother hears the cry, but Alfie's mother turns a deaf ear.

Katherine Paterson and Betsy Byars clearly show the bitterness a child can feel in a foster home. Whereas the narrow interest of Bauer's *Foster Child* lay in the sexual advances of Mr. Beck, Byars's *The Pinballs* (1977) and Paterson's *The Great Gilly Hopkins* (1978) go beyond a particular problem to broad conceptions of the nature of trust and love. In *The Pinballs*, Carlie has to be in a foster home because she cannot get along with her new stepfather. Gilly Hopkins is in a foster home because no one knows where her mother is. Gilly clings to the hope that her mother will come and find her, whereas Carlie has given up on the adult world. Both girls find themselves when they try to help another child in the foster home. Carlie nicknames her group "the pinballs" because she believes they are as powerless as pinballs; they get pushed around all the time. But in the conclusion to the novel, Carlie tells Thomas J that she was wrong.

> Pinballs can't help what happens to them and you and me can. See, when I first came here, all I thought about was running away, only I never did it. I know that doesn't sound like much, but it was me deciding something about my life. . . . And as long as we are trying, Thomas J, we are not pinballs.[5]

Paterson ends *The Great Gilly Hopkins* on a more somber note. Gilly, through the failure of her own plot to make her mother come for her, has to leave Mrs. Trotter, whom she has learned to love, and go to live with her grandmother. When Gilly calls Mrs. Trotter on the phone, she says,

> "Trotter, it's all wrong. Nothing turned out the way it's supposed to."
> "How you mean supposed to? Life ain't supposed to be nothing, 'cept maybe tough. . . . all that stuff about happy endings is lies. The only ending in this world is death. . . . you just fool yourself if you expect good things all the time."
> "If life is so bad, how come you're so happy?"
> "Did I say bad? I said it was tough. Nothing to make you happy like doing good on a tough job, now is there?"[6]

Gilly cries as she says goodbye to Mrs. Trotter, and for the first time says the words "I love you." Carlie and Gilly have both learned that loving someone makes life a little easier; they always felt the need to be loved but never realized they themselves needed to return love. Unlike *Foster Child*, where Renny is more confused, frightened, and bitter as the books ends, Carlie and Gilly have started on the long, hard road toward a life of understanding.

Paul Zindel shows the effects of a parent's alcoholism on a teenager in *Pardon Me, You're Stepping on My Eyeball* (1976). Marsh's favorite time of day is about 7:00 p.m., when his mother usually passes out. Marsh can then watch whatever he wants on television while his mother lies on the floor by the piano. If she doesn't pass out, Marsh is in for verbal abuse. "You're a rotting, disgusting, revolting little son! And if you ask me, I should have had an abortion. That's what I think everytime I look at you."[7] Marsh clings to the letters he has received from his father, who will be coming to get him one day. It is not until Marsh himself faces the bitter truth that the reader realizes Marsh's father is already dead. He was also an alcoholic, and Marsh was with him the day he staggered out of the bar and into the street in front of an oncoming bus. Marsh saw his father killed but repressed the memory of it; once he is forced to look at the truth he starts to accept it. Zindel leaves the reader knowing that Marsh has a long road yet to travel before he reaches the end, which seems to hold some happiness.

Paul Zindel in *My Darling, My Hamburger* (1969) deals forthrightly with the subject of teenage sex. Sean and Liz are close to having sex, but Liz is scared. Sean is getting frustrated: "Nature arranged it so that we have the equipment. And the need. So we'd better find a way, or we're going to do something as bad as suffocating. If you ask me, that's why there're so many sickies in the world. Everybody gets suffocated as teenagers."[8] Although Zindel's characters talk with teenage frankness about sex, Zindel uses an adult's discretion in the description of sexual activity, unlike Judy Blume in *Forever*. However, his book is an illustration of how rapidly changing social attitudes can date a book. Sean finally succeeds in getting Liz to have sex, but neither of them is prepared, and Liz gets pregnant. In *It's Not What You Expect* (1973) by Norma Klein, written four years later, Ralph and Sara Lee find themselves in the same predicament as Sean and Liz. Both girls have abortions. Liz wants only to die: the guilt and the pain are too much to handle. Liz is never seen again in the book.

Sara Lee has her abortion, then goes home and eats dinner. Shortly after, she goes off to college with Ralph; the abortion never mattered, either emotionally or physically. However, is Zindel in fact less realistic than Klein here? While abortions are treated much more casually with each passing year, there is still a twinge of guilt, sorrow, remorse, or confusion, at the very least about the initial decision.[9]

In the following three novels, the depiction of death and the emotional adjustments of the grieving survivors is more realistic and complete than in the novels that treat death as a one-dimensional problem. The sorrow caused by a death is not the only emotion that needs time to heal. Often a death evokes feelings of confusion, anxiety, and guilt. The guilt may be unwarranted, but sometimes, as the New Realistic novel shows, a thoughtless action has large effects, and one must bear the guilt of having caused a death.

Paul Zindel's *The Pigman* (1968) is written as "a memorial epic" to Angelo Pignate by John Conlan and Lorraine Jenson. The two teenagers formed an unexpected friendship with old Mr. Pignate, whom they called the Pigman. Their relationship was built on trust; for the first time John and Lorraine trusted an adult and were trusted in return, until they betrayed that trust. As a result, Mr. Pignate died, and the two teens were left to deal with the harsh reality that they could not escape the responsibility for their actions.

In Katherine Paterson's *Bridge to Terabithia* (1977), Jess and Leslie create the secret world of Terabithia, where they are King and Queen; in order to reach their secret world they have to swing across the creek on a rope. Jess does not meet Leslie as planned when he finds out that Miss Edmunds, his teacher, wants to take him to the Smithsonian in Washington. Leslie, tired of waiting for Jess, goes to Terabithia alone, but the rope breaks and she hits her head and drowns. Jess feels guilt and then anger at her for leaving him. He feels shock, denial, fear, and grief. Paterson portrays these feelings very realistically. Eventually Jess comes to accept Leslie's death, as she would have wanted him to. "Now it was time for him to move out. She wasn't there, so he must go for both of them. It was up to him to pay back to the world in beauty and caring what Leslie had loaned him in vision and strength."[10]

In Cynthia Voigt's moving novel *Tell Me If the Lovers Are Losers* (1982), three girls from different environments form a close relationship at Stanton College. Ann is intelligent and introspective, Niki is competitive and brash, and Hildy is oddly innocent and strangely

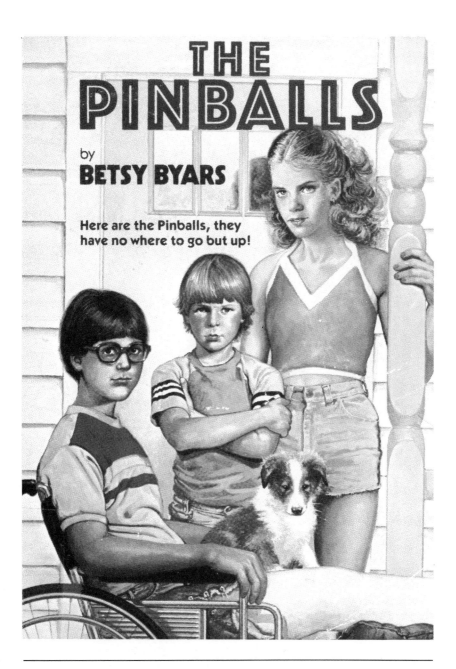

The Pinballs, Betsy Byars, cover art by Tom Newsom

Bridge to Terabithia, Katherine Paterson,
illustrated by Donna Diamond

wise. The three girls share their ideas and their feelings on and off the volleyball court; they try to help each other in school, family, and everyday situations. This beautifully written novel shows the three girls becoming deeply involved with one another while growing as individuals. Hildy is from a poor farm; she is on a scholarship and has no money. When it becomes obvious that Hildy cannot see well yet is too proud to admit she cannot afford glasses or to accept money from them, Ann and Niki arrange with the dean for Hildy to be paid for coaching the volleyball team, and they persuade Hildy to wear the glasses, although she finds this new way of seeing bewildering. The glasses become a symbol; without them, Hildy insists, she saw more. With them, the world has too much detail. Ann likes to borrow the glasses, although they turn the world into a colored blur for her; she wants some of Hildy's inner vision. After Hildy and Niki have an argument, Hildy abandons the glasses and goes by bicycle to the observatory. A car hits Hildy and she dies instantly; the driver had been drinking, but Hildy was in the middle of the road. Ann and Niki are left to help each other deal with the shock and loss.

In Lois Lowry's *Autumn Street* (1980), seven-year-old Charles is murdered in the big woods near Elizabeth's grandmother's house. Elizabeth comes home because she is scared to go into the woods; Charles gets mad and goes in alone. Elizabeth is worried about Charles yet does not want him to get into trouble, so she doesn't tell. She is put to bed with a fever but gets up when she hears the talking downstairs. She learns that Charles's body has been found and that Ferdie Gossett, the half-mad derelict who wanders the streets searching the garbage cans, has been charged.

> In my own anguished delirium I could see Charles, so small; and I could see the man into whose furtive-eyed face I had sometimes glanced with timid curiosity as he stood alone, a victim himself. . . . And the man had carried with him a knife. He had cut Charles' throat from one side to the other.[11]

Elizabeth's description of Charles's murder in *Autumn Street* is very different from the description of Katie's murder in *The Truth Trap*. Lowry chooses to be straightforward, vivid, and simple, whereas Miller chooses to be sensational, pounding home the horrible death with detailed description. *Autumn Street* is a moving story that takes place during World War II. Charles is black and is Elizabeth's best friend, the grandson of Tatie, the cook at Elizabeth's grandparents' house. Charles is not allowed in front of the house; ironically, it is because of this petty discrimination that the children must walk the long way around to go sledding. Thus, Charles notices the woods and wants to play there, and it is there that he dies.

Unleaving (1976) by Jill Paton Walsh is similar to Wells's *When No One Was Looking* in that it focuses on a murder committed out of love. There the similarities end, because Walsh creates a believable, poignant struggle of conscience. The motive is love of the victim, a kind of mercy killing. Patrick pushes his retarded sister Mollie off the cliff. He wants to save her from cruelty and insensitivity. He thinks he should be willing to suffer the guilt of killing Mollie for her sake. Their father is a professor of philosophy who believes that souls resemble bodies. Mollie's deformed body repels the professor. His reaction to her is part of what convinces Patrick that all her life Mollie will be hurt by people's recoiling from her. She is a loving child with just enough intelligence to understand that people feel revulsion for her. Later Patrick says,

> "I expected to feel dreadful. I expected to feel crushed by guilt. . . . I knew I would. And I thought that was nothing, nothing compared to what she would suffer as she grew to know dimly what other people felt about her."[12]

Where *Unleaving* raises complex moral and ethical questions about quality of life versus length of life and whether anyone has a right to make that choice for someone else, *When No One Was Looking* has next to no complexity of idea or character.

One of the characters in *Unleaving* is Patrick's friend Madge, whom we first meet in an earlier Walsh novel, *Goldengrove* (1972). Madge always spends her summers with her cousin Paul at Gran's house, Goldengrove. During the last summer of her childhood she meets the blind professor, a bitter man who tells her, "Some wounds cannot be healed, some things are beyond helping and cannot be put right."[13] The professor will never trust again. Madge thinks this is a sick and wicked view of the world until she learns the truth about Paul and herself; Paul is really her brother. Madge feels deeply wronged by the deception her family has perpetrated, and as the novel ends she admits that the professor's view of life has more truth than she had realized. In *Unleaving*, Madge has grown as a person but is still compassionate and sensitive to others. She is ready to be a friend to Patrick, who needs her trust and support.

John Rowe Townsend's *Cloudy-Bright* (1984) is a first-person narrative seen through the eyes of both protagonists. Sam and Jenny meet while Jenny is taking pictures with her father's expensive Hasselblad camera; Sam has just lost the Hasselblad he had borrowed from Barhampton Polytechnic, where he is a visual arts student. Sam arranges to meet Jenny for day outings so that he can use her father's camera to enter the school's photography contest. Meanwhile, Sam is falling in love with a fellow student, Elaine, who is using him in much the same way he is using Jenny. Jenny is falling in love with Sam. After Sam finds the original Hasselblad camera and equipment, which he had thought lost forever, he realizes that he needs Jenny for more than just her father's camera. While Sam is practical, Jenny is dreamy, and together they take winning photographs. Townsend shows that everything is not as it seems as he develops the teenage love triangle from both Sam's and Jenny's point of view.

In *Good Night, Prof, Dear* (1970), Townsend again deals with the contrasts between characters' perceptions of reality, although this book has a single narrator and a unified point of view. As the character matures and his understanding of the meaning of events changes, we learn that what Graham initially believes is very different from what he knows really happened by the end of the book. His love for an older woman and what he considers his betrayal by her for money both take on a radically different meaning when he finally has all the facts. What he thought of as undying passion for Lynn looks immature and shallow in comparison to Lynn's concern for him, which went so far as to give him up and to accept blame and the appearance of wrongdoing rather than take the potentially profitable step of marrying him to his own harm and ultimate sorrow. When Lynn returns the money with which Graham's father had thought to buy her off, her integrity and honor are established beyond a doubt.

Australian Ivan Southall's *Ash Road* (1965) is an exciting story about children coping with potential disaster. Harry, Graham, and Wallace finally have their parents' permission to go camping on their own for a week. The first night is frightening for Graham, who gets up to make a cup of coffee and carelessly starts a fire that the winds blow out of control very quickly. The three boys escape the fire, but it spreads rapidly toward the foothills, where everything is tinder-dry. All of the adults go to help with the fire, leaving a handful of children and two old men to cope as the fire surges toward town. Old Mr. George has a stroke, and despite the efforts of the children he dies. The children know that the fire is coming and that there is no way in or out of town. They are completely blocked off by the flames. The children are all very courageous, but in the end it is the rain that saves their homes. Southall shows the panic, confusion, and kindness of all these children as they meet each crisis and try to help each other even though they are all scared. After the rain comes and Graham thinks about all that has happened among his new friends, he decides that he is strong enough to admit the truth: he started this fire.

The importance of honest interaction between children and adults is one of the major themes of the modern realistic novel for children. Unlike the problem novel, in which the adult is nearly always wrong and never able to change or see his or her error, the realistic novel with the universal theme shows that if an adult is made aware of the conflict, he or she is sometimes capable of change. The child sometimes needs the support and guidance of an older, wiser someone in order to survive. The ingenuity and courage of children are not lost in their acceptance of help from the adult world.

New Realism not only deals with subjects that were once considered inappropriate for children, it also treats of universal themes. Lowry's *Autumn Street* is about much more than the murder of Charles, just as Paterson's *Bridge to Terabithia* is about much more than the death of Leslie. Only those novels that have some touch of universality are likely to be remembered in the next century.

Notes

1. Linnea A. Due, *High and Outside* (New York: Bantam, 1980), p. 128.

2. John Donovan, *I'll Get There. It Better Be Worth the Trip* (New York: Harper & Row, 1969), pp. 143, 151.

3. Mary Pope Osborne, *Run, Run, As Fast As You Can* (New York: Dial Press, 1981), p. 148–49.

4. Frances A. Miller, *The Truth Trap* (New York: Fawcett Juniper, 1980), p. 16.

5. Betsy Byars, *The Pinballs* (New York: Scholastic Book Services, 1977), pp. 136–37.

6. Katherine Paterson, *The Great Gilly Hopkins* (New York: Avon, 1978), pp. 147–48.

7. Paul Zindel, *Pardon Me, You're Stepping on My Eyeball* (New York: Bantam, 1977), p. 10.

8. Paul Zindel, *My Darling, My Hamburger* (New York: Harper & Row, 1969), p. 38.

9. Sheila Egoff draws a similar comparison between these two novels in "The Problem Novel," in *Only Connect: Readings on Children's Literature,* eds. Egoff et al. (Toronto and New York: Oxford University Press, 1980), p. 362.

10. Katherine Paterson, *Bridge to Terabithia* (New York: Avon, 1979), p. 126.

11. Lois Lowry, *Autumn Street* (New York: Dell, 1980), pp. 164–65.

12. Jill Paton Walsh, *Unleaving* (New York: Avon, 1976), p. 123.

13. Jill Paton Walsh, *Goldengrove* (New York: Farrar, Straus & Giroux, 1972), p. 119.

Black Images in American Children's Literature

James A. Miller

As RECENTLY AS 1965 NANCY LARRICK characterized the children's book industry in the United States as "The All-White World of Children's Books."[1] In her survey of children's books published between 1962 and 1964, she discovered that over 93 percent of them did not include a single black character. In the handful of works where black characters did appear, they were generally removed from contemporary American society, located in the past or in another country, and the illustrations tended to portray them as physically indistinguishable from their white counterparts. Larrick's comments are reinforced by the research of Jane Bingham, whose analysis of the portrayal of Afro-Americans in children's books published between 1930 and 1968 yielded only forty-nine books containing illustrations of blacks. Bingham also discovered that blacks appearing in children's books published before 1945 were portrayed in terms of the popular racial stereotypes of the period.[2]

While Larrick's study was confined to a three-year period, her comments could be extended to the history of the children's book industry in general. Since the emergence in the early nineteenth century of a body of literature written specifically for American children by American writers, Afro-Americans have—until fairly recently—either been excluded as subjects unworthy of literary treatment or portrayed as objects of caricature and racist sterotypes.

Lydia Maria Child, a pioneer figure in American children's liter-

99

ature and a committed abolitionist, recognized this problem early in her career and sought to address it in the pages of *The Juvenile Miscellany,* the children's periodical she edited from 1826 to 1834. Child sought to undermine racial prejudice and combat racial stereotypes through gentle appeals to her young readers. As long as she confined her views to the pages of the *Miscellany,* adults seemed willing to accept them. Apparently, adults were less tolerant when Child expressed her opinions more directly. In the months following the publication of her abolitionist manifesto, *An Appeal in Favor of That Class of Americans Called Africans,* in 1833, mass cancellations of subscriptions forced her to cease publication of the *Miscellany.* In spite of the efforts of nineteenth-century writers like Lydia Maria Child, and of other journals such as *The Slave's Friend* (1836–38), the dominant trend in American children's literature until well into the twentieth century was shaped by American social, economic, and political practices towards the black community.

Significantly, it was the distinguished Afro-American historian and civil rights leader W. E. B. Du Bois who launched the first serious effort to create positive images for Afro-American children in the twentieth century. As editor (1910–32) of *The Crisis: A Record of the Darker Races,* the official journal of the NAACP, Du Bois designated the October issue each year as a special children's number. By 1919 he had concluded that more effort must be devoted to the cultural needs of Afro-American children. With the assistance of the business manager of *The Crisis,* Augustus Granville Dill, and its literary editor, Jessie Redmon Fauset, Du Bois formed a publishing company and, in January 1920, produced the first issue of *The Brownie's Book: A Monthly Magazine for the Children of the Sun.*

Published from January 1920 to December 1921, *The Brownie's Book* was a memorable venture in Afro-American children's literature and a prototype for subsequent developments in the field. The goals of the magazine, as Du Bois expressed them in the inaugural issue, spoke directly to the challenge of developing a sense of self-esteem among black children:

> To make colored children realize that being colored is a normal, beautiful thing, to make them familiar with the history and achievements of the Negro race, to make them know that other colored children have grown into beautiful, useful, famous persons, to teach them delicately, a code of honor and

actions in their relations with white children, to turn their little hurts and resentments into emulation, ambition and love of their own homes and companions, to point out the best amusements and joys and worthwhile things of life, to inspire them for definite occupations and duties with a broad spirit of sacrifice.[3]

Through the pages of *The Brownie's Book,* Du Bois sought to demonstrate that Afro-Americans had a rich cultural and historical legacy and a wealth of living writers and artists as well. Cover artwork and illustrations were contributed by noted black artists Laura Wheeler, Albert Smith, Marcellus Hawkins, and others. In each issue of *The Brownie's Book* there were stories, folk tales and legends from around the world, poems, games, puzzles, riddles, music, biographies, and current events. Appearing as it did during the early stirrings of the Harlem Renaissance, *The Brownie's Book* attracted contributions from many well-known Afro-American writers: Arthur Huff Fauset, James Weldon Johnson, Effie Lee Newsome, Jessie Fauset, and Georgia Douglas Johnson, among others. Langston Hughes contributed some of his early work to *The Brownie's Book,* as did Nina Yolanda Du Bois, Du Bois's daughter.

Most issues of *The Brownie's Book* featured biographies of notable black heroes and heroines. Samuel Coleridge-Taylor, Alexandre Dumas, Crispus Attucks, Denmark Vesey, Phillis Wheatley, Toussaint L'Ouverture, Harriet Tubman, Frederick Douglass, and others were among the subjects of these sketches. Du Bois contributed a regular column on international events, called "As the Crow Flies," with himself as the Crow. In this role, Du Bois never failed to remind his young readers that black was beautiful:

> I like my black feathers—
>   don't you?
> Whirl, whirl, up, whirl and fly
> home to my sweet, little, black
> crowlets . . . Ah, but they're black
> and sweet and bonnie.[4]

Du Bois's column interpreted current events for young readers, reporting on the problems faced by the League of Nations as well as the struggles for freedom by oppressed groups in the United States.

Other features of *The Brownie's Book* were "The Judge," a lively advice column for young children, edited by Jessie Redmon Fauset; "The Jury," devoted to letters from young readers; and "The Grown-ups Corner," directed to parents. Advertising was kept to a minimum and was always directed towards the promotion of books and self-improvement through education.

A noble experiment, *The Brownie's Book* ran for twenty-four issues before it ceased publication in December 1921, a casualty of the economic slump in the years following World War I. In spite of its collapse, *The Brownie's Book* was a serious attempt to create a body of "literature adapted to colored children and indeed to all children who live in a world of varied races."[5]

The Brownie's Book was a milestone in the history of American children's literature. In its emphasis on African and Afro-American history, inspirational biographies, the richness of Afro-American culture, and the necessity of fostering a sense of black pride among Afro-Americans, it anticipated by several decades the explosion of black consciousness during the 1960s. Like Lydia Maria Child's experiment with *The Juvenile Miscellany* almost a century earlier, however, *The Brownie's Book* apparently had little impact on the racial climate of American society during the 1920s—or the dominant practices of the children's publishing industry during the next decade.

The popular Dr. Dolittle books, beginning with *The Story of Dr. Dolittle* in 1920, were replete with racial stereotypes and epithets. In *Dr. Dolittle's Zoo*, for example, Hugh Lofting created Prince Bumpo, a fat, ignorant African prince. Spurned by a fair-skinned princess because of his blackness, Prince Bumpo appeals to Dr. Dolittle—a captive in his kingdom—to turn his skin white. Dr. Dolittle agrees, if the prince will help him escape, then covers Bumpo with a white ointment, outwits him, and flees. The Nancy Drew series, introduced in 1930, continued the long-established literary tradition of portraying black characters as menials who spoke barely understandable dialect.

Illustrations, too, reflected many of the stereotyped perceptions whites held of blacks. The cover of Annie Vaugh Weaver's *Frawg*, published in 1930, portrayed a black boy holding a watermelon, while the concluding pages of the book depicted the black road to heaven lined with watermelons—illustrations that received praise from the *Library Journal*.[6] Indeed, racist illustrations often received high praise from reviewers. The *New York Times* review of *Nicodemus*, published

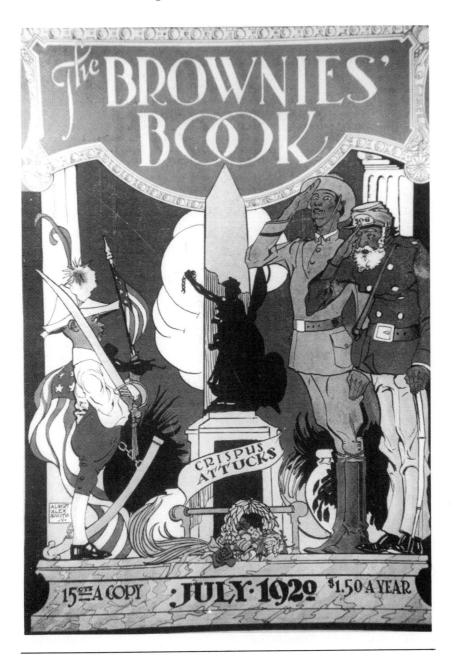

The Brownies' Book magazine
cover art by Albert Alex Smith

Mr. Kelso's Lion, Arna Bontemps, cover art by Len Ebert

in 1934, concluded that "there is humor in the presentation of pigs and pickaninnies."[7]

During the 1930s, some of the writers associated with the Harlem Renaissance of the preceding decade attempted to build on the legacy established by *The Brownie's Book,* most notably Arna Bontemps and Langston Hughes. Writer, critic, biographer, anthologist, librarian, and teacher, Arna Bontemps (1902–73) played an active role in bringing the Afro-American heritage to schoolchildren and in collecting documents, art, and artifacts in libraries and museums at Fisk University, Syracuse, and Yale, among other institutions. In 1932 Bontemps and Langston Hughes, one of black America's most popular and prolific writers, collaborated on *Popo and Fifina, Children of Haiti*— the beginning of a literary partnership that continued until Hughes's death in 1967.

In 1937 Bontemps published *Sad-Faced Boy,* which he described in a letter to Hughes as "the first Harlem story for children"[8]—that is, the first attempt to use Harlem as a locale for children's fiction. These early works avoided direct social commentary, choosing instead to locate black children in the context of experiences associated with all children. In 1941 Bontemps compiled *Golden Slippers,* an anthology of black poetry for young readers, followed by *The Fast Sooner Hound* (written in collaboration with Jack Conroy), the story of a long-legged, lop-eared hound who could outrun the Cannonball Express, and *Sam Patch* (1942; also written with Jack Conroy), the "high, wide and handsome jumper" who defeated Hurricane Hank, the Kaskasi Snapping Turtle.

Although Bontemps's fiction for children often explored nonracial themes, his historical works were dedicated to recounting Afro-American history. *Chariot in the Sky* (1941) is a full-length study of the Fisk Jubilee Singers, while *We Have Tomorrow* (1945) is a series of biographies of twelve Afro-Americans who succeeded in unusual fields. His *Story of the Negro* (1948) received very favorable reviews and was mentioned as a runner-up for the Newbery Medal. During the 1950s, Bontemps continued to produce biographies of significant Afro-Americans, including *Story of George Washington Carver* (1954) and *Frederick Douglass: Slave, Fighter, Freeman* (1959). During the same period, Langston Hughes produced *Famous American Negoes* (1954), *Famous Negro Music Makers* (1955), and *Famous Negro Heroes of America* (1958).

Arna Bontemps and Langston Hughes were an important bridge

between the 1920s and post–World War II developments in American children's literature, and their success in the field provided the foundation for the emergence of a generation of talented Afro-American writers during the 1960s.

In the final analysis, of course, changes in the portrayal of Afro-Americans in children's literature occurred not as a result of the efforts of talented writers like Arna Bontemps and Langston Hughes but as a consequence of the shift in social climate in American society in the years following World War II. The increased militancy of the black community in the postwar years, the first stirrings of the civil rights movement in the United States, and the struggle for African and Third World independence abroad forced a new social awareness onto American society, and publishers of children's books responded accordingly.

One important breakthrough occurred in 1945 with the publication of Lorraine and Jerrold Beim's *Two Is a Team,* a Dick-and-Jane-type story with a black boy replacing Jane. Written for very young children, *Two Is a Team* describes the youthful escapades of two young boys. The illustrations of a white and black child playing together were noteworthy for a 1945 children's publication, and in spite of the innocuous story, a number of communities violently objected to this assault on the racial status quo.[9]

Although the controversy over *Two Is a Team* reflected the vehemence with which some Americans continued to cling to racist beliefs, the 1940s witnessed the publication of a spate of works designed to arouse the social consciousness of Americans about the problems facing the black community. Jesse Jackson's *Call Me Charley* (1945) is a pioneer effort in this vein.

The story of a black family that has moved into the white suburbs, *Call Me Charley* revolves around the difficulties twelve-year-old Charley has in gaining acceptance at school. Eventually, he manages to win over Tom, a white classmate, as his first real friend in the community. Charley and Tom collaborate on a school project and are delighted when they win first prize, a free pass to the local swimming club. Their triumph is quickly shattered, however, when Charley's prize is replaced with cash because the club does not admit blacks. This is only one of many trials Charley must face throughout the novel. He is harassed by George, a young bigot, encounters racism in the classroom, and must overcome his father's skepticism about the value of pursuing an education. When a teacher refuses to give

Charley a part in a school play, however, white parents rally in his support, and he eventually achieves his place in the community.

Call Me Charley depicts for its readers glimpses of the discrimination faced by black children in American society, a racial bigotry personified most clearly in the character of George. A basic message of the novel is that people like George will ultimately fail in the face of good will and justice. Charley's mother articulates this optimistic message when she tells him, "As long as you work hard and try to do right . . . you will always find some good people like . . . Tom and his folks marching along with you in the right path. And fellows like George may come along too, sooner or later."[10]

In the years following the 1954 Supreme Court decision outlawing segregation in public schools, the trend initiated by Jesse Jackson picked up added momentum. The optimistic message of *Call Me Charley* is echoed in Natalie Savage Carlson's story about the integration of a parochial school in Louisiana, *The Empty Schoolhouse* (1965). Carlson's book recounts the experiences of Lullah Royal, a ten-year-old black girl who helps her mother maintain a motel. She leaps at the opportunity to attend St. Joseph's school because her best friend goes there. When she integrates the school, however, whites stop sending their children and even her best friend deserts her. The boycott is brought to a head when two racial bigots, outsiders to the community, go beyond heckling and shoot Lullah. Fortunately, she receives only a superficial wound, but the shot galvanizes the conscience of the white community. Opposition to integration ends, and the story concludes on a positive note.

Call Me Charley and *The Empty Schoolhouse* share some striking structural similarities. In their commitment to a vision of an integrated society, both works take it for granted that blacks are striving to become completely absorbed into American society. Issues of black identity are therefore subordinated to the quest for acceptance by white society. In both books the obstacles to integration are represented by whites outside the mainstream American traditions of fair play and justice—George in *Call Me Charley,* the outside agitators in *The Empty Schoolhouse.* The white community is generally portrayed as passively in favor of racial integration, but it usually takes a dramatic event—such as the shooting of Lullah Royal—to win its active support. In the meantime, black characters are urged to practice the virtues of hard work and forbearance. Social change, when it occurs, must take place within the heart of the white community.

Lorenz Graham (the brother-in-law of W. E. B. Du Bois) explores themes similar to those of Jesse Jackson and Natalie Savage Carlson but takes a somewhat more critical view of the American mainstream. In three novels published between 1958 and 1969, Graham explores the experiences of the Williams family as its members struggle for a place in American society. *South Town* (1958) examines the overt racism the Williams family experiences in the South. Unable to endure the violence and bigotry of the South, the family moves north.

North Town (1965) explores the problems of living in an integrated society. Like Charley in *Call Me Charley*, David Williams, the son, encounters problems at school. He, too, struggles for acceptance and acquires a white friend who teaches him how to play football. Just when David seems to have achieved a place for himself in his new community, his father is hospitalized and David is forced to work to support his family. Through the care of a sympathetic Jewish doctor, Mr. Williams regains his health. At the end of the novel, the American Dream seems to be within everyone's grasp. David has become a football star and plans to be a doctor, Mr. Williams is back at work, and the family is living in a new house. All of the hopes of integration seemed to be captured by David during a moment when he looks up from the football field:

> ... the late afternoon sun had broken through the clouds lighting a row of American flags silhouetted against the sky. David knew his father was there, and Jeannette. . . . He could not pick out faces, white or black or brown, but he knew they were all there. This, he thought, was like America.[11]

In Graham's *Whose Town?* (1969), however, we discover that many lingering questions remain unanswered. Racial tensions pervade this novel. During his last year of high school David is beaten up by some white teenagers, but he is singled out for assault charges by the police. In the aftermath of the fight, one of David's friends is shot by a white man. David's father and other blacks are laid off at a local foundry. *Whose Town?* captures the mood of black frustration and anger during the late 1960s, as David develops a heightened sense of black pride and considers black separatism as an alternative. Although David finally chooses a more moderate course, Graham suggests that racial integration in the North may not be the answer to the problems facing blacks in American society—a message underscored by the title of his most recent work in this series, *Return to South Town* (1976).

Two Is a Team, written and illustrated by Lorraine and Jerrold Beim

The Snowy Day, written and illustrated by Ezra Jack Keats

Another significant trend during the post–World War II years was the emergence of a group of books that included black characters but usually avoided racial issues. Like the Beims' *Two Is a Team,* these works are based on experiences common to children of all races. In some of them, the race of the characters is only incidental to the plot; in others, the only clue to racial identity is conveyed through the illustrations.

One of the key authors in this group is Ezra Jack Keats, whose series of books about the joys and trials of a young black boy named Peter has received high praise in many circles. Beginning with *The Snowy Day* (1962; winner of the 1963 Caldecott Medal), Keats created a cycle of stories revolving around simple challenges in Peter's life. *Whistle for Willie* (1964), for example, deals with Peter's efforts to learn how to whistle for his dog. Throughout the series, Keats displays a warmhearted and light touch. Ann Herbert Scott's *Sam* (1967) portrays a black middle-class family. Sam, the youngest child, feels excluded from the various activities of his household. His dilemma is resolved when his mother invites him into the kitchen to make raspberry tarts. Grete Mannheim's *The Two Friends* (1968) is a pictorial treatment of the bond between a black girl and her white friend, revolving around simple daily events. Joan Lexau's *Benjie* (1970) explores the relationship between a young black boy and his grandmother.

Just as Lydia Maria Child sought to minimize the racial and cultural differences between whites and blacks in her nineteenth-century stories, the writers of these stories emphasize universal experiences over specifically racial ones. Generally, the stories concern characters who happen to be black and whose experiences are set within secure middle-class environments. Although many of these works were highly praised for offering a bridge between the black world and white readers, they were also criticized—particularly by some black writers—for presenting a romantic view of black life and ignoring significant racial and cultural differences.

Against the backdrop of this criticism there emerged during the social and political turbulence of the 1960s a generation of black writers who sought to create a body of children's literature rooted in Afro-American cultural traditions, sensibility, and world view.

One theme among these writers was the exploration of poverty, racism, and violence as integral features of urban life. Their works, written primarily for young adults, offered realistic explorations of the hopes and frustrations of young blacks in the ghetto—a trend initiated by the sensational success of Kristin Hunter's *The Soul Brothers and Sister Lou* (1968). Fourteen-year-old Lou Hawkins is determined to escape from the grim realities of ghetto life. She persuades her older brother to provide recreational space in his print shop to keep neighborhood youth out of trouble, and then she and her friends organize a singing group. After a confrontation with brutal police ends in the death of one of the group, another member composes a eulogy with the help of a high school teacher and former blues singer. The Soul Brothers and Sister Lou cut a record and become an overnight success. Hunter's novel, too, became virtually an overnight success, selling over one million copies and winning the 1968 Council on Interracial Books for Children prize.

Where Kristin Hunter's novel celebrates one of the traditional formulas for escaping the ghetto, the works of Sharon Bell Mathis stress the ties of familial and personal responsibility and the saving power of love. In *Sidewalk Story* (1971) nine-year-old Lilly Etta Allen learns that her best friend's family is facing eviction and no one seems willing to stop it. She disobeys her mother, confronts the indifference of institutions, and braves a thunderstorm in order to help her friend's family. Although Lilly Etta's heroism leads to a happy ending, Mathis seems to suggest that such conclusions are not usual for sidewalk stories.

Louise Merriweather's *Daddy Was a Numbers Runner* (1970) offers a bleak view of black urban life. Detailing one year in the life of twelve-year-old Francie Coffin during the Depression, the novel explores the disintegration of her family in the face of economic insecurity and racism. Francie, too, realizes that her prospects for a better future are extremely limited and ends up cursing life at the novel's end.

Walter Dean Myers, another prominent voice to emerge during the late 1960s, explores similar territory in his first novel for young adults, *Fast Sam, Cool Clyde and Stuff* (1975). Set in Harlem, the novel relates the experiences of a group of preteen males confronting problems facing many young black males. During the course of the novel, they are mistakenly arrested several times; one father dies, another deserts his family; a friend who turns to drugs is shot and killed. In spite of these adverse circumstances, Myers emphasizes the bonds linking the group and suggests that such ties may help each individual survive.

These attempts at forging a more realistic portrayal of Afro-American experience, one shaped by the realities of black urban life, pointed to a new development in American children's literature during this period. As Rudine Sims has pointed out, from 1965 to 1979 there was a marked decrease in books aimed at promoting racial harmony and a corresponding increase in books charting new directions in the exploration of Afro-American life and character.[12] Beyond their preoccupation with the social and economic realities of contemporary Afro-American life, the generation of black writers that emerged during the late 1960s placed a renewed emphasis on the African and Afro-American heritage.

Virginia Hamilton, one of the most prolific of these writers, launched her career with *Zeely* in 1967. The novel revolves around Elizabeth Perry, who, with her brother, is spending the summer at her uncle's farm. She becomes fascinated with Zeely, the daughter of a neighboring farmer, who bears a striking resemblance to a photograph of a Watusi queen. Elizabeth incorporates Zeely into her dream life, even imitating her, until the two women have a talk and Zeely explains to Elizabeth the importance of accepting oneself. In *Zeely*, Virginia Hamilton skillfully balances the question of pride in one's African identity with the necessity of living in the present.

Tom Feelings's *Black Pilgrimage* (1972) recounts his own experiences growing up as a child in Bedford-Stuyvesant, his travels to the South, his evolution as an artist, and his decision to leave the United States and live in Africa. In collaboration with Muriel Feelings, he also produced *Moja Means One: Swahili Counting Book* (1971) and *Jambo Means Hello: Swahili Alphabet* (1974), both Caldecott Honor Books. During the early 1970s, Feelings's commitment to the African continent was absolute. As he wrote in *Black Pilgrimage*, "I am an *African,* and I know now that Black people, no matter in what part of the world they may live, are one African people. And in terms of natural resources and potential, and a culture that built the base of humanity, we belong to the richest continent on earth—Africa."[13]

Lucille Clifton's *All Us Come Across the Water* (1973) echoes the "We are an African People" theme, while Sharon Bell Mathis's *Listen for the Fig Tree* (1974) places a strong emphasis on pride in one's African identity. Mathis's novel explores the world of Muffin Johnson, a teenager who loses her sight at the age of ten and loses her father— who was murdered—at the age of fifteen. Muffin must cope with the hardships of her own blindness, life in the ghetto, and her mother's tenuous grasp on sanity. During the celebration of Kwanzaa (an Afro-American alternative to the commercialism of Christmas), Muffin gains a greater understanding of the traditions of self-respect, self-determination, and shared love that have allowed the black community to triumph over adversity.

During the same period there was a proliferation of works that tapped the rich legacy of Afro-American history. In *To Be a Slave* (1964) and *Long Journey Home: Stories from Black History* (1972), Julius Lester draws upon historical documents to present graphic eyewitness accounts of the horrors of slavery. After the publication of *Daddy Was a Numbers Runner,* Louise Merriweather turned her attention to writing biographies of famous blacks for elementary school readers, including *The Heart Man: Dr. Daniel Hale Williams* (1972) and *Don't Ride the Bus on Sunday: The Rosa Parks Story* (1973). Virginia Hamilton published biographies of W. E. B. Du Bois (1972) and Paul Robeson (1974).

The period 1965–79 can therefore be defined as a high point in the portrayal of Afro-American characters in American children's literature, a period of high visibility, marked by the quest for a new realism free of the negative stereotypes of the past, the reassertion of the African and Afro-American cultural legacy, and the vigorous examination of Afro-American history. The result was the emergence of an exciting and diverse body of works that significantly altered the boundaries of American children's literature.

Since this period, however, there has been a steady decline in children's books dealing with black life. Rudine Sims reports that "only about 1 percent of the children's books published in the first half of the eighties focused on black experience in the United States."[14] Consistent with the historical pattern, this shift reflects the social, economic, and political atmosphere of the 1980s: the status of the black community is no longer a burning issue on the national agenda, as it was during the domestic turbulence of the late 1950s and the 1960s. This shift in mood is inevitably reflected in the cultural climate.

Nevertheless, the 1980s do not portend a return to the invisibility of the past. Many of the writers who emerged during the heyday of the 1960s continue to be productive: Lucille Clifton, Eloise Greenfield, Virginia Hamilton, and Walter Dean Myers. And new voices have emerged: Mildred Pitts Walter, who has published four books since 1979; Mildred Taylor, whose second novel in the continuing

Zeely, Virginia Hamilton, illustrated by Symeon Shimin

Zamani Goes to Market, Muriel L. Feelings, illustrated by Tom Feelings

chronicle of the Logan family, *Roll of Thunder, Hear My Cry* (1976), received the 1977 Newbery Medal; and Joyce Carol Thomas, co-winner of an American Book Award for her novel *Marked by Fire* (1982).

At the same time, the issues of racial stereotyping are still matters of sharp and heated debate in the children's literature industry, as two recent episodes make clear.[15] In 1982 Margot Zemach, the U.S. nominee for the 1980 Hans Christian Andersen Medal for illustration, published *Jake and Honeybunch Go to Heaven,* a children's book that freely improvised on a popular Afro-American folk tale. The controversy began when fourteen librarians at the Chicago Public Library criticized the book for perpetuating racially offensive illustrations, singling out Zemach's depiction of a black heaven where the residents fry fish, barbecue spareribs, and listen to jazz. Other librarians and critics entered the debate, and charges of racism and censorship were hurled back and forth across the country. Similarly, Mary Calhoun's *Big Sixteen,* illustrated by Trina Schart Hyman, was accused of perpetuating gross caricatures of black people. In both cases, the issues of racial stereotyping and the distortion of Afro-American historical and cultural traditions once again flared up. Even so, the past several decades have witnessed a sustained assault on the historical legacy of racist images in American children's literature, one that has hopefully cleared the path for a richer vision of American life.

Notes

1. Nancy Larrick, "The All-White World of Children's Books," *Saturday Review,* September 11, 1965, pp. 63–64, 84–85.

2. Jane Bingham, "The Pictorial Treatment of Afro-Americans in Books for Young Children, 1930–1968," *Elementary English* 48 (November 1971): 880–85.

3. Elinor Desverney Sinnette, "*The Brownie's Book:* A Pioneer Publication for Children," in *Black Titan: W. E. B. Du Bois,* eds. John Henrik Clarke et al. (Boston: Beacon Press, 1970), p. 164.

4. Ibid., p. 171.

5. Ibid., p. 174.

6. Myra Pollack Sadker and David Miller Sadker, *Now Upon a Time: A Contemporary View of Children's Literature* (New York: Harper & Row, 1977), p. 131.

7. Ibid.

8. Charles H. Nichols, ed., *Arna Bontemps–Langston Hughes: Letters, 1925–1967* (New York: Dodd, Mead, 1980), p. 47.

9. Sadker and Sadker, *Now Upon a Time,* p. 140.

10. Jesse Jackson, *Call Me Charley* (New York: Harper & Row, 1945), p. 156.

11. Lorenz Graham, *North Town* (New York: Crowell, 1965), p. 213.

12. Rudine Sims, *Shadow and Substance: Afro-American Experience in Contemporary Children's Literature* (Urbana, Ill.: National Council of Teachers of English, 1982), p. 104.

13. Tom Feelings, *Black Pilgrimage* (New York: Lothrop, Lee & Shepard, 1972), p. 50.

14. Rudine Sims, "Children's Books About Blacks: A Mid-Eighties Status Report," *Children's Literature Review,* vol. 8 (Detroit: Gale Research, 1985), p. 9.

15. See Sims, ibid., p. 12.

Twentieth-Century Children's Fantasy

Mary E. Shaner

THE GENRE OF FANTASY is difficult to define adequately, as Ruth Nadelman Lynn points out in her perceptive introduction to *Fantasy for Children*.[1] Even the *Oxford Companion to Children's Literature*, while effortfully specific, ends on a vague note: "[Fantasy is] a term used (in the context of children's literature) to describe works of fiction, written by a specific author (i.e. not traditional) and usually novel-length, which involve the supernatural or some other unreal element."[2] The last clause is the important one, and it ends (admittedly, of necessity) with a phrase sufficiently broad to include not just *Peter Rabbit* and *Peter Pan* but most of the books of the Bible.

More satisfying definitions that describe fantasy conceptually can be even less concrete. Sheila Egoff, in her fine critical study of children's literature, *Thursday's Child*, flounders a bit: "Fantasy is a literature of paradox. It is the discovery of the real within the unreal, the credible within the incredible, the believable within the unbelievable."[3] Aside from being redundant, this does describe one common element of fantasy: there is in fantasy the constant paradox created by one or more elements that contradict some of the known rules of the natural universe while operating alongside other of those rules. Yet this contradiction is rarely the significant focus of the fantasy; no one reads Beatrix Potter with a constant sense of the tension between the real and the unreal created by human clothing on animals. In the talking beast story, the mind is more likely to be engaged by the way the animal characters' behavior illuminates, even satirizes, human behavior: the revelation of the unreal within the real, the false in the fact.

Perhaps fantasy is the art of the impossible, ordering the chaos of the imagination; but this is done by all fiction. Yet fantasy orders the chaos of the *fringes* of the imagination, the outermost reaches of dream. It holds the mirror up to the farthest-in and the farthest-out possibilities of the human mind, deepest nightmare and wildest hope. Although fantasy certainly is not realism, neither is it the antithesis of realism. Fantasies are constructed upon a substratum of reality, and any good fantasy must have, as good realistic fiction must, a modicum of verisimilitude. Despite this, it is fair to say, paraphrasing Ursula Le Guin, that fantasy is more concerned with truth than with fact. Therefore, it provides us with "a different approach to reality. . . . Fantasy is nearer to poetry, to mysticism, and to insanity than naturalistic fiction is."[4]

The search for a definition of fantasy that would include all types and satisfy all readers may have no conclusion, or perhaps only a conclusion the length of the unabridged *Oxford English Dictionary*. In the end, the meaning of fantasy is best shown by illustration, a rich sampling of the variety of actual fantasies. Even in such a sample, controversy is unavoidable, for there is a great deal of overlap from category to category. Is Agnes Smith's remarkable *An Edge of the Forest* more an allegory than a talking animal story? Where should one place L. M. Boston's Green Knowe books, mythic fantasy or adventury fantasy? Is Elizabeth Marie Pope's *The Perilous Gard* a fantasy or a historical novel? It feels like a fantasy, but there is no *real* operation of magic or the supernatural in the entire book. The answers to these questions cannot be absolute.

The following survey of fantasy types is necessarily broad and incomplete—the twentieth century has been prodigal with fantasy. To avoid the simple dichotomy often made in discussions of fantasy (works that are "high fantasy" and those that aren't), we have imitated some of Lynn's divisions, although we use fewer than she and are not always in agreement with her placement of a particular book. (Science fiction, which often overlaps with fantasy, is discussed in Thomas J. Weber's "Children's Science Fiction," below.)

Folk Tale and Fairy Tale

The twentieth century does not have the equivalent of the great nineteenth-century folklorists who produced, to the delight and ben-

The Farthest Shore, Ursula K. Le Guin, illustrated by Gail Garraty

The River at Green Knowe, L. M. Boston, illustrated by Peter Boston

efit of children, the great fairy and folk tale collections. The Brothers Grimm, Andrew Lang, Joseph Jacobs, and others performed services of inestimable value to children's literature, and their collections are not likely to be superseded in this or any other century. The twentieth century has produced, however, new editions and/or translations of the work of these men, some of which are in themselves classics. For instance, in the two-volume *The Juniper Tree and Other Tales from Grimm* (1973), beautifully illustrated by Maurice Sendak, Lore Segal and Randall Jarrell have translated selections from Jakob and Wilhelm Grimm's books into fine prose. The stories are unbowdlerized, true to the originals. Ralph Manheim's translation of *Grimms' Tales for Young and Old* (1977) may be one of the best now available: true to the tales in both word and incident, as unembarrassedly frank as the originals. Brian Alderson's annotated edition of Lang's *The Blue Fairy Book* (1978) provides some cultural context and background for the tales. Other good collections of the early folklorists' material have been made by Peter and Jørgen Asbjørnsen, Roger Lancelyn Green, Ruth Manning Sanders, and Seon Manley and Gogo Lewis, among others.

This is not to say that the twentieth century has not produced new collections of folk and fairy tales. The twenties and thirties showed a lively interest in oral traditions from many lands and produced notable collections of traditional materials from all over the world. Parker Fillmore retold Czech folk tales in *Czechoslovak Fairy Tales* (1919) and *The Shoemaker's Apron* (1920); Russia was represented in Ida Zeitlin's *Skazki: Tales and Legends of Old Russia;* Padraic Colum, besides his fine retellings of Irish myths such as *The King of Ireland's Son* (1921), collected Hawaiian folk tales in *At the Gateways of the Day* (1924) and *Bright Islands* (1925). The stories in Charles Finger's award-winning *Tales from Silver Lands* (1924) were collected from South American Indians during his travels on that continent. African folk tales collected from the Haussa in Nigeria were retold by Erick Berry in *Black Folk Tales* (1928), and French author Blaise Cendrars's unfortunately titled *Little Black Stories for Little White Children* (translated in 1929 by Margery Bianco) contained a wide variety of African tales.

In the forties, Pura Belpré's *The Tiger and the Rabbit and Other Tales* (1946) represented Puerto Rican folk culture. Harold Courlander collected Haitian folk tales in *Uncle Bouqui of Haiti* (1942). A Chinese author, Lim Sian-Tek, gave us *Folk Tales from China* (1944), and Arthur Waley translated *The Adventures of Monkey* (1944). Frances

Carpenter's *Tales of a Korean Grandmother* (1947) and Yoshiko Uch-
ida's *Dancing Kettle and Other Japanese Folk Tales* (1949) provide further
evidence that the 1940s, despite or maybe as a result of World War
II, were years in which interest in the culture and traditions of other
nations was strong.[5]

Stories from the heritage of Native American tribes of both con-
tinents have also formed part of the strong folkloric tradition of the
twentieth century. Among the best early collections of these are Cyrus
MacMillan's *Canadian Wonder Tales* (1918) and *Canadian Fairy Tales*
(1922), probably better known in the combined edition, *Glooskap's
Country and Other Indian Tales*. These stories of Glooskap, the supernatural hero of the Micmacs, are retold in strong, simple prose; they
have perhaps been somewhat bowdlerized but are nonetheless myths
of power and have some flavor of authenticity. Much the same can
be said of *Skunny Wundy and Other Indian Tales* (1925), a collection of
Seneca stories by Arthur C. Parker (Gawaso Wanneh).

Some modern treatments of Native American materials show an
especial interest in the "trickster" tales, which are so clever and often
so amusing. *Raven the Trickster: Legends of the North American Indians*
(1981) by the Canadian poet Gail Robinson is a wonderful combination of the truly terrifying ("Cannibal") and the truly funny ("The
Man Who Sat on the Tide"). A splendid selection of the tales collected
from the Pawnee, Blackfeet, and Cheyenne by George Bird Gunnell
in the 1870s has been edited by John Bierhorst: *The Whistling Skeleton:
American Indian Tales of the Supernatural* (1982). These have the au-
thentic chill of the traditional ghost story but are also a mine of
information on tribal beliefs and customs. B. Traven's retelling of
Mexican Indian myth, *The Creation of the Sun and the Moon* (1968), is
a vivid and moving account of how the young hero Chicovaneg, with
the aid of the Feathered Serpent, creates a new sun to replace the
one put out by evil spirits; in the second half of the legend, Chicovaneg's son, aided by the rabbit Tul, creates the moon. Jamake Highwater's *Anpao: An American Indian Odyssey* (1977) is a quest story constructed from elements drawn from the traditional tales of the
Indians of the Great Plains and the Southwest.

The Appalachian folk tales collected by Richard Chase in *The Jack
Tales* (1943) and *Grandfather Tales* (1948) are now considered classics.
They are American retellings of much older tales, most of them from
traditional European folklore, but they are flavored by the colorful
mountain idiom and a strong sense of local setting.

Interest in traditional folklore has continued to the present. Some notable retellers and editors of the last twenty years include Alan Garner, Virginia Haviland, and Helen Cresswell. Verna Aardema's retellings of African tales are justly famed, especially *Why Mosquitoes Buzz in People's Ears* (1975). Terry Berger's *Black Fairy Tales* (1969) are from South Africa, from Swazi, Shangani, and m'Suto oral traditions. The American Indian collection edited by Richard Erdoes, *The Sound of Flutes and Other Indian Legends* (1976), features stories told by Native Americans such as Lame Deer and Leonard Crow Dog. *The Magic Orange Tree and Other Haitian Folktales* (1978), collected by Diane Wolkstein, gives off a pervasive atmosphere of island culture. *The Stone Statue of an Ancient Hero and Other Chinese Tales* by Ye Shengtao and others (1983) is translated into readable English prose by Betty Ting (Liu Yi Fang).

The most striking impact of social change upon collections of traditional tales is shown in the emergence of feminist collections of fairy tales. In these collections, the emphasis is upon strong, positive images of women; therefore, they do not include any of the traditional fairy tale heroines who are so passive and so dependent upon the good services of a prince. In Rosemary Minard's *Womenfolk and Fairy Tales* (1975), Molly Whuppie, Kate Crackernuts, Cap o'Rushes, and Clever Grethel are representative heroines: they are strong, competent, and independent. "Three Strong Women," a Japanese tale in which a famous wrestler is shown to be pitifully weak in comparison to a family of three incredibly strong women, defies all expectations: not only are the women stronger, the strongest is the grandmother. Most of this collection is European or Oriental in origin; one tale is African. In *The Maid of the North: Feminist Folk Tales from Around the World* (1981), selected by Ethel Johnston Phelps, there is also an international flavor. There are two African tales, three North American Indian tales, and a number of lesser-known European tales. Phelps has also collected nonsexist folk and fairy stories in *Tatterhood and Other Tales*. The feminist collections highlight stories that, although as exciting to read or hear as "Rapunzel" or from a tradition quite as long as that of "Sleeping Beauty," have never had the fame the more passive heroines' stories have had. But Mollie Whuppie and her ilk may be characters whose time has come.

Traditional materials are often excluded from discussions of fantasy because they have no specific author, just editors, collectors, retellers, and adapters. If they are fantasies, they are not the fantasies of a single, unique imagination but of all the imaginations that have retold them. Perhaps they are products of a cultural collective unconscious. Certainly, they are the stuff on which literary fantasy builds.

The Literary Fairy Tale

The literary fairy tale has a specific author who uses the conventions of the traditional fairy tale to create a new story. Although there are serious, even "high serious," literary fairy tales, many are humorous, often deriving their humor from mild parody of the traditional tale. Although the literary fairy tale is not peculiar to the twentieth century (Andersen, MacDonald, Ruskin, and Wilde, among others, contributed to it in the nineteenth century), it is well represented there. Indeed, the century begins with the publication of the comic fairy tales of E. Nesbit (Edith Bland), *The Book of Dragons* (1900) and *Nine Unlikely Tales* (1901). Most of these tales are in the mold of Kenneth Grahame's "The Reluctant Dragon" (*Dream Days,* 1898): humorous, whimsical, and contradictory of some of the expectations we normally bring to a fairy tale. In *The Book of Dragons,* for instance, there is the Manticora ("The Book of Beasts"), which eats milk and pussycats and is terrified of dragons; or there is the wicked Prince Tiresome with his hunting pack of hippopotami ("The Fiery Dragon"); or the princess of "The Island of the Nine Whirlpools," who, during her long years of imprisonment on the island, "lived on her income."

Nesbit's fairy tale characters usually have all the vividness of real individuals. But her special talent for creating real characters in fantastic situations is never fully exploited in her short stories. It is in her fantasy novels that this aspect of her genius is most fully realized. These works are discussed later under "Magic Adventure Fantasy."

Another writer of literary fairy tales was Rudyard Kipling, with *Puck of Pook's Hill* (1906) and *Rewards and Fairies* (1910). In these books, Puck arranges for Dan and Una to meet characters from English history of the past three thousand years. The stories are very fine, if somewhat unduly chauvinistic about the excellence of all things English. The central theme is necessity: when fate leads to a particular choice, the right-thinking person can do only the honorable, responsible thing. From the slave boy reared by fairies, accepting his slave collar, to the early tribesman selling his eye to buy the secret of iron for his people, these characters are moved by an interior necessity that overrides personal desire. "What else could I have done?" they ask repeatedly; and though they could in fact have done otherwise, they could not have done so while remaining true to themselves.

The tales of Eleanor Farjeon are somewhat lighter, although she has her more serious themes. *Martin Pippin in the Apple Orchard* (1921) and *Martin Pippin in the Daisy Field* (1937), *The Little Bookroom* (1931), *Jim at the Corner* (1958; originally *The Old Sailor's Yarn Box*, 1934), and *The Old Nurse's Stocking Basket* (1931) are but a few collections of her memorable stories. But the prolific Farjeon was not a very disciplined writer. Some of the stories seem to go on and on through unnecessarily repetitious convolutions. Even the great "Elsie Piddock Skips in Her Sleep" (in *Martin Pippin in the Daisy Field*) is too long.

Barbara Leonie Picard tells very traditional fairy tales in which the good-hearted and pure of spirit do live happily ever after. She is rarely comic in the Nesbit vein and, although somewhat whimsical, is never precious. Her collections are *The Mermaid and the Simpleton* (1949), *The Faun and the Woodcutter's Daughter* (1951), *The Lady of the Linden Tree (1954)*, and *The Goldfinch Garden: Seven Tales* (1963).

Rootabaga Stories (1922) and *Rootabaga Pigeons* (1923) by Carl Sandburg are marvelous original tales in the tradition of the American folk tale and tall tale. Humorous, exuberant, idiomatic, and poetic, these tales provide shifting perspectives on reality. Even the titles give a sudden, quirky twist to the world we know: "The Wedding Procession of the Rag Doll and the Broom Handle and Who Was in It," "How the Animals Lost Their Tails and Got Them Back Traveling from Philadelphia to Medicine Hat," "The White Horse Girl and the Blue Wind Boy." This last is a mythic quest story of beauty and simplicity, perhaps the best in the collection.

The fairy stories of Nicholas Stuart Gray are similar in style to Farjeon's but have a more mordant humor. Particularly amusing are his demons, who view human endeavors with amusement, irony, and annoyance. *Mainly in Moonlight: Ten Stories of Sorcery and the Supernatural* (1965) contains "The Reluctant Familiar," in which the demonic familiar thoroughly fouls up a mission to win a princess for John Dee and leaves Dr. Dee confronting a djinn who has by mistake swallowed Dee's love potion. *A Wind from Nowhere* (1979) and *The Edge of Evening* (1976) continue Gray's combination of wit and high sorcery.

Joan Aiken's hilarious *Armitage, Armitage, Fly Away Home* (1965), *A Small Pinch of Weather* (1971), and *Smoke from Cromwell's Time and Other Stories* (1970) are fine collections by a very inventive writer. The stories dealing with the Armitage family are particularly pleasing, especially "The Land of Trees and Heroes."

The fairy tales of Jane Yolen are less humorous, more bittersweet, after the fashion of Andersen or Wilde. *The Girl Who Cried Flowers and Other Tales* (1974), *The Hundredth Dove and Other Tales* (1977), and *The Moon Ribbon and Other Tales* (1976) are collections of stories in which often the strange and marvelous has some difficulty finding acceptance in the world.

The short stories of Isaac Bashevis Singer are in the tradition of tall tales and also of the allegorical fable. The Fools of Chelm figure in more than one of his collections, but they also have their own delightful volume, *The Fools of Chelm and Their History* (1973). *Naftali the Storyteller and His Horse, Sus, and Other Stories* (1976) and *Zlateh the Goat and Other Stories* (1966) provide a good representative sampling of Singer's wise laughter.

Virginia Hamilton's *The Time-Ago Tales of Jahdu* (1969) and *Time-Ago Lost: More Tales of Jahdu* show one of the most imaginative of black American writers creating in the folk tale mode. Mama Luka tells stories of Jahdu, a young boy with magical powers, to Lee Edward, whom she is babysitting.

Like the traditional fairy tale, the literary fairy tale has undergone some changes in response to political and social change. In Gray's and Aiken's stories in particular, the heroines are much less passive than in most traditional tales. Jay Williams's *The Practical Princess and Other Liberating Fairy Tales* (1978) is perhaps too self-consciously revisionist to be altogether effective. The stories are somewhat more liberationist-didactic than magical. Rather better is Beverly Kellar's *A Small, Elderly Dragon* (1984), in which the intellectual, liberated princess is a bit of a pain in the neck but has courage and intelligence.

Living Dolls and Other Toys

The fantasy of the living toy is a natural outgrowth of the observation of children's play. Probably the most famous single example of this type of fantasy was written in the nineteenth century: Andersen's "The Steadfast Tin Soldier." But the twentieth century has made some striking contributions to this subgenre. Many, like Frances Hodgson Burnett's *Racketty Packetty House* (1905) or Abbie Farwell Brown's *The Lonesomest Doll* (1901) are almost forgotten, perhaps unjustly. Others, like Margery Williams Bianco's *The Velveteen Rabbit; or, How Toys Become Real* (1922) have become cult books, enjoying a bigger vogue among college students than among children.

Johnny Gruelle (John Barton Gruelle) produced the first of many Raggedy Ann books in 1918, *Raggedy Ann Stories.* This red-haired rag doll with her shoe-button eyes and her candy heart has adventures with her companion doll, Raggedy Andy, and other toys of the girl Marcella. Although the villains they encounter are not very villainous, the adventures sometimes entail some genuinely upsetting moments. Because of identification with the rag doll as a living thing, the loss of her shoe-button eyes (which are replaced), the washing off of her facial features (which are painted back on), and other admittedly reparable mutilations, as well as squeezings, twistings, tearings, and dowsings in water, are somehow more distressing than amusing.

Winnie-the-Pooh (1926) and *The House at Pooh Corner* (1928) are so convincing in their picture of the personalities and lives of Winnie-the-Pooh, Eeyore, Piglet, and the others that one forgets they are toys. Indeed, they live more independent lives than most "living toys": they are not confined to a nursery or a house. They live in their own territory, a wood, a meadow, a tree, and Christopher Robin comes to this simple fantasy world to visit them. Their adventures are gently comic. Their personalities are clearly defined by a few outstanding and never-varying qualities: Tigger bounces, Piglet is timid, Eeyore is morose. These are comfortable, safe, charming fantasies redolent of security. "Endearing" is the word for A. A. Milne's stuffed toys.

Rachel Field's *Hitty: Her First Hundred Years* (1929; British title, *Hitty: The Life and Adventures of a Wooden Doll,* 1932) gave children's literature a good picaresque novel in which the adventuring first-person narrator is a doll. The style in which Hitty expresses herself is charmingly formal—rather like that of a nineteenth-century lady writing in her journal. Hitty is a keen observer of everything from changing fashions to local customs as she is carried about the world by her owners.

Miss Hickory (1946) by Carolyn Sherwin Bailey is something out of the ordinary in doll books. No human characters appear in Miss Hickory's world. She is tough, tart, and independent, and her adventures are with the animals in the forest where she lives. Although sometimes frightened and defensive, she is the ultimate survivor, becoming part of a blossoming apple tree even after Squirrel has eaten her head.

Of Rumer Godden's many doll fantasies, the best is *Impunity Jane: The Story of a Pocket Doll* (1954). This story, about a gutsy doll who longs for adventure and is bored in the doll's house of the little girl who owns her, broke with convention by showing Gideon, the little boy who "borrows" Impunity Jane but finally comes to own her, playing with a doll and enjoying it. Unfortunately, Godden had to have Gideon worry about being thought a "sissy," as indeed he is called by a rough gang of boys. He escapes humiliation by calling Impunity Jane "a model," so that the other boys decide to play with her too.

Pauline Clarke's *The Twelve and the Genii* (1962; American title, *The Return of the Twelves,* 1963) is based on the delightful hypothesis that the toy soldiers that once belonged to Branwell Brontë might be rediscovered and brought to life by a young boy. The wooden soldiers are still loyal to the Brontë children ("the Genii" of the title), and their determined trek by night to the Brontë Museum, formerly the parsonage at Haworth, has both a poignancy and a rightness to it. Although the living soldiers are reminiscent of the Old One, the magical toy soldier in Edward Eager's *Knight's Castle* (1956), they are more individualized. Since the action of the book focuses not upon play with the soldiers but rather upon the accomplishment of their goal, the return to their proper place, they have a dignity and human purposefulness unusual (although not unique) in living toy stories.

The Mouse and His Child (1967) by Russell Hoban, a quest story about wind-up toys, has levels of meaning and implications that make it suitable for an older audience than is usually attracted to living toy stories. The mouse and his child are searching for a process by which they can become self-winding; the child, however, wants something further: a family and a home. The characters include a tramp who is a kind of deus ex machina; a villainous rat who pursues the pair relentlessly; a theatrical troupe, the Caws of Art, who perform a play that is a not-unkind parody of Samuel Beckett's late works; a fortune-telling frog; and other mechanical toys. Hoban is a writer at once witty and serious. The seemingly hopeless quest of the two mice is almost a parable of the individual's search for independence from the coercion of circumstance, yoked with the theme of interdependence through love freely exchanged.

Although there have always been living toy fantasies that make use of the material of reality—human characters to interact with the toys, human settings for the toys to move about in—a recent novel by Sylvia Cassedy, *Behind the Attic Wall* (1983), blends the themes of modern realism and the fantasy of living dolls in a most effective fashion. The child protagonist, Maggie, is an orphan, bitter, withdrawn, angry, and badly behaved, who has been thrown out of nine foster homes and boarding schools because of "poor adjustment." When she comes to stay with her great-aunts in their huge house that was once a nineteenth-century boarding school, the stiff, unaffectionate, cranky aunts come no closer than any previous adults to reaching the real Maggie who is hidden so deep inside this unprepossessing exterior. Only Great-Uncle Morris, with his strange inconsequential chatter and odd jokes, seems to like Maggie and to take her bad behavior lightly. And Maggie's behavior is genuinely bad; she is not a merely mischievous child. But her rudeness, hostility, and dishonesty are the products of deep-rooted fear.

When she first hears the strange voices in the house, she is puzzled; when she learns that the aunts cannot hear them, she is frightened and angry. She notes that Uncle Morris seems to hear them, but he turns her questions aside with his daft jokes. "When it is time" the voices call her to come to tea; she finds her way to a hidden room behind the attic wall where two living dolls, Miss Christabel and Timothy John, wait with their live china dog, Juniper. At first Maggie behaves as hatefully to them as she does to the rest of the world; in fact, she knocks them down. But later she begins to enjoy their company and the tranquility of their room. Their conversation is very like Uncle Morris's, but with them Maggie's latent imagination and wit blossom; she, too, can toss off airy persiflage. She does not understand the rules that govern the dolls' lives and limit their sphere of action, but she tries to observe them, especially the rule that no one else must see the dolls or something terrible will happen.

One day through Maggie's carelessness the aunts see the dolls, and suddenly they are not alive anymore. Maggie puts together details from the dolls' conversations and Uncle Morris's meanderings and realizes that the dolls are reincarnations of the people who built the house and founded the early boarding school. She is desperate to bring them back, slipping up to the attic to try to revive them, having pretended conversations with them in which she does all the voices, finally begging Uncle Morris to bring them back, for she is sure he knows how. He says he will "when it is time," but then he dies, and

Maggie, who is being sent away to yet another home, goes to say goodbye to the dead dolls. She, the "impossible" child, the unlovable child, tells the dolls she loves them. It is this new-learned capacity for loving that will enable her at last to have a permanent home with her new family. Still the dolls do not live. When she is packed, minutes before she must leave, she hears them calling her. She rushes to the attic, having only time to say a *real* goodbye. They are indeed alive again, and another doll is with them: Uncle Morris.

The poignancy of Maggie's grief and the long, slow struggle of her stunted emotions to come to the surface make this one of the most touching of modern fantasies. Maggie is an absolutely believable emotionally damaged child, a child straight out of the New Realism. But the dolls, strange as they are, have their own convincing reality. The combination is strikingly effective.

Magic Adventure Fantasy[6]

In magic adventure books, the child protagonists encounter, acquire, or themselves become magic. Most commonly, the magic is embodied in a talisman of some sort (a ring, a book, even a bedknob). The tone of this subgenre is generally humorous; some of the best comic writing in fantasy occurs here. Much of the comedy derives from the interaction between the magical and the real; realistic characterization and setting counterpoise bizarre events. Structurally, magic adventures are usually episodic. Problems, such as keeping adults from noticing the magical happenings, are inherent in the mixture of reality and magic, and usually plague the protagonists throughout the book. The past mistress of this category of fantasy is E. Nesbit.

Nesbit's singular talent lay in her creation of vividly real children and her almost uncanny understanding of how they think, feel, and behave. She also had a fertile imagination for the magical. Her ability to combine realistic children and magical events believably has rarely been equaled. Her fullest expression of this talent was not in her short stories but in her children's novels, especially in the trilogy *Five Children and It* (1902), *The Phoenix and the Carpet* (1904), and *The Story of the Amulet* (1906), and in what many consider her masterpiece, *The Enchanted Castle* (1907). This last work is quintessential Nesbit. Four children, neither perfectly good nor perfectly bad, bright, imaginative, and resourceful, acquire a magical talisman, a ring. Initially unaware of its magical properties and later uncertain of the rules that govern it, they work out the uses of the ring by trial and error.

If it sometimes seems mostly error, that, too, is typical of magic in Nesbit's works: it is a troublesome thing, setting its possessors at odds with the mortal world. Of course, to get what one wishes for is not always good; magic, at least in Nesbit, takes wishes very literally and seems indifferent to consequences. When a careless wish gives life to the Ugli-wuglies, dummies the children have made from old clothes, walking sticks, golf clubs, and other such items, the comedy has a tinge of nightmare. But in addition to being perilous, magic is also beautiful. The children in *The Enchanted Castle* can see the statues in the Duke's grounds come to life; they can play and swim with marble gods and feast upon divine food.

Nesbit's realistic characterizations of children—something she may have learned from Grahame's *Dream Days* and *The Golden Age* (1900)— were especially influential. At long last, children in books for children could be neither prudes nor prigs but normally, healthily mischievous. Although Nesbit's plots integrating magic convincingly with the real world were often imitated, her most successful followers have appeared in the latter half of the twentieth century. Of these, the most consistent is Edward Eager, who has a similar deft humor, a similar eye for the incongruities of magic in the modern world.

Eager's characters frankly acknowledge the preeminence of Nesbit's works:

> This summer the children had found some books by a writer named E. Nesbit, surely the most wonderful books in the world. . . . And now yesterday *The Enchanted Castle* had come in, and they took it out, and Jane, because she could read fastest and loudest, read it out loud all the way home, and when they got home she went on reading, and when their mother came home they hardly said a word to her, and when dinner was served they didn't notice a thing they ate.[7]

In fact, in one book (*The Time Garden*) Eager's children briefly glimpse Nesbit's characters flying on the magic carpet from *The Phoenix and the Carpet*.

Despite all this homage, Eager is not a mere carbon copy of Nesbit. Her work is the model, but his plots are his own. His settings are American, his period the 1950s, and his realism gently colored by a fifties American idealism and optimism. Like Nesbit, he has some social awareness; especially in *The Well-Wishers* (1960) he shows his children's concern for social problems. But the problems are presented in soft focus, and the solutions are too simple, the villains too easily converted or overcome, the general populace too good-hearted to be true. Nesbit's portrayals of wretched poverty, in, say, *Harding's Luck,* are brief but memorable, and she does not encourage complacency about the status quo when, in *The Story of the Amulet,* the children visit a future to which early twentieth-century Britain seems a barbaric, primitive Dark Age. Eager lacks this toughness. But his sense of magic is quite as powerful, and his imagination nearly as inventive as Nesbit's. *Knight's Castle* (1956), with its living toys who reenact *Ivanhoe* in accordance with the children's play, is the liveliest; *Magic by the Lake* (1957) is perhaps the most nostalgic. *The Time Garden* (1958) is a time-travel fantasy set in Massachusetts. *Magic or Not?* (1959) and its sequel, *The Well-Wishers,* are patterned after such works as Nesbit's *The Wonderful Garden; or, The Three C's* (1911), in which the real magic is in the loving hearts of the children.

Mary Poppins (1934) by P. L. Travers and its sequels, *Mary Poppins Comes Back* (1935), *Mary Poppins Opens the Door* (1943), and *Mary Poppins in the Park* (1952), may be among the most outstanding fantasies for children ever written. (The abecedarian *Mary Poppins from A to Z,* 1962, and *Mary Poppins in Cherry Tree Lane,* 1982, are mere footnotes to the canon.) They are only superficially in the Nesbit tradition: the magic personage, Mary Poppins, is as prickly as the Psammead, Nesbit's sand fairy; the children, especially Jane and Michael, are as realistically curious, fun-loving, and occasionally naughty as any of Nesbit's characters; the magic is not merely malicious but dangerous if the children activate it while being naughty when Mary Poppins isn't nearby. But *Mary Poppins* is really sui generis. The apparent mixture of realism and fantasy—the world of Cherry Tree Lane and the park mixed with Mrs. Corry's shop and Mr. Twigley's wishes—is really not a mixture at all; the adult characters, Mr. and Mrs. Banks, the Lord Mayor, the Park Keeper, may one and all participate in and be touched by the magical events. Unlike the children, they may not really remember the magic when it's over, but for a short time the children within them are called out by the magic. In Travers's world, the great gulf between adults and children is bridged, and the real world—the lane, the park, the shops—is filled with magical people and events. Mary Poppins is the medium, not just through which magic enters the real world, but through which the magic of the real emerges.

Each book except *Mary Poppins in the Park* follows a similar pattern, although the order of events differs: Mary Poppins arrives, unexpectedly and by extraordinary means; she promises to stay until some specific improbable or impossible event occurs; she takes the children with her to visit one of her eccentric but gifted relations; she tells the children a story that is somehow linked to their real lives (their handyman is really "The Dirty Rascal"; Michael's china cat is "The Cat That Looked at a King"); one of Mary Poppins's odd (and sometimes frightening) friends proves to have extraordinary powers (the gilt stars from Mrs. Corry's gingerbread become stars in the sky; the peppermint canes bought from Miss Calico fly; Nellie-Rubina brings spring); one of the children has a bad day, gets into terrible trouble, and must be rescued by Mary Poppins (only in the first two books); the children, by magic escort or invitation, are taken to some grand celebration attended by supernatural beings (talking animals, the constellations, characters from fairy tales and books, etc.) honoring Mary Poppins; the condition for Mary Poppins to leave is fulfilled, and she departs.

Like Nesbit's, Travers's books are episodic; each chapter contains a complete event. But this pattern of episodes is not a mere formula. It is a construct, almost a maze, that the children walk each time, coming in each book a little closer to the heart of the matter, the secret of magic in themselves. Near the conclusion of *Mary Poppins Opens the Door* (the last of the patterned books, for *Mary Poppins in the Park* is a collection of discrete adventures and stories) Michael asks Mary Poppins,

> "Shall we, too, Mary Poppins?". . . .
> "Shall you, too, what?" she enquired with a sniff.
> "Live happily ever afterwards?" he said eagerly.
> A smile, half sad, half tender, played faintly round her mouth.
> "Perhaps," she said, thoughtfully. "It all depends."
> "What on, Mary Poppins?"
> "On you," she said, quietly. . . .[8]

Mary Norton's *Bed-knob and Broomstick* (1957; originally two books, *The Magic Bed-knob; or, How to Become a Witch in Ten Easy Lessons,*

1944, and *Bonfires and Broomsticks,* 1947) has particularly charming characters: a self-taught witch who is prim and proper, with flashes of a real desire to be wicked; three bright, observant children; and an incompetent seventeenth-century wizard. The magic talisman is an enchanted bedknob.

Black and Blue Magic (1966) by Zilpha Keatley Snyder, Roald Dahl's *Charlie and the Chocolate Factory* (1964), L. M. Boston's *The River at Green Knowe* (1959) from her Green Knowe series, Nicholas Stuart Gray's *The Apple Stone* (1969) and *Down in the Cellar* (1961), *The Ogre Downstairs* (1975) by Diana Wynne Jones, *The Midnight Folk: A Novel* (1927) by John Masefield, *A Grass Rope* (1957) by William Mayne, and *The Genie of Sutton Place* (1973) by George Selden are some other very good examples of this popular subgenre.

Talking Animals and Other Beast Tales

The talking animal fantasy exists in a variety of forms, depending upon the degree of realism of the depictions of the animals *qua* animals, upon the nature and type of interaction the animals have with humankind, and upon the extent of the animals' "humanization." Increasingly, in novels featuring otherwise realistic animals who talk among themselves and think like humans, there has been a shift to serious themes relating to real-world issues. The animals are frequently trying to escape or alleviate evils caused by mankind. Such books usually have at least some didactic purpose and show a keen awareness of ecological issues.[9]

One of the first such books was *Bambi* (1928; 1923 in Germany) by Felix Salten. Although not originally intended for children, it is one of those books enthusiastically adopted by them, and few people nowadays think of it as an adult novel. It has its sentimental elements, but it also shows Nature as sometimes "red in tooth and claw." Man as hunter is of course the great enemy, even more deadly than the natural predators.

In *Mrs. Frisby and the Rats of NIMH* (1971) by Robert C. O'Brien, a group of superintelligent laboratory rats comes to the aid of Mrs. Frisby, a field mouse. Here again man is the enemy: Mrs. Frisby must move before her present nest is destroyed by a farmer's plowing. The scientists and technicians whose experiments have produced the rats are working on potentially destructive projects. Mankind's commitment to technological progress without concern for the harm it can do is contrasted with the wisdom of the animals (see also Weber, "Children's Science Fiction," below).

The works of Richard Adams have demonstrated the human threat to the natural world most effectively. In *Watership Down* (1974; 1972 in Britain), the odyssey of the band of rabbits is caused by Fiver's premonitions of disaster. The disaster does come and is described in realistic but horrific terms: the entire rabbit warren is destroyed by men, evidently land developers. The animals' sense that mankind and all its works are destructive is well founded.

In N. M. Bodecker's *The Mushroom Center Disaster* (1974), human litter is the problem; in Sandy Clifford's *The Roquefort Gang* (1981), animal experimentation threatens mice. These books are asking human sympathy for our fellow creatures and make a serious case in entertaining fashion.

E. B. White's *Charlotte's Web* (1952) shows farm animals in a relatively realistic light; in fact, the dilemma of Wilbur the pig's impending doom is caused by his being *just* a pig to the farmer, however much he may be a pet to the farmer's young daughter. When the spider Charlotte alters the human perspective on Wilbur through the messages she weaves into her web ("Some pig!"), the farmer spares Wilbur. He and the general public suddenly see that Wilbur is special. Despite the realism of the animal characters' relationship to humans, White is not directly commenting on that relationship; he is apparently not criticizing meat-eaters, nor does he suggest that the works of man upset the ecological balance and damage the environment. The focus of *Charlotte's Web* is the friendship between the pig and the spider, the death of Charlotte as part of a natural cycle, and the continuance of her life and friendship for Wilbur through her offspring. Thus, White's animals teach a philosophical truth that is applicable to the lives of the human audience.

The more fantastic, less realistic talking animals are often featured in comic tales. But this is not always true: these characters are often merely humans in disguise and are capable of the full range of human emotion and experience. And all that range can be found in the works of Beatrix Potter, perhaps the greatest inventor of talking animal tales in this century. She had, of course, the advantage of being an artist as well as a writer. She did not have to rely upon words alone to create her characters; yet the words alone will do it.

> Her print gown was tucked up, and she was wearing a large apron over her striped petticoat. Her little black nose went

sniffle, sniffle, snuffle, and her eyes went twinkle, twinkle;
and underneath her cap—where Lucie had yellow curls—
that little person had PRICKLES! . . . .

The little person made a bob-curtsey—"Oh, yes, if you
please'm; my name is Mrs. Tiggy-winkle; oh, yes if you
please'm I'm an excellent clear-starcher!"[10]

Graham Greene in his fine essay "Beatrix Potter" uses this last sen-
tence to illustrate the economy with which Potter could draw a character's portrait.[11]

Greene (perhaps ironically) divides Potter's work into comedies
and tragedies. The great comic period begins in 1904 with *The Tale
of Two Bad Mice* and lasts until 1908, when *The Tale of Jemima Puddle-
Duck* introduces what Greene calls her "first smiling villain." The
climax of this darker period comes with the publication of *The Tale
of Mr. Tod* (1912), with its repellent villain the badger Tommy Brock.
The Tale of Pigling Bland the next year ends on an optimistic note.
Potter wrote but little after that (*The Tale of Little Pig Robinson*, published in 1930, had been written very early).

Potter's stories are witty and ironic. She has often been compared
to Jane Austen, but the narrow society from which she elicits universal
truth is peopled by rabbits, hedgehogs, mice, squirrels, and toads.
Her animals do behave like animals in many respects, but they are
human in more respects. Through them, Potter comments on human
behavior. There is a human villain, Mr. MacGregor, but he is nowhere
near so sinister as Tommy Brock. Potter's animals are not particularly
at odds with human technology and ways. In fact, they dress and live
like humans, with most of the furnishings of the human world.

Another author whose talking animals live quite human lives is
Kenneth Grahame. *The Wind in the Willows* (1908) is one of the best-
loved children's books in English, a book at once comic and serious,
dreamlike and real. It is a profoundly consolatory story, showing
repeated episodes of losing, then recovering, home.[12] Mole, lost in
the Wild Wood, is found by Rat, and then, both lost, they find the
door to Badger's home and are welcomed in to food, warmth, and
pleasant companionship. In the chapter "Dulce Domum," Mole recovers briefly his literal home. When Mole and Rat go adventuring
with Toad in his caravan, Rat is wretchedly homesick for the River,
to which they eventually make a safe return. But in "Wayfarers All"
Rat is tempted to leave home and become a wanderer. Mole prevents

him, and eventually the writing of poetry soothes Rat's wanderlust. In "The Piper at the Gates of Dawn," the lost baby Otter is found safe at the feet of the God and returned to home and family. Finally, the climax of the book is the forcible recovery of Toad Hall from the stoats and weasels.

This is not, of course, all there is to the novel. The portrayal of a vanishing rural world of natural beauty gives a poignancy to the beautiful descriptions of river, field, and wood. The unquenchable Toad's comic adventures in the world of men give us a view of humanity as essentially alien to the natural world of the Riverbank. Humans are not especially enemies to it; indeed, it would seem that they do not even know about it, and their power does not extend there. Toad is safe when he reaches the Riverbank. When Badger shows Mole the tunnels of his home, he tells Mole that once there was a city of men there. But the men went away; the Badgers remain.

In *The Wind in the Willows* the animals can assert, as Badger does, that the comings and goings of mankind do not concern them; whatever happens to men, the animals will endure. But in 1986 what the human race does unquestionably affects animals; and when the human race goes, it will not go alone.

An unusual animal fantasy in the *Bambi* tradition, but more allegorical, is Agnes Smith's *An Edge of the Forest* (1959). A small black lamb is chased into "The Children's Forest" by a mad (psychotic, not rabid) sheepdog and is there adopted by a young black leopardess. But the lamb needs milk, so the leopardess forces a doe to feed the lamb in return for the safety of her fawn. Traveling with the deer herd is hard for the lamb, whose short legs cannot keep up. Finally, the lamb decides to return to Man, and the deer, the leopardess and her mate, and the owls, who love the lamb, follow her to see that Man does her no harm. The young shepherd and his grandmother are frightened at the sight of the leopards, and the grandmother wants the boy to kill the lamb to distract the leopards so they can get away. Fortunately, he does not; the wild beasts turn back into the forest at the sight of the lamb safe in his arms.

The lamb, a mild, helpless, domestic animal, is a very disturbing element among the wild beasts. "Are you death?" she asks the young black leopardess, and this is not the hardest of the questions she asks. For her, both the leopardess and the deer try to change their natures, and partially succeed. The wild animals fear Man, with reason; but the lamb remembers the shepherds as symbols of safety and protection. She cannot survive in the wilderness forever, however much the wilderness tries to accommodate her. Yet briefly, for her sake, there is peace between enemies; even the Great Enemy, Man, in his role of shepherd and protector, is for a moment not the enemy but just another of the ill-assorted friends of the small black lamb.

Michael Bond's *A Bear Called Paddington* (1960; 1958 in Britain), *Tales of Olga Da Polga* (1973; 1972 in Britain) and their many sequels have made this little bear and guinea pig almost as familiar to the nursery as Winnie-the-Pooh. Paddington lives in London with the Browns, who found the little Peruvian bear abandoned in Paddington Station. Olga Da Polga, the fat and vain guinea pig, is somewhat less well known. Both Paddington and Olga are highly comic characters, obstinate and idiosyncratic. They get into trouble with humans occasionally, but not because they are animals. There is little awareness of humanity's threat to the environment. Paddington, especially, is a very urban bear.

Joan Aiken's *Arabel's Raven* (1974; British title, *Tales of Arabel's Raven,* 1972) and its sequels, *Arabel and Mortimer* (1981) and *Mortimer's Cross* (1984), may not properly be talking animal fantasies, since Mortimer the raven says only "Nevermore" or "Aark!" However, he prefers walking to flying, sleeps in a coal scuttle, and likes to drive lawnmowers. Aiken's humor is sometimes satirical, as when, in *Mortimer's Cross,* she involves Arabel and Mortimer with a kidnapped punk-rock star. There is an awareness of environment in these books, especially of the monstrous disruptions caused by man and machinery, but it appears mostly through Aiken's realistic depiction of the urban-suburban setting. Mortimer loves machinery, the noisier the better.

Secondary Worlds and Alternative Histories

In his essay "On Fairy-Stories," J. R. R. Tolkien considers the "true" fairy story to be one set in a world other than the real one that we know. He calls such a world a "secondary world," and the art of making it, "subcreation."[13] The making of such fantasy worlds may be the activity in which humanity most clearly demonstrates its likeness to God. Such fantasies are sometimes called "high fantasy." This category is probably the one most people mean when they say "fantasy."

Paddington's Story Book, Michael Bond, illustrated by Peggy Fortnum

Charlotte's Web, E. B. White, illustrated by Garth Williams

Alternative histories are versions of life in this world, but a world whose history has so changed that it has little correspondence to factual history. For instance, magic may operate as an ordinary aspect of day-to-day life in an alternative history.

Oz is the first fully developed secondary world of the new century. *The Wizard of Oz* by L. Frank Baum (originally *The Wonderful Wizard of Oz*) was published in 1900, and Baum wrote thirteen sequels to it, ending with *Glinda of Oz* (1920). There are a number of later sequels by other authors. Baum was an inventive and original fantasist, especially skilled in the art of naming. But his plots in the later books are often strained, and the characters, while still lovable, less individual than the early characters in everything but name.

Because of the popularity of the movie starring Judy Garland, Oz may be the secondary world best known to American children. As Jordan Brotman points out in "A Late Wanderer in Oz," this fantasy kingdom is backed by "the hardness of real experience."[14] Although there are many little utopias in Oz, there are also little Kansases, or Kansas-type characters, scattered throughout the books. Yet for all the drabness of the Kansas that Baum depicts, the essential quest in *The Wizard of Oz* is Dorothy's search for a way to return home. It is in this quest to recover her home and in the consolation of the quest's satisfactory completion that *The Wizard of Oz* most closely conforms to Tolkien's description of the "eucatastrophe," the happy ending after struggle and pain.

J. M. Barrie's famous secondary world, Never-Never Land, first appeared in the play *Peter Pan; or, The Boy Who Wouldn't Grow Up* (1904). A novelization of the play also appeared in 1904, and in 1906 *Peter Pan in Kensington Gardens* (an abridgment of *The Little White Bird*, 1892) confirmed the lasting appeal of the ageless boy. Various abridgments of the novel *Peter Pan* followed. The full-text edition of *Peter Pan and Wendy* (1921) is probably the most useful for scholarly purposes.

Never-Never Land has become a permanent part of the English-speaking world's mythology. This land where boys never grow up and where all the elements necessary for adventure are readily available (pirates, Indians, fairies) has become a symbol on the one hand of an unattainable paradise and on the other hand of irresponsible escapism, just as Peter Pan himself has become a symbol of both the eternal boy and the immature, irresponsible man. From a woman's viewpoint, poor Wendy gets a raw deal: unlike the boys, she must at once assume the responsibilities of maturity and be a mother to the Lost Boys. And of course, Captain Hook, the threatening mature male with his phallic hook-hand, is a Freudian critic's delight; however, even he and his pirates are childish. Only the females show a sense of responsibility and potential for growth.

Interestingly, Barrie's vision of the perfection of eternal immaturity has attracted few imitators. As a matter of fact, although in most children's books adults are to a degree the enemy, the authority figure, it is also a convention that the child wants to become one. This is both psychologically right—we have by nature a desire to grow as well as an imperative to do so—and (one hesitates to say it) morally right. In Natalie Babbitt's *Tuck Everlasting* (1975; see "Mythic Fantasy," below), Winnie Foster has the opportunity to remain eternally young and to live forever; it is her triumph that she chooses instead to mature, to grow old, and to die. However, Barrie does have a follower among modern writers, and the Lost Boys do have direct descendants: the Borribles! How horrified Barrie would be.

Michael De Larrabeiti's *The Borribles* (1978; 1976 in Britain) is the story of apparent children with pointed ears who live free and wild in the urban environment, and who will remain children as long as they are not caught by the adults, particularly the police, who would clip their pointed ears and make them go to school and *grow up*! Why they prefer their feral existence is puzzling; they live with almost continuous violence and carry on running warfare with their enemies, the Rumbles. Several of them die violently; but a Borrible apparently prefers death to maturity. The barbaric Borribles may be, however, a more realistic vision of what such children would be like than Barrie's Lost Boys were.

In 1937, J. R. R. Tolkien's *The Hobbit* appeared, and readers were introduced to the world of Middle Earth, a world inhabited by dwarves and dragons, elves and men, and other denizens of faerie. Hobbits are short and usually stout; they look like children of men, but they have substantial, hairy feet. The hobbit of the title is Bilbo Baggins, a very conventional, comfort-loving hobbit who suddenly plunges into adventure, accepting a position as a burglar with a band of dwarves who plan to steal an ancient treasure from a dragon. Bilbo matures and changes on his journey, and his adventures set in motion events described in Tolkien's great romance for adults, *The Lord of the Rings*.

Tolkien's influence on twentieth-century fantasy is difficult to overestimate. It shows not so much in direct imitations of his work (though some have been written, most of them bad), or even in the spate of hobbitlike creatures, talking, walking trees, cranky wizards, elaborate fantasy languages, and so forth, but rather in the sudden expansion of the mythic scope of fantasy. Perhaps the words of Fred Inglis, despite his dislike of *The Lord of the Rings* and its influence, best describe this change. "After Tolkien, a whole new galaxy of writers has emerged to write for children out of a deep, swelling sense that the world has been stripped of its magic, the throat of poetry cut, the cherished individual severed both from his own significance and the chance of action which will make a difference to things."[15]

C. S. Lewis's Narnia series started with *The Lion, the Witch, and the Wardrobe* (1951) and ended with the seventh volume, *The Last Battle* (1956). Narnia is a kingdom in another world visited by children from our world; in fact, only a Son of Adam or Daughter of Eve can rule in Narnia. The country is populated by talking animals and trees, and Lewis borrows creatures from mythology freely. Father Christmas drops by in *The Lion, the Witch, and the Wardrobe,* and Silenus and Bacchus lead a bacchanal in *Prince Caspian.* Lewis's children are modeled after Nesbit's and have the same naturalness and believability. They embark upon higher adventures than Nesbit's children do, but they have the same necessary equipment: courage, ingenuity, and goodness of heart (although this last is demonstrated with far less abandon than in Nesbit's books). Lewis's themes are Christian, and he has there been somewhat influenced by George MacDonald's fantasies in which the magical being (the great-great-grandmother in the Curdie books, for instance) has some level of divine meaning.

There is much to admire in these books. For one thing, we often see the action from the point of view of one of the girls. Lucy in the first three books and Jill Pole in the last two of the series are competent, brave, intelligent girls, and we get to know their inward thoughts. The central characters of the other two books, *The Magician's Nephew* (1955) and *The Horse and His Boy* (1954), are boys. However, it is troubling that in *The Last Battle* Susan, who no longer believes in Narnia, is spoken of as if she were damned. Edmund, a traitor in the first book, repented and was forgiven; in *The Voyage of the Dawn Treader* (1952) Eustace, a troublemaker, repented and was forgiven. Why is Susan so roundly condemned?

Another worrisome element is the obvious Semitic origin of the great villains of Narnia, the Calormenes. They are dark-skinned, wear clothing out of the Arabian Nights, and have religious and social customs that in our world, at least, are generally to be found in the Middle East. Although one of them is portrayed in *The Last Battle* as courageous, devout, and good, the others are cruel, destructive, dishonest, and hypocritical. And the special trappings of their culture make them not an exotic imaginary species but clearly another of Lewis's borrowings from Earth's culture. One cannot but conclude that this is an undesirable racial image.

Strangely, Lewis destroyed Narnia in *The Last Battle*. This apocalyptic novel is a rarity in children's fantasy: the end of a secondary world. Sometimes such a world may be cut off from further contact with outsiders, but never destroyed. Yet Narnia ends. The children die. There is even a Last Judgment and an afterlife. This last, to be sure, turns the conclusion into a "eucatastrophe," a happy ending after great grief. Although the frightening events of *The Last Battle* have a truly mythic grandeur to them, Lewis's motive for thus ending the series remains puzzling. It may be that it is the necessary conclusion to the underlying Christian mythos of all of the books.

Ursula K. Le Guin's Earthsea trilogy, *A Wizard of Earthsea* (1968), *The Tombs of Atuan* (1971), and *The Farthest Shore* (1972), takes place in a world where magic is a high art. Ged, the dark-skinned hero,[16] goes to the school for mages on the island of Roke to be educated as a wizard. In *The Tombs of Atuan*, he recovers the Lost Rune of Peace; in *The Farthest Shore*, Ged, now Archmage on Roke, conquers the dead wizard who is draining the magic out of the world, and identifies the boy who is to be the long-awaited High King. These novels have all the elements of other high fantasy: magic, wizards, dragons (the best since Tolkien), quests, opportunity to do good, temptation to do evil. But there is also something new: a philosophy almost Buddhist in its quietude and restraint, a concern for peace, and an emphasis on the balance that must be maintained among all things in nature.

The most successful of the three books is the first. *A Wizard of Earthsea* shows us Ged as a boy of great talent and great pride. On Roke, he allows himself to be goaded into calling up a spirit from the dead; the black shadow that comes with it claws him savagely but is driven away by the Archmage. Ged recovers but is no longer quick to learn or quick to anger. His face is scarred, and his future holds little promise. The shadow is abroad in the world and will pursue him wherever he goes. He evades it for a time but finally, on the advice of the old wizard on his native island, turns to confront it—and it flees. Ged does not think he can overcome it, for true magic gains its power from the true names of things, and the shadow seems to have no name. But when at the end of a long pursuit Ged forces the shadow to face him, it has come to look like him. He calls it "Ged" and grasps the shadow, and they merge into one. He had called his own death and fear of death out of the land of the dead. When he acknowledges and accepts it, it has no power over him.

The parallels between this novel and "Tom-Tit-Tot," the old British version of "Rumpelstiltskin," are striking. The mother who changes her complaint of her daughter's greed ("My daughter has eat five pies today") to a boast when the king rides up ("My daughter has spun five skeins today") creates an opening for the black thing out of pride, and the daughter by her silence endorses it. In order to save herself after the black impet has done the spinning for her, she must name it truly. And when the king overhears its boasting chant ("Nimmy, nimmy, not, / My name's Tom-Tit-Tot") and mentions it to the girl, she is able to name the creature, and he vanishes. *The Wizard of Earthsea* is rooted in the tenets of very old myth; both it and the frightening little folk tale tell us of the need to know what our shadows truly are.

Lloyd Alexander's Westmark trilogy (*Westmark*, 1981; *The Kestrel*, 1982; *The Beggar Queen*, 1984) and Diana Wynne Jones's Dalemark books (*Cart and Cwidder*, 1975; *Drowned Ammett*, 1978; *The Spellcoats*, 1979) share a modern awareness of political reality and a concern for the poor and oppressed. Alexander has lively debate among his revolutionaries; ultimately, his hero rejects violence and his heroine rejects her throne in order to place the government in the hands of the people. Jones shows a similar conflict and confusion in the mind of the young revolutionary in *Drowned Ammet*.

In *The Blue Sword* (1982) and *The Hero and the Crown* (1984), Robin McKinley creates the kingdom of Damar, which, in *The Blue Sword*, bears a strong resemblance to India under the colonial rule of the British; and she explores sympathetically the mistakes and actual wrongdoing that stem from the colonizers' failure to understand the native population. A very likable heroine, Harry Crewe, is kidnapped by the Damarian tribesmen and trained as a warrior to fight with them against the not-human enemy whose army is approaching the border. Harry, who unbeknownst to herself has a Damarian ancestor, has the supersensory powers of the Damarians, and with the help of visits from the spirit of the long-dead Damarian hero-queen Aerin Dragonslayer, she defeats the enemy forces by pulling a mountainside down onto them. *The Hero and the Crown* goes back to a much earlier period in Damarian history to recount the exploits of Aerin Dragonslayer.

Patricia McKillip's *The Riddle-Master of Hed* (1976), *Heir of Sea and Fire* (1977), and *Harpist in the Wind* (1979) take place in a world in which the solving of riddles has become a high art, and Morgan, Prince and Riddle-Master, bears upon his forehead three stars that constitute a riddle more important than any other in the world. This is very serious fantasy about identity and the uses of power.

On a lighter note, four of the Minnipins in Carol Kendall's *The Gammage Cup* (1959) are outlawed from their village of Slipper-on-the-Water in the Land Between the Mountains because of nonconformity. When they rouse the villagers to combat a band of mushroomlike invaders, all is forgiven and the value of individualism somewhat understood.

Alternative histories are somewhat less common than secondary world fantasies and can be quite amusing as well as adventurous. In her series that takes place in an England in which the Stewarts were never driven from the British throne, Joan Aiken satirizes the Gothic novel, Dickens, *Moby Dick,* and whatever else takes her fancy. Her extravagant imaginings (a cannon in the Hidden Forest on Nantucket big enough to shoot to England, a plot to put St. Paul's on rollers and push it into the Thames during the coronation, and so forth) are in themselves hilarious. Her villains are outrageously sinister, but her heroines and single hero are uncommonly real, despite the impossibility of some of their actions. Especially vivid is the unquenchable Dido Twite. The books are, in order, *The Wolves of Willoughby Chase* (1962), *Black Hearts in Battersea* (1964), *Nightbirds on Nantucket* (1966), *The Cuckoo Tree* (1971), and *The Stolen Lake* (1981).

Diana Wynne Jones's *Charmed Life* (1977) and *The Magicians of Caprona* (1980) take place in an alternate world in which the practice of magic is the norm and the great enchanter Chrestomanci is responsible for seeing that all magical activities are performed responsibly and with due care. Although each book has its serious theme, there is also much humor and extravagant adventure. *Witch Week* (1982), in which Chrestomanci also appears, is set in yet another alternative world in which magical activity of any sort is forbidden

The Lion, the Witch and the Wardrobe, C. S. Lewis,
illustrated by Pauline Baynes

The Hobbit; or, There and Back Again,
written and illustrated by J. R. R. Tolkien

upon pain of death. The terrors of literal witch-hunting are brought out, while the adventures of the young witches who are trying to hide their natures are nonetheless essentially amusing.

More serious is Peter Dickinson's The Changes trilogy, *The Weathermonger* (1968), *Heartsease* (1969), and *The Devil's Children* (1970). In an England that has mysteriously reverted to the thinking of the Middle Ages, any memory of the modern world or any interest in machinery is dangerous. In each of these books, two very valuable themes are explored: the nature of bigotry and intolerance, and the value or danger of technology.

Mythic Fantasy[17]

This category comprises fantasy based upon traditional myth and new stories that are mythic in nature. Mythic fantasy novels are sometimes also secondary world fantasies and include some of the most powerful of modern fantasies.

Alan Garner's *The Weirdstone of Brisingamen* (1960) may be a landmark in children's literature, not because it is a masterpiece (actually, it has the predictable weaknesses of a first novel), but because it is the first novel for children to tap the wealth of primal myth, especially Celtic folklore, as a source for fantasy, and to allow real children while still in the real world to have "frightening (rather than comic) adventures."[18] The influence of *The Weirdstone* and its sequel, *The Moon of Gomrath* (1963), can be seen in the works of Penelope Lively and Susan Cooper, among others.

What many consider Garner's best fantasy artistically came in 1967: *The Owl Service*. Again, Garner uses the stuff of ancient myth, in this case the medieval Welsh *Mabinogion,* as the cause of terrifying events involving modern teenagers. An old set of china on which the pattern seen one way is flowers, another way, an owl, carries a curse. When the three young people, two boys and a girl, unpack the china, the curse begins to work, and they seem impelled to relive an ancient tragedy. The human emotions brought out by the curse are not created by it, however. Resentment, jealousy, anger, and even love are already there under the surface. The interactions of these powerful feelings would make this a moving novel even if the fantasy element were removed.

Penelope Lively's fantasies are also firmly grounded in myth, especially local folklore. Like William Faulkner, she is acutely aware of the relationship between the past and the present, and the impact of the past on the present. In her books, the past often reawakens into the present, sometimes with comic, sometimes with tragic effect. In *The Ghost of Thomas Kempe* (1973), the ghost of a seventeenth-century sorcerer decides that the boy who lives in what was once his room must be his apprentice. The problems arising from this are very funny, and complicated by the impossibility of convincing anyone of the truth. In *The House in Norham Gardens* (1974) an old shield from New Guinea brought to the house by Clare's great-grandfather gives her visions of the life of the tribe and a sense that the shield should go back to them.

The five books that make up Susan Cooper's *The Dark Is Rising* sequence are based on Arthurian myth and recount a long-running struggle between the powers of good and evil, the Light and the Dark. The first book, *Over Sea, Under Stone* (1965), is the weakest, really just a summer holiday story with a bit of magic thrown in. It is in the second book, *The Dark Is Rising* (1973), that Cooper's writing and the series really take off. *Greenwitch* (1974), *The Grey King* (1975), and *Silver on the Tree* (1975) complete the set. It is sadly true that for all the breadth of conception of the fantastic, Cooper's fantasy is flat and unconvincing when dealing with real characters without magical powers. And within the realms of the fantastic itself, the reader is not always convinced that the powers of the Light are really morally and ethically better than the powers of the Dark. Both are totalitarian and demand unquestioning obedience; the representatives of both deceive mortals as to their true nature; both are ruthless in the pursuit of their cause; both manipulate mortal minds and memories to suit their purposes. Although the plots are interesting and the action exciting, the underlying philosophy is dubious.

Lloyd Alexander's Prydain series is loosely based on Welsh mythology. *The Book of Three* (1964), *The Black Cauldron* (1965), *The Castle of Llyr* (1966), *Taran Wanderer* (1967), and *The High King* (1968) tell the story of Taran, the Assistant Pig-Keeper, and how he matured and changed and was finally chosen to be the High King. Taran's quest for a father and an identity is a theme throughout, as is the wastefulness and ugliness of war in comparison to the crafts of peace. Alexander is sometimes openly didactic on this latter theme, and his techniques of characterization are heavy-handed. Characters talk in the catchphrases attached to them ("crunchings and munchings," "A

Fflam is always . . .") and sometimes have objects that seem a part of their identities (the Princess's bauble, Fflewddur Fflam's harp).

A mythic fantasy that seems almost a realistic novel and really defies classification is Natalie Babbitt's *Tuck Everlasting* (1975). The Tucks have drunk from a spring that gives immortality and halts aging. When Winnie learns their secret, they kidnap her long enough to explain why she, too, must keep the secret. As Tuck explains to Winnie, life is useless if you cannot grow and change, and growing and changing means dying when the time comes. On the other hand, Tuck's seventeen-year-old son begs Winnie to drink the water when she becomes a teenager, so that there will be an immortal girl to be a companion to him. When Mae Tuck is arrested for killing the wicked stranger before he can force Winnie to drink, Winnie sees as much as the Tucks the necessity of freeing Mae, so she helps with the escape. Many years later, the Tucks return to the town and find Winnie's grave.

The wisdom of *Tuck Everlasting* is well matched by Babbitt's unselfconsciously rhythmic and simple prose. She deals with motifs that have fascinated humanity since earliest times, eternal life and eternal youth. Like Le Guin in the Earthsea trilogy, Babbitt rejects this cherished human dream, intimating that it would devalue rather than enhance life. The acceptance of death as a natural part of life is presented very positively but without distortion or preaching. The spokesperson for this view, Angus Tuck, is eloquent but uneducated; his simple, earnest plea for Winnie's understanding is both moving and convincing.

Patricia Wrightson's *The Nargun and the Stars* (1973) is one of several of this Australian author's books to utilize aboriginal myth in a fantasy. The Nargun is a creature made of stone, born in the morning of the world. It hates the noise of machinery, which drives it away from its longtime lair. Eventually it comes to the sheep station in the outback where the orphaned Simon Brent has just come to live with his elderly cousins. The Nargun is dangerous but not malicious. In its own strange way it loves even the things it kills. But the humans are frightened and oppressed by its presence nearby. With the aid of the prankster Potkoorok, another ancient spirit, Simon and his cousins entrap the Nargun in a cave deep within the mountain. When the mountain falls, the undying Nargun will again see and yearn toward the stars.

Wrightson's work is important because, besides the fact that she writes well, she uses the unfamiliar mythology of a little-known culture to illuminate, even criticize, modern technological culture. Her treatment of the delicate balance of nature as not merely a complex ecological structure but also a complex spiritual structure has no tint of sentimentality or romanticism because of the thoroughly nonromantic characters of the mythological creatures, the astringent Potkoorok of the swamp, the wispy, grieving Turongs of the trees, the aggressive Nyols of the caves.

Philippa Pearce's *Tom's Midnight Garden* (1958) is technically a time-travel fantasy, but time, too, is the matter of myth. This superb fantasy, which John Rowe Townsend considers "a masterpiece,"[19] contains mythic truth about the workings of time, of youth and age, and of friendship. Tom goes to visit his uncle and aunt in their flat in a grand old house. He finds that on nights when the grandfather clock strikes thirteen he can go out into a beautiful garden that is not there in the daytime and play with Hatty, a sad and somewhat neglected orphan. Hatty and the garden belong to the old house in the past. Long periods of time elapse in the past between Tom's visits, and he is still a boy when Hatty is quite clearly becoming a young lady. At last a night comes when the garden is not there; Tom, frantic and grief-stricken, rouses the house calling for Hatty. The landlady, old Mrs. Bartholomew, whom Tom has never seen, sends for Tom the next morning: *she* is Hatty, and her dreams of the lonely childhood in which she desperately wanted a friend have called the Midnight Garden of the past into being.

A mythic conception that has long had a strong grip on the human imagination is that of miniature people. In Greek mythology, the pygmies who battle the cranes are a notable example. The most famous literary use of this conception occurs, of course, in Book I of Jonathan Swift's eighteenth-century satire *Gulliver's Travels*. But the Lilliputians have their twentieth-century chronicles too. In T. H. White's *Mistress Masham's Repose* (1946), the descendants of some Lilliputians brought to England by Gulliver are discovered by Mavis living on the grounds of her ruined estate. She has not only to control her personal "Yahoo-ish" tendency to treat the Lilliputians like dolls and play with them but also to protect them from the plots of her wicked governess to sell them to a circus.

The most notable use of miniature people in twentieth-century children's fantasy, however, is in Mary Norton's series about the Borrowers: *The Borrowers* (1952), *The Borrowers Afield* (1955), *The Bor-

rowers Afloat (1959), *The Borrowers Aloft* (1961), *Poor Stainless* (1971), and *The Borrowers Avenged* (1982). Borrowers are tiny people who live by "borrowing" from human beings. They have great ingenuity, which they need, for they are vulnerable to almost every living thing that is larger than they are. Despite their reliance on man-made materials, mankind is the greatest danger in their world, and the most shameful thing a Borrower can experience is to be seen by a human being. Despite this, Arrietty Clock, daughter of Pod and Homily, is strongly attracted to humans and has a lamentable tendency to become friends with them. As emerges in the course of the series, there are two significant dangers to Borrowers from association with humans: one is exploitation, as when the wicked Mr. and Mrs. Platter, in *The Borrowers Aloft,* cage the Clocks, intending to use them as an attraction in their touristy model village; the other is loss of self-reliance when a kind human being becomes aware of the Borrowers' existence and begins making things for them and giving them an excess of material goods. In the last volume (which, despite the thirty years that elapsed between it and the first volume, is quite up to the standard of the other books), the Platters are effectively routed. But as Pod points out, despite the willingness of Mr. Potts and Miss Menzies to protect them, the Borrowers must move once more. They cannot rely upon the protection of human beings, however kind, without losing their independence and self-reliance. Arrietty, reluctantly, at last sees the force of this.

Arthurian legend has been an important source of mythic fantasy in this century and has figured peripherally in many works of other fantasy subgenres as well. It supplies the villain in Lively's *The Whispering Knights* (1971), the magic behind The Changes in Dickinson's trilogy, the time-disrupting candle in William Mayne's *Earthfasts* (1966), and one adventure in Eager's *Half Magic* (1954), to name but a few. The most striking use of the Arthurian materials, however, was made by T. H. White in *The Sword in the Stone* (1938), the first book of *The Once and Future King*, his retelling of Malory's *Morte d'Arthur.*

The Sword in the Stone is the story of Arthur's childhood as a presumed illegitimate foster child in the castle of Sir Ector. Ector's son Kay lords it over "the Wart," as Arthur is called, more or less unconsciously and without malice. Still, the Wart is a child without family or a real place of his own in the world, and his existence, while not miserable, is nonetheless somewhat sad and insecure. But when Merlin agrees to tutor the Wart and Kay, Arthur begins to learn without knowing why the necessary lessons of manhood and of kingship. Merlin's methods are unusual: the Wart is changed into a fish, a hawk, a wild goose, a badger, and so on; he learns to value nature by being a part of it, and he learns courage, tenacity, fidelity, and compassion against the day when, as king, he will need all these traits.

Magic, wizardry, and witchcraft are themselves the stuff of myth, and recently, perhaps influenced by the upsurge of occult novels for adults, there have been a number of novels for young people that touch upon the dark and dangerous side of magic and magical beings. Meredith Ann Pierce's *The Darkangel* (1982) and *A Gathering of Gargoyles* (1985) feature a slave girl, Aeriel, who becomes the thirteenth bride of a vampire whom she must kill in order to free the wraiths of his other wives and to prevent his attaining his full powers. But because she loves him, as he is dying she exchanges hearts with him, thus not merely saving his life but also restoring him to humanity. He and she must then begin to gather the material to fulfill the prophetic verse that will accomplish the downfall of the witch who made him a vampire.

Margaret Mahy's *The Changeover* (1984) is an unusual story on several levels. It features a genuinely frightening villain; a warm and affectionate single-parent family; an abused and alienated young man with occult powers; a teenage heroine who is courageous, natural, and vividly real; and a moving and gently erotic love story.

The materials of the early English and Scottish ballads are redolent of primeval myth and speak, as all myth does, to elements deep in the core of the human heart and mind. One early ballad, "Tam Lin," has been used more than once as a basis for Young Adult novels, including Dahlov Ipcar's *The Queen of Spells* (1973), Elizabeth Marie Pope's *The Perilous Gard* (1974), and Diana Wynne Jones's *Fire and Hemlock* (1985). Of these works, the best is the most recent, Jones's novel, because it is rather more complex and fully developed than the earlier ones.

In *Fire and Hemlock,* nineteen-year-old Polly Whittacker discovers that she has two contradictory sets of memories of her past. The surface, apparently real memories of quite an ordinary life are mere camouflage intended to insure that she forgets Thomas Lynn. As Polly recovers her true memories, she also gains an understanding of her past, her love for Tom, and the impending crisis of the coming Halloween on which Tom is doomed to die.

The richness of *Fire and Hemlock* stems, first, from the gritty portrayal of Polly's real life. Her wretchedness and confusion during her parents' divorce; her despair when her paranoiac mother throws her out of the house and her weak, charming father fails her; her joy in her tough, spunky grandmother's stability and love, all combine to provide a substratum of firm reality upon which the supernatural fantasy is built. Second, Jones has drawn an intricate network of mythic and literary interconnections that keeps the reader aware that the events of the plot are part of a pattern running not merely deep in time but deep in human nature. Thomas Lynn knows Polly is his hope of salvation but is forbidden to tell her the truth about himself, his condition, and her role. Therefore, he tries to tell her indirectly through the countless books he sends her: *The Oxford Book of Ballads*, a collection of fairy tales, *The Golden Bough*, and so on. When Polly finally draws things together, the reader does, too, and sees, like Polly, that all the clues make sense: that the story Polly and Thomas Lynn are living is an old story, terrible and beautiful and somehow known by us throughout all our years.

Fantasy in all its forms may well be the largest genre of children's literature in the twentieth century. Certainly it contains a striking number of "classics," books that seem likely to outlast the shifts of tastes and trends. Modern fantasy is notable for fully developed characters (e.g., Maggie in *Behind the Attic Wall*), serious themes (e.g., Le Guin's Earthsea trilogy), grandeur of conception (e.g., White's *The Once and Future King*), and mythic scope and resonance (e.g., Garner's *The Owl Service*). Although still vulnerable to the pragmatist's charges of escapism—for one can easily lose oneself in these bright other worlds (or brighter visions of this world)—modern fantasy, like most modern writing for children, is generally firmly based in the realities of our world, even in the most bitter and disillusioning of those realities. Like the oldest fairy tales, the best of the newest fantasy shows life as both dangerous and promising, and happiness as at once impossibly costly and also in every mortal's grasp.

The children in these books are more original and less patently virtuous than their nineteenth-century predecessors, but they are also clearly descended from Alice, Curdie, and Tom the Chimney-sweep. The tradition of fantasy is strongly rooted in the nineteenth century, but many of its flowers and fruits are products of our own time, at once sweet and tart.

Notes

1. Ruth Nadelman Lynn, *Fantasy for Children: An Annotated Checklist and Reference Guide*, 2d ed. (New York and London: Bowker, 1983), pp. 1–3.

2. Humphrey Carpenter and Mari Prichard, *The Oxford Companion to Children's Literature* (New York: Oxford University Press, 1984).

3. Sheila Egoff, *Thursday's Child* (Chicago: ALA, 1981), p. 80.

4. Ursula Le Guin, "From Elfland to Poughkeepsie," in *The Language of the Night: Essays on Fantasy and Science Fiction* (New York: Putnam, 1979), pp. 84, 93.

5. A fuller survey of folk tale editions in the early decades of the century can be found in Cornelia Meigs et al., eds., *A Critical History of Children's Literature*, rev. ed. (New York: Macmillan, 1969).

6. Category title taken from Lynn, *Fantasy for Children*, p. 164.

7. Edward Eager, *Half Magic* (New York: Harcourt, 1954), p. 7.

8. P. L. Travers, *Mary Poppins Opens the Door* (New York and London: Harcourt, Brace & World, 1943), pp. 205–6.

9. Sheila Egoff makes a similar point in *Thursday's Child* (Chicago: ALA, 1981) although she includes less realistic animals, some who wear clothing, for instance, in her discussion.

10. Beatrix Potter, *The Tale of Mrs. Tiggy-winkle* (New York: Warne, 1905), pp. 23, 25.

11. In *Only Connect: Readings on Children's Literature*, eds. Sheila Egoff et al. (Toronto and New York: Oxford University Press, 1980), p. 262.

12. Idea from a lecture presented by Samuel Pickering to the NEH Institute on Children's Literature at the University of Connecticut, August 2, 1983.

13. In *Tree and Leaf* (Boston: Houghton Mifflin, 1965), pp. 3–84.

14. In *Only Connect*, eds. Egoff et al., pp. 156–69.

15. Fred Inglis, *The Promise of Happiness* (Cambridge, England: Cambridge University Press, 1981), p. 200.

16. Although Le Guin places no emphasis on it, the only white people in Earthsea seem to be the cruel and savage Kargs of the warmongering Kargad Empire.

17. Category taken from Lynn, *Fantasy for Children*, p. 187 (characteristics described are different, however).

18. Carpenter and Prichard, *Oxford Companion*, s.v. Fantasy.

19. John Rowe Townsend, *Written for Children: An Outline of English Children's Literature* (Harmondsworth, Middlesex: Penguin, 1976), p. 247.

Children's Science Fiction

Thomas J. Weber

LIKE CHILDREN'S LITERATURE, SCIENCE FICTION is a marketing category. The commercial science fiction genre was created in 1926 by Hugo Gernsback, when he published the first issue of *Amazing Stories*. Since then the field has grown into a major American marketing genre, along with mysteries, romances, and adventure fiction. Yet SF is not definable entirely in terms of what is published within the genre itself; even before the first science fiction magazines, Jules Verne and H. G. Wells wrote popular novels that are clearly science fiction. In his historical survey *Billion Year Spree*, Brian Aldiss traces the beginnings of SF back to Mary Wollstonecraft Shelley's *Frankenstein* (1818).[1] Some trace it back farther than that. And mainstream writers such as C. S. Lewis, Kingsley Amis, and Thomas Pynchon have continued to adopt the tropes of science fiction for their own works.

Science fiction, then, is not just a commercial marketing genre but a collection of themes, traditions, and methodologies as well. It is difficult to establish a definition that includes everything readers habitually identify as "science fiction" and at the same time is specific enough to exclude works that are generally considered "mainstream." One of the broader theoretical definitions, one that also divides science fiction from fantasy, was proposed by Darko Suvin, who defines science fiction as literature that achieves its aesthetic effects through cognitive estrangement.[2] Estrangement (relocating the reader from

159

his or her present reality into one that is different and unusual, thus provoking what science fiction readers call "sense of wonder") differentiates science fiction from the "realistic" literary mainstream. This also applies to fantasy. However, science fiction sees the norms of any age (including its own) as unique, changeable, and therefore subject to a cognitive view. Fantasy similarly doubts the laws of the author's empirical world but does not use imagination as a means of understanding the tendencies latent in reality; instead, it uses it as an end in itself, cut off from real contingencies. It posits a world different from one's own where some carpets do, magically, fly, and into which one crosses purely by an act of faith and fancy. Fantasy is inimical to the empirical world and its laws. Science fiction works within them to achieve a similar effect.

Because SF exists both as a marketing category and as a field of literature, it can be expected that works within the marketing category share certain characteristics, resembling each other more than they resemble works of SF from outside the genre. This is true of children's SF as well. Within the boundaries of the science fiction genre is a subcategory of juveniles with their own shared history. Yet mainstream children's literature, like the adult mainstream, has recently found the tropes of science fiction very useful. In fact, some children's books published as early as the late nineteenth century are now identifiable as science fiction. The traditions of the juvenile within the SF genre and the SF book within children's literature are distinct and separate, however, and will be treated separately within this essay.

If it is impossible to study science fiction accurately without defining it and identifying its place in the market, it is likewise impossible to consider science fiction in children's literature adequately without first examining science fiction *as* children's literature. Thomas M. Disch argues persuasively in his essay "The Embarrassments of Science Fiction" that science fiction is primarily a children's literature, aimed at children and dealing with themes traditional in children's books.[3] Many of science fiction's most distinguished works feature children as protagonists. Most of science fiction's ardent readers are children or began reading it as children. It has been said and frequently repeated by those inside the field that "the golden age of science fiction is twelve," reflecting many readers' firm belief that the best science fiction they have ever read was that being published when they were young.

It is necessarily difficult, then, to make distinctions between juvenile science fiction and adult science fiction. There are books within the field aimed specifically at juveniles, but most children advance to "adult" science fiction with little difficulty. It is only in recent years, with the arrival of stylistic experimentation and adult themes (particularly sexuality) in the genre that any clear distinction between juvenile and adult science fiction has begun to be evident. Even so, the majority of the readership continues to be children and adults who started reading science fiction as children.

Even the marketing distinctions between juvenile and adult science fiction are inconsistent and unreliable. The juvenile works of Robert A. Heinlein and André Norton, who are by far the most prolific and influential writers of children's science fiction, have frequently been reissued in paperback as "adult" science fiction; in Heinlein's case they were often serialized in magazines as adult novels before they were published as juveniles. Nevertheless, marketing distinctions are important, as those works specifically marketed as juveniles end up in the children's section of libraries and are generally the first science fiction that children encounter. Any attempt to separate juvenile and adult science fiction through thematic distinctions is hopeless, as there is far too much overlap between the two. Even an attempt to distinguish them by the age of the protagonist results in such clearly "adult" science fiction novels as Edgar Pangborn's *Davy* or Theodore Sturgeon's *More Than Human* being classified as children's books. For works within the genre itself, marketing distinctions, however inconsistent, are the only criteria that can be effectively used, so with one exception, only works specifically marketed as "juvenile" will be considered in this essay. Nevertheless, it should be kept in mind that the entire field is read and enjoyed by, and to some extent aimed at, children.

Children's Literature Within Science Fiction

The Dime Novels started by Erastus Beadle in 1860 probably marked the first appearance of science fiction in literature specifically written for children. These were in large part concerned with the technological ingenuity of young men and their consequent adventures and inventions. *Frank Reade, Jr.* was the best-selling of the Dime Novel series, and the most science fictional, featuring numerous submarine and airplane adventures. Dime Novels declined and disappeared around the turn of the century, partly because of public outcry against their supposedly evil effects on boys, and partly because of competition from the pulp magazines. Juvenile science fiction continued in the new format of illustrated hardcover juvenile book series, the most important of which were the Great Marvel series by Roy Rockwood (house name used by publisher Cupples and Leon of New York) and the Tom Swift stories of Victor Appleton (house name of the American Stratemeyer Syndicate; first thirty-five written by Howard R. Garis), the former featuring interplanetary exploration and the latter featuring the teenage inventor Tom Swift. These early children's science fiction works were poorly written and characterized, and served largely as vehicles for the ideas contained within them. Nonetheless, they were very popular and stimulated children's imagination and ingenuity in ways that had not previously been explored. The Tom Swift series in particular helped pave the way for the early Gernsback science fiction magazines, which primarily emphasized scientific extrapolation, with literary merit at best a secondary consideration.

In 1947, with *Rocket Ship Galileo,* Robert A. Heinlein pioneered the writing of books for children that were specifically and primarily science fiction. Despite the fact that his period of writing juveniles was a relatively brief one (sixteen years) and that the last of them was published over twenty years ago (*Podkayne of Mars,* 1963), Heinlein remains the most important and distinguished of juvenile science fiction writers. His direct style, solid science, and the naturalness and ease with which he creates a societal background in just a few strokes all help to make his juveniles among the best in the field, and even among the best of his own work. They are crisp, imaginative, and involving; and while they are excellent escape novels, they are also intellectually challenging. Heinlein is exceptional among science fiction writers in that there was no drop in quality when he wrote for children. Alexei Panshin, author of the most perceptive full-length study of Heinlein (*Heinlein in Dimension,* 1968), places five of Heinlein's juveniles (three of which were originally published in adult magazines) among his seven best stories overall.[4]

Rocket Ship Galileo, the first of Heinlein's juveniles, is generally considered the first American children's science fiction work to merit serious critical attention. Nevertheless, it does not stand up to his later efforts; it is condescending, as though it were written for a younger audience than the rest of his juveniles, and the plot and characters are not particularly noteworthy. Its critical and popular success at the time is mainly attributable to the low standards then prevailing, which Heinlein would shortly help raise.

Red Planet (1949), the third Heinlein juvenile, was the first to display the originality of idea and thoroughness of background that characterize his adult fiction. The red planet of the title is Mars, complete with the "canals" observed by astronomer Percival Lowell. A private Earth-based company has begun to colonize Mars. The colonists (all of whom work for the company) avoid the deathly cold of the Martian winter by migrating from pole to pole, using ice boats that travel along the canals. They are working to make Mars a livable place for humans, primarily by attempting to extract oxygen from the Martian soil, but for the time being people survive with special suits and breathing masks. The people who run the company back on Earth, however, have no idea of the hardships facing the colonists, and through ignorance and corporate stupidity they decide to end the seasonal migrations and import more colonists. The original colonists learn of the plan, rebel against the company, and proclaim their independence.

At the same time, the colonists have to deal with the native Martians, whom they find mysterious and impenetrable. The Martians disapprove of the actions of the company and are contemplating radical measures when the revolution occurs. Events are seen through the eyes of a boy colonist who is less involved in the action itself than are the adolescents in some later Heinlein juveniles, but who is nonetheless (typically for Heinlein) the one human wise or perhaps imaginative enough to make the key conceptual breakthrough: that the Martians are more complicated than previously thought, and that dealing with them would perhaps be easier than dealing with the company. His actions are ultimately responsible for saving the colony from annihilation by the Martians, who have grown tired of fighting the humans.

Red Planet's main faults lie in its rather slow pace and the protagonist's removal from much of the action (while resentment and revolution are building among the colonists, he is busy befriending a native Martian). As a result the Martians are more fully characterized than the average science fiction aliens, and the intrigues among the Earth people come to seem secondary, less immediate, and somewhat unreal.

Tunnel in the Sky (1955) is simultaneously Heinlein's most thrilling

164	MASTERWORKS OF CHILDREN'S LITERATURE

adventure novel and one of his most trenchant commentaries on the nature of society and adulthood. It is also relentlessly dark in mood, which was unusual for children's science fiction at the time. It concerns a group of adolescents and the final test of their Advanced Survival course: they are dropped on a randomly selected planet with their choice of weapons and equipment, to be picked up again in two to ten days. Their mission is simply to survive. Only after the allotted time and then some has passed do they realize that they have been lost, or forgotten, perhaps forever; they then set about slowly and painfully building a society. After some violence between various factions of the adolescents, the central fifteen characters succeed in setting up the rudiments of a working organization, build relationships, and even have children. Two years later Earth relocates them and returns most of them to society as if they were still children, ignoring their obvious success in surviving on adult terms. Despite the encapsulation of two years of plot into the space of a juvenile science fiction novel and the sometimes stereotyped characterization (particularly of women), *Tunnel in the Sky*'s fascinating premise and its examination of the way adult society recognizes only chronological age and treats youth accordingly make it one of Heinlein's most subtle and provocative books.

Subordination of character and plot to an examination of the way societies work has often been a primary characteristic of Heinlein's adult fiction, and *Tunnel in the Sky* displays that predilection to some degree. *Citizen of the Galaxy* (1957), however, is the most thoroughgoing example of this tendency among his juveniles. On the surface, it is a relatively straightforward rite of passage story. The protagonist begins the novel as a slave, becomes a space trader and a member of the military, and eventually assumes his rightful place as heir to an Earth-based financial corporation. Along the way, he learns about himself, his place in society, and the lot and fortunes of others. But the novel is not primarily about him; it is an examination of the societies he moves through, and he serves as the reader's eyes. Heinlein contrasts various modes of structuring society and investigates several opposing economic theories. The protagonist's rise also allows Heinlein to comment on slavery, freedom, and the responsibilities of power. Unlike several of his adult novels that examine societal power structures, *Citizen of the Galaxy* largely manages to avoid attacking straw men; Heinlein has taken pains to create believable characters with real motivations and interests. Admirably, the main

Ballantine/30103/$2.25

SCIENCE FICTION ADVENTURE

Robert A. HEINLEIN

HAVE SPACE SUIT-WILL TRAVEL

Kip was willing to give up a lot to
get to the Moon—but he never
expected it to be his life!

Have Space Suit—Will Travel, Robert A. Heinlein,
cover art by Darrell K. Sweet

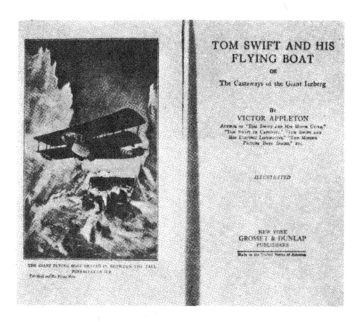

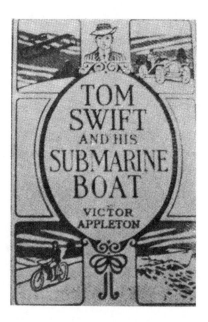

Two Tom Swift adventures by Victor Appleton,

character retains the memory of his time as a slave and upon achieving power works to change society for the better.

Unfortunately, the effectiveness of the characterization is diminished by the omniscient viewpoint Heinlein employs, which plays on the reader's interest in ideas at the expense of identification with the protagonist. Also, it is readily apparent that the societies Heinlein studies were designed before the plot, much of which is jerry-rigged and rife with coincidences that are difficult to accept. Still, *Citizen of the Galaxy* is a strong work, and an unusually serious one for children's science fiction.

Despite the fact that *Have Space Suit—Will Travel* (1958) is primarily an adventure story, lacking most of the adult themes and seriousness of other Heinlein juveniles, it is among his most successful. An eighteen-year-old boy who wants to go to the moon is the protagonist, and he is Heinlein's most thorough job of sympathetic characterization. The novel is about *him* rather than the scenery, and as he builds his own spacesuit, travels to the moon on his own initiative, goes on to Pluto, then Vega, then a near galaxy, the reader is right there with him, breathless and waiting for the next show. For good measure, Heinlein throws in a kitchen sinkful of special effects: flying saucers, aliens, Powerful Galactic Civilizations; yet the focus of the book is never lost. *Have Space Suit—Will Travel* is probably the primary example to date of the pure "sense of wonder" juvenile science fiction novel. Of course, it is not completely without thought or messsage; it has much to say about the value of brains, perseverance, and courage (a theme of primary importance in Heinlein's work), but for once Heinlein demonstrates these qualities by implication instead of lecturing about them. And the main character is so likable and believable that, as Alexei Panshin has pointed out, only a misanthrope could dislike *Have Space Suit—Will Travel*.[5]

Apart from a penchant for occasionally allowing his backgrounds to overwhelm his stories, Robert A. Heinlein has consistently displayed a fine sense of the proper synthesis in the science fiction juvenile: genuinely original and imaginative ideas combined with believable adolescent characters faced with young adult concerns. Whatever becomes of his reputation for adult science fiction, he will remain one of the most important figures in juvenile science fiction in both historic and literary terms.

Aside from Heinlein, certainly the most influential and prolific writer of juveniles within the field of science fiction has been André

Norton. Norton is in fact the single significant author in the genre whose reputation rests almost entirely upon juveniles. She is neither a skillful prose stylist nor a thematic innovator, though her novels are remarkable for their fast action and evocation of strange places. Norton writes straightforward adventure stories in which the conflict is between good and evil, and the qualities of courage, endurance, friendship, unselfishness, loyalty, and resourcefulness are assumed in her heroes and heroines. Good will and effort are consistently rewarded in the Norton universe, and if this tends to negate the effectiveness of her conflicts and villains, it has not significantly affected her popularity: most readers of science fiction began with either Heinlein or Norton, and the majority of her work remains in print.

The scale of Norton's output (over one hundred books) makes it impossible to sum up her career briefly; however, she regularly employs themes and motifs that can be considered the core of her appeal to children. Norton mixes the tropes and images of science fiction and fantasy, frequently creating a somewhat muddled overall mood: medieval and future technologies vie with one another, or coexist peacefully; space-age vehicles are drawn by animals; powerful, incomprehensible machines left by previous races are found and utilized. Yet despite this intermingling of themes, very little of Norton's work is actually fantasy; fantastic elements such as magic or telepathy are usually explained in scientific terms or set against a background of science and rationality in which what seems incomprehensible or irrational is still assumed to have a rational basis. Norton gets tremendous mileage out of Arthur C. Clarke's dictum that "any sufficiently advanced technology is indistinguishable from magic."

Norton is greatly interested in animals and their relationships with people. Cooperative and even equal relationships (frequently telephathic) between humans and animals are common in her work, and she often portrays animals as morally superior to human beings. She has sometimes achieved evocative effects by turning human beings into animals and imaginatively describing the resulting physical sensations.

Norton is also the first writer of juvenile science fiction to utilize convincing female protagonists. Until Norton, female readers of science fiction for children had to content themselves with the unexciting traditional female roles, or with mentally substituting a female version of the sympathetic male protagonist. As a result, juvenile science fiction understandably held little appeal for females and, like adult science fiction, was read almost exclusively by males until the 1960s and the broadening of the themes employed within the genre. Norton, with her uncompromising portrayals of girls performing the heroic actions previously reserved for boys, deserves much of the credit for the greatly increased number of women currently reading and writing science fiction.

Perhaps Norton's most significant contribution to children's literature has been the *Witch World* series (1963 onwards). Because magic (witchcraft) is a primary motif, these books resemble fantasy more than the rest of her novels. They are nonetheless solidly science fiction, taking place on an imaginatively rendered alien planet, with the magic presented as a scientific phenomenon. The *Witch World* stories are richly told with verve and color, and little of the sloppiness that frequently characterizes her output. The supernatural elements are lively and convincing, and tempered by a firm grounding in anthropology. The early volumes in the series are particularly fresh, moving satisfyingly from conflict to conclusion with little of the cobbled-together sense that frequently pervades her writing.

Also significant among Norton's works are *Catseye* (1961) and *Quest Crosstime* (1965). In the former, a young boy who works in a pet shop discovers that he can communicate with animals. He stumbles upon the fact that several pets in the shop are being used as secret weapons in a plot against the rulers of the planet. He is forced to flee into the Wild, and only close cooperation with several exotic animals enables him to survive and become a member of the Rangers who patrol the Wild. The latter novel is set in a future where it is possible to move "crosstime" to parallel universes. One group on a planet devastated by nuclear war proposes crosstiming so that their society can rebuild itself. The protagonists (two female and one male) are swept into a revolt organized by those opposed to crosstiming. Before the revolt is quashed, the adventure spills over to E625, a crosstime world embroiled in a tense stalemate modeled upon the conflict between the American Plains Indians and the pioneers. Both books are notable for avoiding the easy answers Norton usually provides. They are thoughtful and somewhat ambiguous, *Quest Crosstime* particularly.

Even the best of Norton's work has shortcomings in style and plotting. Her straightforward style is well designed for the type of fast-paced adventure she prefers to write, and her alien worlds are often skillfully evoked, but her characters tend to be of a piece, whether male or female. Her works are primarily escapist, and the prose rarely transcends the material. Her plots, like those of adult science fiction author A. E. Van Vogt, depend heavily upon recomplication, or what some critics refer to less kindly as the "kitchen sink technique"; that is, throwing in a fantastic new development whenever the author thinks the reader's interest may be flagging. Nonetheless, Norton's works have proved enduring, and her themes are very appealing to young readers. She is among the most significant and influential writers within the genre.

John Christopher has been the most skilled practitioner of juvenile science fiction in recent years, though his influence has been more strongly felt in Britain than in the United States. His major contributions to the form have been ambiguity and ambivalence in a literature replete with clearly definable conflicts and pat answers. His typical protagonist is a young adolescent boy, intelligent but somewhat unwise and impetuous, who is not gifted with patience, courage, judgment, or other traditional heroic virtues but must learn them in order to mature and properly accomplish his goals. He is generally faced with a tyranny to be escaped or circumvented. Technology plays an important role in Christopher's juveniles, usually as a means of destruction or social control, but also as something crucial that has been lost in his regressed futures. The main character will find himself faced with tough ethical choices in which lives, friendships, and freedom hang in the balance and no choice is wholly attractive. Christopher's tyrannies are large, frightening, and powerful, but the individuals involved in them are complex, well defined, and frequently even sympathetic. The typical Christopher juvenile book or series ends with the protagonists achieving the goals they began with, and yet the resolution will be ambiguous and the results not entirely what they had in mind: there are contingencies that had not been considered. Perhaps there is still more work to be done.

The most important of Christopher's works for children is the series that begins with *The White Mountains* (1967). Earth of the relatively near future has been taken over by aliens who appear to Earth people as huge metal tripods. The aliens dominate the humans by means of caps that are sewn on at puberty as part of a child's rite of passage. These caps control their thoughts and keep them docile. Will, a young boy approaching capping, is having doubts about the procedure, particularly as his best friend has just been through it and emerged a wholly changed person with whom Will can no longer communicate. Still, Will sees no alternative and is resigned to the inevitability of capping, until he meets and befriends one of the vagrants (feebleminded victims of unsuccessful cappings). The man then reveals himself as not a vagrant at all but a recruiting agent for the free people who live, uncapped, in the White Mountains (Switzerland), where the tripods cannot go.

After some agonizing over his place in life, Will decides to leave his family and run away to the White Mountains, propelled by fear more than anything else. He is joined by his former worst enemy, his cousin Henry, and by young Jean-Paul, a boy genius who has reinvented spectacles in a world where technology has largely been quashed by the tripods. They encounter various dangers and temptations along the way, and eventually, in one of the most evocative passages of the book, they stumble into one of Earth's old great cities (which have been entirely depopulated). There they find underground trains, huge buildings, and technological marvels, and wonder at the former glory and strength of Earth people. They take some grenades from a weapons cache, and Will uses one to accomplish the unheard-of: he kills a pursuing tripod. He and the members of his party are awestruck; they realize for the first time that they can do more than run away: they can fight back. At the close of the first book, they finally reach the White Mountains and willingly choose a life of hardship and freedom.

The second and third books, *The City of Gold and Lead* (1967) and *The Pool of Fire* (1968), relate the struggle of the free Earth people to overthrow the tripods. It is in these books that the ambiguities of the series truly begin to be felt. The free humans are quarrelsome and often less than admirable. The aliens are presented as lords and tyrants who treat humans as we do animals, yet they are capable of thoughtfulness and even kindness. In *City of Gold and Lead,* Will and his new companion Fritz become slaves in one of the tripods' great domed cities. Fritz's master is tyrannical and abusive, while Will's is considerate, treating him as a pet and even expressing curiosity about the details of human life. Will is still not wholly mature; he remains impetuous and impatient, and each of his vices is matched by a corresponding virtue on the part of slow, taciturn Fritz. Ultimately it is Will who escapes, purely by luck. He is forced to kill his kindly master after it is revealed that Will's cap is a fake one. Fleeing via the city water system, he brings vital information back to the free humans. In *The Pool of Fire* the humans use this information to destroy the various great cities. The series ends, appropriately enough, on a perfect note of ambiguity: the aliens have been overthrown, and the victorious humans immediately begin to bicker among themselves. They have solved their problem, they have won; and yet they have learned little.

Christopher's other major work for children is *The Guardians*, which appropriately won the *Guardian* prize for best children's book of 1970. It tells of an England divided into two parts: the Conurb, a technological megalopolis rife with injustice and unrest, and the County, where the gentry pursue a rural lifestyle. Rob is a Conurban whose father has died mysteriously. He has been placed in a strict orphanage where he is routinely abused and tortured by the older boys and neglected by the uncaring adults in charge. Escaping to the County, he is befriended by a resident family and passed off as gentry. Rob gradually learns of the systematic repression of dissident elements by the ruling elite. He is given the opportunity to become a Guardian, one of the elite police force who root out malcontents and maintain order. After some soul-searching, he decides instead to return to the Conurb and join the revolutionary movement. *The Guardians* is a study in tyranny and the potentially evil implications of behavioral modification and mind control, and also an examination of ethical choices, particularly individual well-being versus the common good. It is tempting to see it as a polemic against technology as well, but that would be a misreading: while technology is used by the ruling class as a tool of repression and most of the injustice in the book takes place in the highly mechanized Conurb, the agents of repression include the wealthy residents of the County. Christopher is never a simple writer, and his answers are not easy.

The extraordinary popularity of Robert A. Heinlein and André Norton, coupled with the economic boom of science fiction in the mid-1950s, led to a peak in production of science fiction juveniles in the late 1950s, barely ten years after Heinlein had pioneered the form with *Rocket Ship Galileo*. An overwhelming majority of this material was hackwork, featuring all the worst aspects of both science fiction and children's literature, and publishable only because of a perceived niche in the marketplace. After 1960, publication of science fiction novels specifically marketed as juveniles dropped precipitously, though production of children's literature with science fiction elements (and of fantasy juveniles) markedly increased.

The decline of science fiction juveniles was largely due to two

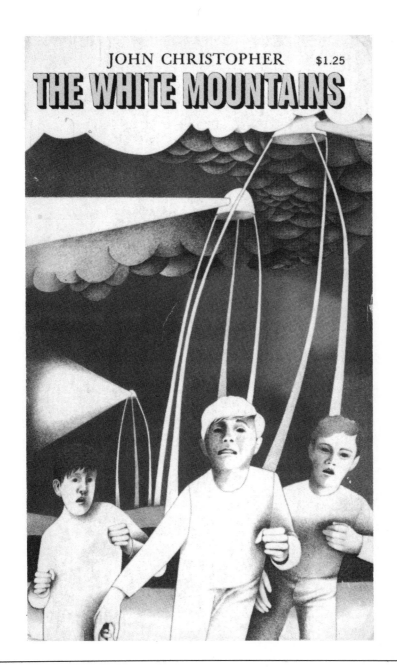

The White Mountains, John Christopher

Rite of Passage, Alexei Panshin, cover art by Leo and Diane Dillon

factors: the divestiture of the major distributor of science fiction magazines in the late 1950s, which left many of the magazines without distribution and nearly killed the entire field; and the hazy distinctions between juvenile and adult science fiction. The field had become saturated with bad juveniles; publishers discovered that people were buying fewer juveniles, that the people who bought juveniles were generally the same people who bought adult science fiction, and that the market would not bear as much bad science fiction as they had thought it would. Consequently, for a time publication of genre science fiction juveniles fell to almost nothing.

The situation has been somewhat remedied recently, with SF writers such as Gregory Benford and Laurence Yep including juveniles among their regular work, and with the growth of the fantasy juvenile field, which largely overlaps science fiction and is often marketed by the same publishers. Throughout the 1960s, however, the only regular writers of juvenile science fiction within the genre were Norton, Christopher, and Alan Nourse, and the other notable juveniles of the period tended to be single efforts by primarily adult writers. The most significant of these, and indeed the most unusual and provocative book to be published as a juvenile in science fiction, was Samuel R. Delany's *Empire Star* (1966).

Delany is a highly articulate and experimental writer. He published his first novel at the age of twenty and almost immediately became one of science fiction's major voices. He is particularly noted for complexity of structure, creative use of myth, and speculation on the meaning and nature of language. *Empire Star* was his earliest significant novel, preceding his most celebrated work (though one of his award-winning adult novels, *Babel-17*, was actually written earlier). It is the first of his books that combines his characteristic depth of thought with a skillful and interesting narrative.

David G. Hartwell points out in his excellent introduction to the Gregg Press edition of *Empire Star* that it is on one level a textbook, an instruction manual for Delany's audience.[6] The book has a story (a fairly standard journey-from-innocence-to-experience plot), but it is deliberately distanced from the reader by the systematic destruction of the plot as an element in the construction of the work. It is narrated by an alien being who is literally an embodied point of view, omniscient via time travel. In other words, the story is told from first-person omniscient point of view, something possible only in a work of science fiction (or perhaps theology).

Empire Star is written on several levels (a fact frequently noted by the narrator, making it a work of metafiction as well), yet those levels are not necessarily too difficult for Delany's young audience; he provides clues and overt instruction for the reading and interpretation of the novel, attempting to educate the reader into an intuitive state of multilevel reading. Delany is a rare animal indeed in children's literature: not only does he refuse to condescend to his audience, he attempts to bring them up to his level. This is a difficult feat, full of pitfalls, and a lesser writer might only have succeeded in frustrating or (worse) boring the reader. But the uses of language are Delany's primary fictional concern, and there is probably no one in science fiction who spends more time sorting out connotative and denotative detail in his own work: every word is chosen with care. The closing passage in *Empire Star* reads: "It's a beginning. It's an end. I leave to you the problem of ordering your perceptions and making the journey from one to the other." I doubt that his readers are disappointed.

Empire Star shares themes with many of Delany's adult novels; among the more important are the young adolescent male on a quest for an individual identity, and the lack of a solid antagonist. The latter is rare in children's science fiction, which usually requires a tangible menace or obstacle to be overcome. Delany's conflicts are rarely concrete. The "antagonists" his characters must vanquish are usually internal. In *Empire Star* the protagonist contends with his own innocence, ignorance, and desire to know what makes him special. These are mundane problems that most adolescents can readily identify with, and are in seeming opposition to the fantastic nature of Delany's settings, indeed to the settings of all science fiction. Delany's work suggests that to distance mundane "real world" considerations from fantastic literature strains credibility. His science fiction is unusual both in the scope of its speculation and in the relevance and verisimilitude of its subject matter—qualities strongly present in *Empire Star*, perhaps juvenile science fiction's most thoughtful work to date.

Alexei Panshin's *Rite of Passage* is not strictly a juvenile, in that it was never marketed specifically for children; nevertheless it deserves consideration here because of its extensive use of themes traditionally associated with children's science fiction, and because it is a loving homage to Heinlein's juveniles (making it in many ways the best novel Heinlein never wrote). It employs a common science fictional device that has yet to make its way into mainstream literature: the generation starship, bearing a society built and maintained to last the hundreds or perhaps thousands of years required to travel from one star system to another at sub-light speed. Handled cleverly, the generation starship enables the author to examine in microcosmic form the complexities of societal structure and maintenance, from law to myth-making and religion.

Panshin's generation starship is one of eight that escaped from Earth when it was destroyed a century and a half earlier. Life is increasingly rootless, and education in the form of a survival test (echoing Heinlein's *Tunnel in the Sky*) provides the starship society's initiation rite. Mia, the protagonist, is not only a prototype Heinlein heroic character, she is also a believable and sympathetic adolescent female, a trick Heinlein was never able to pull off. Her progress from childhood to adulthood is expertly portrayed as she struggles to survive in the wilds of an alien planet. When she completes her trial, she is abruptly (in her society) a full adult, providing an interesting contrast to the denouement of *Tunnel in the Sky*, in which the protagonists are forced to revert to childhood merely because of their chronological age. Adulthood does not bring Mia surety, however; in fact, she finds that' the more she learns and grows, the more questions she has, and she becomes less willing to accept things as they are. Ultimately she validly questions the stratified society of the ship itself.

Heinlein's juveniles are sometimes remarkable for decrying the twentieth-century American experience of education and maturation; *Rite of Passage* challenges that experience head-on as insufficient and artificial, arguing for an education in which adulthood is a measure of real maturity rather than an arbitrary and universal reward for reaching a certain age. Panshin has managed the difficult feat of portraying a society as a whole and its impact on individuals through the ever-changing eyes and mind of a child growing into adulthood. Simultaneously social description, social criticism, and a character study, *Rite of Passage* is the most exhaustive examination of the traditional juvenile maturation theme that science fiction has yet provided.

Science Fiction Within Children's Literature

There are many ways in which juvenile science fiction outside the marketing genre differs from that within. The most important and pervasive is the relation of the science fiction material to the fiction itself; outside the field, the tropes of science fiction are usually employed as a means to an end, whereas within the genre, the fantastic content is often an end to be explored in itself. The science fiction content of a genre novel is central, crucial to the plot and the characters; without it the story does not exist. If the science fiction content is removed from a nongenre book, however, the bulk of the fiction generally remains; it is merely looking for a new hinge on which to turn.

This removal of the science fiction from the focus is both a weakness and a strength for nongenre science fiction. On the one hand, the author is free to concentrate on character, prose style, and thematic concerns that are frequently subordinated to fantastic elements in genre science fiction. On the other hand, the distancing of the fantastic diminishes its effect and trivializes it. Cognitive dissonance is a delicate thing; if the strange and wonderful is not examined and brought to center stage but left out in the wings, the reader's sense of wonder may wither and die.

Similarly, science fiction written outside the genre is usually innocent of the accumulated tradition that readers of science fiction tend to take for granted. A frequent mistake of nongenre science fiction writers is to place overmuch emphasis on what seems to them an extremely adventurous and wild idea that was actually milked dry sometime in the 1930s. Ignorance of the history of science fiction also leads many writers of mainstream literature with incidental fantastic elements into the Science Fiction/Fantasy Trap: the assumption that all fantastic elements can be mixed together to cumulative effect. This mistake is particularly common in children's literature that employs the tropes of science fiction and fantasy. Fantasy and science fiction are generally *not* compatible; in fact, they tend to cancel each other out. The cognitive dissonance the reader experiences when the hero employs a hyperdrive to speed faster than light, move backwards in time, adjust reality, and save the day is diminished if not altogether obliterated if the villain merely waves a magic wand, says "presto-chango," and the world reverts to its former state. As Philip K. Dick is supposed to have pointed out, in a world where anything can happen, nobody cares what happens. Fiction, no matter how fantastic the elements, must have an intelligible internal logic to be effective, and the intrusion of fantasy upon science fiction or vice versa destroys that logic.

Children's literature has historically dealt much more thoroughly with fantasy than with science fiction. Before the advent of the space race and the sudden usefulness of science fiction tropes as metaphors inside mainstream literature, examples of children's books presenting real human concerns revolving around a science fiction idea were few and far between. Early attempts include the wooden and uninspiring Tom Swift and Frank Reade books discussed earlier; L. Frank Baum's *The Master Key: An Electric Fairy Tale* (1901), which is plodding and lacks the easy whimsy of his fantasies; and Hugh Lofting's *Doctor Dolittle in the Moon* (1929), which is certainly science fiction, but whose peculiarities and sense of wonder are those associated with Dr. Dolittle rather than science fiction.

The first children's novel to succeed thoroughly in both telling a fascinating story and cognitively estranging the reader is William Pène du Bois's tale of the events leading up to the eruption of Krakatoa, *The Twenty-One Balloons* (1946). It is written in first-person oral storytelling style (with interruptions) from the point of view of a retired math teacher who is found adrift in the Atlantic clinging to the wreckage of twenty-one deflated balloons, after having embarked over the Pacific with only one. It transpires that the Professor has in fact been shot down by the residents of Krakatoa, who have built a small utopia they don't want the rest of the world discovering. They agree that the fact that the winds blew him over their island is not his fault and invite him (well, compel him) to stay as their guest. The bulk of the book is spent describing their little "utopia," and it is fascinating: there are twenty family units, each with a mother, a father, a boy, and a girl; each family runs a different sort of restaurant and provides a different service to the other residents of the island. Their houses are technological marvels, incorporating devices such as automatic sheet rollers and washers so that nobody has to wash their sheets, and hydraulic beds that lift out through skylights into the night air. Oh, yes, they are also rich; Krakatoa has a huge diamond mine, and they periodically bring diamonds to the mainland and sell them for supplies. Their lives are spent in a child's dream of endless leisure; in fact, much of their spare time is devoted to thinking up new ways to amuse one another.

Lest we think that du Bois is proposing some kind of achievable utopia, he slyly tempers it with a bit of social comment; being the richest people in the world, the Krakatoans have nothing better to do than to try to outrich each other. Inflation hits all-time highs in

Krakatoa, with the typical dinner tab running, say, a quarter of a person's share in the diamond mines. But du Bois really isn't indulging in much in the way of *serious* social comment; all of the characters are drawn affectionately, and at worst du Bois sees them as a bit ludicrous (as does the reader). Ultimately, of course, Krakatoa blows up and the residents escape (with a healthy supply of diamonds) on a huge platform buoyed by twenty-one balloons. The Krakatoans ditch out family by family, leaving the Professor frantically sprinting from one end of the platform to the other, adjusting balloons to keep the platform level, and finally crashing into the Atlantic.

The Twenty-One Balloons is similar in tone to the rest of du Bois's books for children, most of which are not science fiction. Particularly, they share an amused tolerance for excess in all its forms. His current work for children is an ongoing series of separate studies of the seven deadly sins; four novels have been published thus far, and there is within them (charmingly, for children's fiction) no denunciation of vice. The lightness of du Bois's tone in *The Twenty-One Balloons* should not be mistaken for lightness of content, however; his imagination is vivid, and the book won him the Newbery Medal in 1948.

If du Bois's tone is light, Roald Dahl's in *Charlie and the Chocolate Factory* (1964) is only a shade darker. *The Twenty-One Balloons* and *Charlie and the Chocolate Factory* have much in common; in both of them, the fantastic elements are integral and indispensable to the story, and yet no plot is developed from the fantastic speculation. We are merely taken on a tour of the author's imagination and expected to gape openmouthed in awe. Both authors are skillful enough that the reader largely experiences the desired reaction but at the end is left undernourished, stuffed with rainbow-hued cotton candy. Like du Bois, Dahl views the excesses of his characters with amusement, but his humor is cruel and less tolerant. Still, even the vilest characters come out in the wash mostly unharmed.

Charlie Bucket is a quiet, unassuming, impoverished young boy. Typically for Dahl, Charlie is utterly without fault or vice, and his parents and grandfather are reasonable candidates for canonization as well. Charlie's grandest wishes come true when he becomes one of five lucky winners of a Golden Ticket that will enable him to tour the mysterious chocolate factory of the even mysteriouser Mr. Wonka and return home with all the chocolate he can eat for the rest of his life. The book is two-faceted: it is a tour of the wonderful technological world of Mr. Wonka's huge factory, which resembles nothing

Charlie and the Chocolate Factory, Roald Dahl,
illustrated by Joseph Schindelman

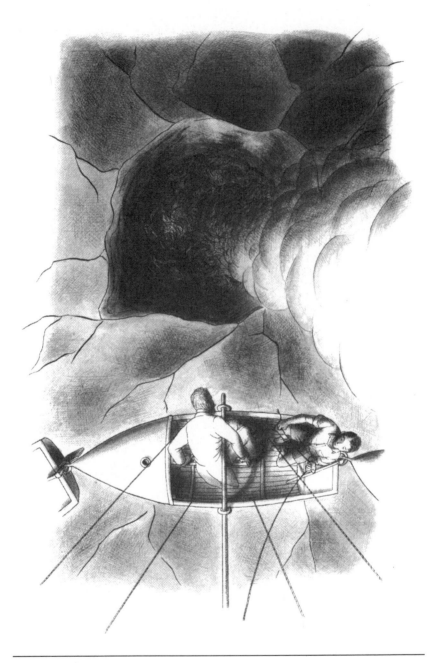

The Twenty-One Balloons, written and illustrated by William Pène du Bois

so much as a miniature version of some of the more bizarre aspects of Oz; and it is a morality tale of sorts, albeit a fairly obvious one. Each of the other four children is loathsome in their own individual way (as are their parents), and each meets a fate in the factory appropriate to their particular loathsomeness. Virtuous Charlie is rewarded at the end by being given the factory: Mr. Wonka is growing old and can no longer run things by himself.

The preachy aspects of the book would be intolerable, particularly given the breadth of the brush with which Dahl paints his obvious stereotypes (neither fat children nor rich children are likely to find much to enjoy here), were it not for Dahl's cleverness throughout. The tour of the factory is marvelous, breathtaking invention piled upon staggering improbability, and the breathless Mr. Wonka is a wonderful character, eccentric and just nonlinear enough in his thinking to convince everyone around him of his utter insanity, when of course he is perfectly sane and even a genius. Given the magnificence of the surface gloss here, it is a shame that Dahl could not have added some depth to his story. Unfortunately, this sort of wild hopping about from fancy to absurdity is characteristic of Dahl's fiction for children; it is a tribute to his considerable understanding of things children find exciting that his books are even coherent. When his imagination flags, as in the sequel *Charlie and the Great Glass Elevator* (1972), the flimsy shell collapses, revealing little within.

Science fiction abruptly came of age in a number of ways in the 1960s. Experimental mainstream writers such as Donald Barthelme, Thomas Pynchon, and William S. Burroughs discovered that the tropes of science fiction could do more than provide social extrapolation (previously the principal use of science fiction by mainstream authors like Orwell and Huxley); they could alter the structure and character of fiction itself. Writers began to use science fictional concepts not as plot devices but as a means of observation and a method of communication. At the same time, the growing literary development within science fiction suddenly blossomed, and the genre produced fascinating new writers like J. G. Ballard, Thomas M. Disch, Ursula Le Guin, and Samuel R. Delany—writers as concerned with language as with idea. It was not long before children's authors became aware of the myriad possibilities available through the devices of science fiction. The first children's writer to make use of science fiction to its full evocative effect was Madeleine L'Engle, with *A Wrinkle in Time* (1962).

A Wrinkle in Time harks back to the early days of pulp science fiction with its universe-wide struggles, but of course the true struggle in *A Wrinkle in Time* is a much older and more stubborn one: the war between good and evil. Furthermore, though the action of the book takes the protagonists to alien planets and even alternate dimensions, its real battles are on a much smaller scale, over individuals.

The story primarily concerns Meg Murry, intelligent but socially awkward adolescent, and her brilliant younger brother Charles Wallace. Their father is a celebrated scientist who has mysteriously disappeared. With the help of Calvin, Meg's classmate and friend, and under the tutelage of three "angels," Mrs. Who, Mrs. Which, and Mrs. Whatsit, they are sent to the planet Camazotz where their father is being held by the Echthroi, the manifestation of evil in the universe. They observe firsthand the terrifying repression practiced by the Echthroi and endure various psychological trials; Charles Wallace is temporarily lost to the Echthroi due to intellectual pride, and eventually it is Meg's love rather than his brilliance that wins back their father.

No plot description can do justice to the beauty and subtlety of *A Wrinkle in Time*. L'Engle creates whole, believable characters with only a few lines of dialogue and makes each of them special and flawed in their own very individual ways. The Echthroi are truly menacing, and the scope and meaning of the ongoing war between good and evil is vividly portrayed. This is a serious novel that unabashedly investigates the nature of good and evil and demonstrates how the actions and decisions of individuals contribute to or detract from society's moral well-being. L'Engle explores such ethical problems as the proper use of knowledge, the rights of the individual versus those of society, and the possibility that evil exists absolutely, without allowing them to detract from her narrative. It is didactic, but skillfully handled.

Of course, the very nature of the conflict (absolute good and evil in material form) is mystical, and mysticism has some trouble blending with the concrete science fiction she employs (aliens, dimensional travel, planets). Nonetheless, the narrative is never forced, and unlike, say, C. S. Lewis's Narnia series, *A Wrinkle in Time* allows the casual reader to suspend disbelief and enjoy the story on its own merits; it is unquestionably a Christian book, but unobtrusively so.

A Wind in the Door (1973) continues the conflict, and matters have gotten worse. Earth is darkening, gradually succumbing to the Echthroi. A battle is waged over Charles Wallace, a key individual in the cosmos. The Echthroi are convincing farandolae in Charles Wallace's mitochondria (the smallest known building blocks of human cells) to join them, and Charles Wallace is slowly but surely dying from the effects. In *A Wrinkle in Time,* the plot canvas spans planets; this time, the key action occurs inside the tiniest of imaginable worlds: Meg and Calvin are sent to one of Charles Wallace's mitochondria, along with Meg's school principal and a multieyed winged creature that calls itself a "cherubim," to battle the Echthroi and win Charles Wallace's life (and, by implication, the life of Earth). But first Meg has to learn to love the school principal she has hated for years, for he too is a key individual under attack by the Echthroi, and they cannot save Charles Wallace without him.

A Wind in the Door is, if anything, even more exciting in its imagination than *A Wrinkle in Time,* and the character development continues to be solid, particularly for Mr. Jenkins, the hated principal, who is fleshed out into a full human being with strengths and weaknesses. However, it is in many ways only a recapitulation of the themes of the first book, and its impact was not as great.

The nature of the primary struggle between good and evil is so overpowering in these books that one can overlook what is perhaps their greatest strength: they are about Meg, her growth, her pain, and the ethical decisions she is forced to make. At the end of the second book, she is still searching for her identity, and it is a lonely search; she does not fit in with her peers or her family, kind though they are, and her experiences serve to alienate her further from the ideal of what a normal teenage girl should be. If she had little in common with her peers before becoming entangled in cosmos-wide conflict, she has less now.

Ultimately, *A Wrinkle in Time* and *A Wind in the Door* are not wholly successful as science fiction. Though the huge conflict and the characters' more personal day-to-day struggles are both imaginatively and believably presented (indeed the characters are some of the most solid children's literature has seen), one has difficulty compassing the two in the same world. They seem mutually exclusive; it is hard to imagine characters involved in cosmic battles remaining essentially unchanged in their mundane concerns. Both storylines stand well on their own; when joined, they don't fall down, but they do lurch around a bit. Even so, L'Engle's achievement in ringing interesting new changes on the tired old theme of universal conflict is impressive in itself, and her prose is masterful.

Sylvia Louise Engdahl's *Enchantress from the Stars* (1970) is a complex, detailed, perhaps overlong novel dealing with relationships between intelligent races at various stages of development. It is based on the notion that cultures have similar histories and evolve predictably and systematically through three stages: childhood, when all is full of wonder, mysterious and supernatural; adolescence, when superstition is discarded in favor of science; and maturity, when it is discovered that the "supernatural" is real and a part of science itself. Each of these stages is represented in the book by a separate culture. A primitive world called Andrecia is invaded and exploited by a starfaring race called Imperials, who in turn are viewed as "Younglings" by the highly advanced Federation. Believing that cultures should be allowed to develop in their own fashion, the Federation attempts to prevent the Imperial takeover without revealing its own identity to either race.

Elana is still in training and not yet officially a member of the Federation's Anthropological Service, but in true juvenile-hero fashion she stows away on the ship taking her father and her husband-to-be to Andrecia. She does this as something of a lark but soon discovers that it is very serious business indeed: a member of their party is murdered by the Imperials. Elana's father devises a plan that involves Elana's teaching the Andrecians "magic" with which to defeat the "dragon"; that is, telekinesis to conquer an Imperial land-clearing machine. His theory is that the Imperials will leave in a panic if confronted with a phenomenon unexplainable through science.

Unfortunately, Elana and a native named Georyn complicate things by falling in love, and Elana foolishly decides to accompany Georyn in his quest against the dragon. They are both captured by the Imperials and carted off to the Imperial planet as scientific specimens. Fearing she will be unable to resist revealing the existence of the Federation, Elana prepares to commit suicide. Instead, she confides in the Imperial doctor Jarel in order to obtain Georyn's release. She then runs toward the dragon to be crushed by rocks falling from its scooper, but Georyn saves the day by stopping the rocks in midair telekinetically, and the Imperials are indeed frightened back to their home planet by this display. The Federation leaves Andrecia to its development, and Elana leaves with them; the cultural gap between her and Georyn is too wide.

One of the more interesting aspects of the book is its examination of myth in relation to history and reality. The Andrecian culture is too underdeveloped to perceive things as they are, and the new fantastic elements in their worldview cannot be comprehended; so they are assigned mythic archetypes. The central images of the book are the ideas that technology's mysteries are aspects of the supernatural and that a fairy tale may refer to actual events beyond comprehension within current paradigms.

Engdahl also comments on the nature of imperialism and the responsibilities of the powerful. The Imperials are clearly an analogue of modern Western culture; they believe in the power of science over the supernatural, they dominate and exploit a weaker race that they fail to see as human, and they perceive themselves as humanitarian. The Federation is a role model of how societies ought to act, and the Andrecians are simple and innocent. The desire to make political points here negates some of the realism of the book. The Imperials are properly balanced, being based on an already extant model, but the Federation is idealized beyond believability.

The novel also suffers from a weakness in the central premise: it would take a great many more common factors beyond mere biological similarity (humanoid) for cultures to follow such identical paths of development. Even on a less than planet-wide scale, one doubts that this kind of simple common evolutionary growth among cultures could be traced.

Still, there is more speculative thought in *Enchantress from the Stars* than in most children's science fiction, and the speculation is central rather than auxiliary to the plot. Engdahl's interest in hypothetical worlds places her firmly in the science fiction field; at the same time she is concerned with, as she says, "man's place in the universe and human values I consider universal,"[7] indicating a desire to comment on society in the context of science fiction. While such an explicitly stated aim frequently results in tracts rather than novels, it is still an admirable synthesis to attempt.

The late Robert C. O'Brien was a serious writer who dealt with complex moral issues in depth. It is a tribute to his skill as an evocative creator of character and background that he was able to produce a serious novel about talking rodents that is not in the least whimsical. *Mrs. Frisby and the Rats of NIMH* (1971) is primarily about Mrs. Jonathan Frisby, widowed fieldmouse driven to heroic efforts to save her sick child, Timothy. Ploughing day is swiftly approaching, and Timothy is not recuperating quickly enough; if he is moved, he will likely die. If they stay, the farmer's plough will destroy their home. Despairing, she tries a last hope: she turns to the strange, reclusive rats who inhabit the rosebush. To her surprise, they agree to help her when they discover she is the widow of Jonathan Frisby, whose disappearance has always been a mystery to her.

Up to this point the book is strictly a talking animal fantasy (though a well-done one), without a hint of science fiction. But then the rats lead Mrs. Frisby into their home, which, to her further surprise, is many times the size she expected, furnished, carpeted, with electric lights and elevators! The rats devise a plan to move her to an area protected from the ploughing, and the head rat, Nicodemus, explains to Mrs. Frisby that the rats are escapees from NIMH (National Institutes of Mental Health, though that is never explicitly stated in the book), where they were experimental subjects for a drug that greatly enhanced their intelligence. They swiftly learned to read and write, unbeknownst to their keepers. Eventually they escaped through the building's ventilation system, along with two mice, one of whom was Mrs. Frisby's husband Jonathan. They then accumulated bits and pieces of technology and, after numerous adventures, holed up behind the rosebush. However, they were unsatisfied with life as they were currently living it; they felt that as intelligent animals they should be generating their own electricity and growing their own food rather than continuing to live off humans. To that end they have been storing up grain and tools and will soon move far out into the wilderness.

First, however, they will move Mrs. Frisby's house. Unfortunately, such a complex operation requires drugging the cat so that it does not patrol the area. Mrs. Frisby volunteers for this job and learns that it was the very operation of trying to slip sleeping powder into the cat's food that led to the death of her husband. She resolves to go ahead anyway; what choice does she have?

While in the kitchen dropping the powder into the cat dish, Mrs. Frisby overhears the humans planning to exterminate the rats in the rosebush. She returns to warn them, and after moving her house, they quickly dismantle their own home and put up a convincing show to satisfy the humans that they are dead. Two of them actually do perish in the escape, but the rest of the rats are free to pursue their goal of a rat civilization.

The most effective passages in the book are those that show the rats acquiring intelligence in the lab, escaping, and gradually civilizing themselves. Under normal circumstances, the imposition of this fantastic science fiction plot upon the already extant standard fantasy plot (talking animals) would dim the effectiveness of both and muddy the book. However, the science fiction motif, which is the main fantastic element in the plot, is not introduced until almost halfway through the story, by which time the talking animals have ceased being wondered at by the reader; they are an established fact of the world of the book. There have been no further fantastic developments, and the reader is expecting none; this added recomplication is a complete surprise, and devastatingly effective. Of course, if the passages dealing with the rats' heightened intelligence weren't so fascinating in and of themselves, the reader would probably be annoyed at the violation of the assumed laws already established in the book. But O'Brien is a skilled writer, and he adds his ingredients judiciously; there are no additional violent surprises. In any case, the fantasy and science fiction elements are not mutually contradictory; an effective book about rats with heightened intelligence almost *demands* that they be able to speak. To O'Brien's credit, he spaced the introduction of the two motifs and achieved a cumulative rather than jarring effect.

An interesting subplot of the book, and apparently a matter of thematic importance to O'Brien, is the rats' debate among themselves over whether to live as they always had, scrounging off humans, or whether to develop a new self-sufficient rat society. One group of rats maintains that it makes no sense to deny their rathood by trying to change their behavior into that of humans. The other, larger group holds that they are no longer rats but a new species, a sort of superrat, and that the interests and activities that ought to concern them are more like those of humans than those of rats. To deny or stifle intelligence and ambition is ultimately to be dissatisfied. The majority of the rats seem to feel that there is no point in not pushing to one's utmost. It is a fascinating debate, and a comment on the nature of ambition for all intelligent creatures.

Also of central concern is the matter of technology. These new superrats are newly confronting the questions that face industrial humanity: whether to use technological expertise to create a competitive mechanized society that exploits and eventually destroys its environment or whether to opt for a civilization that respects individual and natural resources. At first, O'Brien's message is ambivalent; the rats' home is wired for electricity, and technology is after all the means of their intelligence. By the end of the book, however, a renegade protechnology rat faction has, significantly, electrocuted themselves to death trying to move a power motor, and the main rat colony goes off to live in the wilderness with nothing but farming tools and grain.

Mrs. Frisby and the Rats of NIMH was only O'Brien's second novel; he evidenced a delicacy of touch and sureness of characterization unusual for one with so little experience. His prose was evocative and not condescending, and his books can be read and enjoyed by adults as well as children. His premature death was a loss to children's literature.

Children's literature has yet to fully realize the possibilities available to it through the tropes of SF. Science fiction has historically been a literature of inquiry and challenge. Curiously, it has never been a target of the school library censors, despite the fact that its tradition alone is more radical and dangerous than anything J. D. Salinger ever wrote. Science fiction is frequently the twelve-year-old reader's first encouragement to question received norms. The protocols of reading science fiction demand that the mind remain open to previously unthought-of developments and willing to entertain any speculation for the sake of argument. Science fiction teaches the logical development of ideas, and perhaps more important, it encourages free thought, creativity, and invention. More than any other literature, science fiction is—formally!—*subversive.* The children's writer with an honest desire to write fiction that would truly stretch the reader's imagination and encourage the reexamination of firmly held beliefs could do worse than to turn to SF for inspiration.

Notes

1. Brian W. Aldiss, *Billion Year Spree: The True History of Science Fiction* (Garden City, N.Y.: Doubleday, 1973), pp. 7–39.

2. Darko Suvin, *Metamorphoses of Science Fiction* (New Haven: Yale University Press, 1979), pp. 7–10.

3. Thomas M. Disch, "The Embarrassments of Science Fiction," in *Science Fiction at Large,* ed. Peter Nicholls (London: Gollancz, 1979), pp. 141–55.

4. Alexei Panshin, *Heinlein in Dimension* (Chicago: Advent:Publishers, 1968), p. 41

5. Ibid., p. 85.

6. David G. Hartwell, "Introduction" to *Empire Star* by Samuel R. Delany (Boston: Gregg Press, 1977), p. viii.

7. Quoted in Francis J. Molson, "Sylvia Engdahl," in *Twentieth Century Children's Writers,* ed. D. L. Kirkpatrick (London: Macmillan, 1983), p. 264.

Small Wonders: Baby Books and Picturebooks

Anne Devereaux Jordan

CHILDREN LIVE IN A WORLD OF WONDER, a world of discovery. Each day they are confronted by new things that must be explored, learned, and understood. Since the inception of children's literature in the seventeenth century, there have been books designed to help children in their discovery of the world around them, but none have been so successful as those of the twentieth century. For babies and toddlers this has meant simple, appealing, yet durable books with an emphasis on labeling objects and actions and portraying them with a faithful—identifiable—realism. For older children who have passed through this first stage of identifying, there exist books that expand the "real" world to include the realm of story, image, metaphor, and art: picturebooks. While the latter books are striking for their integration of art and story, the former are unique for their function and the skill with which they fulfill that function.

Baby Books

Small children inhabit a world of images and pictures; their experiences with objects and actions often far outstrip their acquisition of words to describe those objects and actions. Publishers and writers of books for babies and toddlers, even in the nineteenth century, took into consideration the child's limited vocabulary and physical

193

size; hence the production in the 1800s of numerous chapbooks, board books, and toy-books—books small enough for even the smallest hands. In the nineteenth century also, artists of note began considering the smallest children, and the quality and quantity of illustrations in books published for babies and toddlers soared. Walter Crane, for example, "set the standard with his first toy-books; [Randolph] Caldecott . . . continued the toy-books and made them more pictorial, expanding a line of text into a sequence of action, a flat statement into high comedy; and [Kate] Greenaway, with *Under the Window,* swept all of Europe, such was the charm of her demure, old-fashioned children."[1] As the nineteenth century declined, books for the very small child became well established as something a parent should buy to start his child on the road to reading, although notice by the literary establishment was negligible.

With the advent of the 1900s and particularly during the 1920s, however, adults began taking note of books for the very young. Writers and artists began experimenting with books for this age group on a limited scale. The 1920s was "the decade of the preschool child as certainly as the twentieth century has been, as Swedish social critic Ellen Key anticipated, 'the century of the child.' "[2] New findings in pediatrics, education, and developmental studies, along with the establishment of formal nursery schools, suddenly focused attention on preschoolers and on the literature being published for them. There was a movement away from the purely imaginary and a stress on the "here and now" of the child's world, the familiar and the immediate, with increased attention to children's use of language and a resultant—unfortunate—attempt, at times, to replicate in the text of a story the way a child speaks.

Many books produced for older preschool children during the 1920s were innovative and fresh. As Anne Carroll Moore notes in *The Three Owls: Third Book,* "Children's books published in the decade between 1920 and 1930 reveal more new forms, both outward and inward, than at any other period in their history."[3] Too often, however, books for the very smallest child were stilted and unimaginative as a result of the overzealous application of the new ideas emerging in the areas of psychology and education. There was an emphasis on "training" the child, and many of the books were mere lists of everyday objects accompanied by easily recognized but quite uninspired pictures. C. B. Falls's *ABC Book,* published in 1923, was a notable exception. Although Falls's artistry suffers in comparison to illustrations of the nineteenth century, small children received his *ABC Book* with enthusiasm because of its bold, bright colors—oranges, greens, russets and blues—colors that stood out in a world of books filled with drab hues and flat tones.

As adults adjusted to the ideas being propounded for books for younger children, so too did the books reflect a sense of relaxation, and imagination was once more permitted. Illustrators began to stray from the mere representation of everyday objects, and everyday activities, while still incorporated into stories, were clothed in whimsy. *The Story of a Little White Teddy Bear Who Didn't Want to Go to Bed* (1931) by Dorothy Sherrill, although still somewhat rigid, reflects a slightly more imaginative application of the principles evolving at that time. The text is written in the present tense and accompanied by very simple, easily identifiable illustrations; both provide for quick recognition of objects and actions, and incorporate reiteration and cumulation. While *Little White Teddy Bear* conveys an innocent, charming sense of intimacy to the child, its simple drawings lack both the skill and color seen in earlier, and later, books for babies.

The 1930s brought forth a number of advances in books for babies and toddlers. Cloth books were improved upon by the use of brighter colors and more whimsical themes, and the concept of books as playthings gained ground. In 1940 one of the most popular books for the very young was published: *Pat the Bunny* (1940) by Dorothy Kunhardt.

Pat the Bunny's drawings are stiff and uninspired, printed in three "babyish" colors (pink, blue, and yellow, with black outlines), and the text is minimal ("Paul can put his finger through Mummy's ring"), but it was received with glee by its many small readers because of all the activities contained in the book. The reader is asked if he or she can "pat the bunny," put a finger through "Mummy's ring," read a small book, feel "Daddy's beard," and so on. Compared with most other books of the period, *Pat the Bunny* was fresh and innovative and a barrel of fun for babies and toddlers.

The post–World War II baby boom created a demand for books for very young children, and just as children were being "mass-produced" at that time, so did mass production intrude into the publication and marketing of books for the smallest child. The early 1940s had already seen the introduction of Golden Books for children. "The immediate effect," comments Barbara Bader, "was an end to cloth books on a par with picturebooks, to playbooks as Creative Playthings and, where 'babies' were concerned, to the innovative impulse altogether."[4] While books for older preschool children continued their artistic climb with such authors and illustrators as Margaret Wise Brown, Roger Duvoisin, and Robert McCloskey, quality books strictly for babies and toddlers declined. Because of mass-marketing techniques Golden Books were easier for parents to obtain, less expensive—a consideration during wartime austerity—and appealing to small children because of the easy stories and gleaming colors. Many established artists were lured to illustrate Golden Books by both the money to be had and the new printing techniques being utilized by Western Publications, which allowed a wider use of color. The problem was, "As diverse as the illustrators were in style and technique, they tend to adopt a common approach, emphasizing, even exaggerating, the crucial action or emotion, minimizing or eliminating incidental detail, flattening the picture space—all in the service of compression."[5] Similarly, in the interest of brevity and the intended audience, texts of traditional stories were severely truncated and simplified, resulting in a loss of individual style.

As the baby boom tapered off during the 1950s, books for very small children languished in a sort of limbo. Publishing houses continued to produce a few new books each year, but this effort, in retrospect, appears to have been more a gesture than an attempt to further the field. During the 1950s and 1960s, books for babies and toddlers received scant attention, and it was not until the late 1970s, when the children of the baby boom started having children themselves, that the publishing spotlight was once again focused on books for the very young.

The baby boom parents of the 1970s and 1980s are very different from their parents: they are determined that their children have every available educational advantage and be better and smarter than other children. While earlier generations of parents harbored similar ambitions, the baby boom parents stand out for the zeal with which they pursue this goal of "better babies." According to a 1983 *Newsweek* article, "Bringing Up Superbaby," they are "older, richer, more combative, and firmly convinced that there are lessons for everything."[6] One result of the attitudes espoused by these new parents has been a revolution in the area of books for babies and toddlers, the development of a "baby literature." Eden Lipson, Children's Book Review editor of the *New York Times Book Review*, attributes this increased interest in books for the youngest children to the rising rate of childbirth, the women's movement, child-rearing as a "project," greater knowledge of child development, and the decline in library funds.[7] These factors, and the growth in knowledge of how language is acquired, have resulted in books that combine innovation in packaging and art with an attempt to meet the needs of even the infant reader.

The parents of the 1980s are starting the reading experience much earlier than did their own parents. Tundra Books of Canada, among others, caters to this trend, producing a series entitled Baabee Books for infants between five months and three years. May Cutler, president of Tundra Books, states that in starting the baby book project, "we worked completely and only with parents and babies, testing things against baby's reaction." One finding, she reports, is that "babies can see far earlier than we realize. We felt a bit *osé* when we suggested our first series for babies as young as five months, but since publication we found that babies like 'to learn to see' on them; they help their eyes focus."[8] The Baabee Books are highly appealing to infants. Series I consists of four accordion-pleated books that can be hung above a crib or tied into a mobile for the baby to look at. Series II, for children up to three years, is bound in traditional book format. Both series are printed on heavy cardboard without text and use "pure" colors—bright reds, blues, and yellows—with strong black lines. They depict objects and actions a baby or toddler is likely to encounter and are an interesting variation on the "board" books that have long been produced for small children.

There exists, in the 1980s, a tremendous variety of books for the smallest child. Basically, however, they fall into three categories, as New Zealand bookseller Dorothy Butler points out in her *Babies Need Books:* "naming" books, "theme" books, and "story" books. "Stories, for any age group, have narrative; the characters are established, and then the action starts. There is a plot, with some sort of climax and resolution. . . . Theme books are less demanding, but are still a step ahead of naming books, which depict unconnected objects. . . . A theme book depicts objects, activities, and situations that are connected in some way."[9] Today very few publishers produce "naming" books; the majority of books for infants and toddlers center around a theme or have a story, however slight. In the words of Margaret Firth, editor in chief of Putnam's children's books, "A happening is essential."[10]

Within each category of book, parents of the 1980s have a wide choice of types of books. Perhaps the most basic is the cloth book, which has been in existence for nearly one hundred years. Dorothy Butler shuns cloth books, stating, "Rag books look, feel, sound and behave like limp dishrags, and before long, smell like *dirty* limp dishrags."[11] Cloth books, however, are durable, washable, and usually simple in content. They are suitably short for a short attention span, soft and appealing to a baby or toddler, and good for learning concepts inappropriate to board or paper books: buttoning buttons, zipping zippers, etc. *Baby Animals,* produced by Random House, is a typical example of a cloth book with a theme appeal for small children. It has a simple text ("Baby chickens are called chicks. Ducklings are baby ducks."), and although the pictures are rather indifferently drawn, they are printed in bold colors.

Peggy Cloth Books by Platt & Munk (Grosset & Dunlap/Putnam) "feature an uncluttered story line and well-drawn pictures in three colors."[12] This series often incorporates a learning concept in the form of zippers, squeakers, or a clock with hands that move. The major problem with such gimmicks is that the parts can sometimes be torn off and eaten by a baby or, as in *Hush Little Baby* (which has a squeaker meant to sound like a crying baby), can be difficult for small children to work.

Perhaps one of the most appealing series is Rand McNally's delightful Critter Sitters. The pictures of various cuddly animals are skillfully and attractively drawn and are printed in gala colors. Each books follows a particular theme. In *Critter Sitters on the Farm,* for example, various farm activities are shown and labeled: "Horsebackriding," "Feeding the chickens."

For the children of the eighties, the next step toward "real" books is the stuffed-plastic book. "These books are soft, huggable and small, easily handled. . . . Relatively new, the stuffed-plastic book is, as a rule, poorly written and illustrated; the printing is inferior and the color registration off."[13] *I'm a Little Tugboat* (Windmill/Simon & Schuster) is a crudely drawn example. The overly simplistic story is about a fish and a tugboat who become friends. The pictures are nearly static; the only change from page to page occurs in the position of the fish and in the tugboat's eyes.

One series of stuffed-plastic books that is an exception is the Soft Spot series produced by Putnam. Using his popular canine character, Spot, Eric Hill has written and illustrated a number of foam-filled vinyl books with bright four-color pictures and a lively text. The Spot

Otto of the Silver Hand, written and illustrated by Howard Pyle

Millions of Cats, written and illustrated by Wanda Gág
Mike Mulligan and His Steam Shovel, by Virginia Lee Burton

books are well made and are on a par with the more traditional types of baby books.

The type of book that perhaps most often comes to mind in connection with the very small child is the board book. Compared with other types, "Board books vary most in size, shape, theme, price and quality. Constructed of heavy cardboard, or laminated, these books withstand hard use and are no problem for little hands to manage since the pages lie flat."[14]

Macmillan publishes the small (3¼" x 3⅜") Strawberry Block Books, which are among the smallest of the board books. The very small board books tend to be very simple in concept and content. Macmillan's Strawberry *Baby Animals,* for example, consists of a series of easily recognizable but somewhat poorly drawn pictures with one-word labels: "Kitten," "Puppy," "Fawn." Golden Block Books (Golden Press), Viking Block Books, and Viking Circus Books (Viking Press) are similar but have more appealing illustrations. All are diminutive in size and made of very heavy board for sturdiness.

Medium-size board books often incorporate a gimmick reflecting the theme or story of the books. *The Pudgy Fingers Counting Book* (Grosset & Dunlap), illustrated by Doug Cushman, for instance, is die-cut in the shape of a child's hand. After counting ten "Pudgies," charming little bearlike creatures, the final two pages show a child's two hands, each finger capped by a finger-puppet Pudgy. Another series by Grosset & Dunlap, Baby's First Books, has "winkers" on the covers—plastic pictures that change as the book is moved.

Several series in the medium-size range of board books that have no need for gimmicks are those by illustrator Kenneth Lilly. His Baby Animal series (Simon & Schuster), for example, consists of four books: *Animals in the Country, Animals in the Jungle, Animals on the Farm,* and *Animals of the Ocean.* With the eye of a naturalist, Lilly captures each animal perfectly and beautifully. Although his superb illustrations need no text, simple labeling is supplied: "cow and calf," "horse and foal."

The large-size board books are perhaps those most often purchased for a very small child. Gimmicks exist in the larger books, but it is here also that an introduction to the literature traditionally associated with the nursery can be found. Rand McNally, for example, has taken an old, popular collection, *The Real Mother Goose,* illustrated by Blanche Fisher Wright, and reproduced it in four volumes in their Husky Books series. None of the charm, color, or delight of the original has been lost in this transformation; the rhymes have merely been rendered in a more durable form to be easily handled by babies and toddlers. Nursery rhymes, simple folk and fairy tales, and childhood songs—all appear in board book form for even the smallest children to savor.

The twentieth century, in particular the latter half, has proven to be a golden age for books for the baby and toddler. Never before has so much care been devoted to the production of these books, and never before have they existed in such variety and number. While most experts in the field of children's literature feel that the recent increase in the number of books for babies and toddlers will level off, a standard has been established upon which to build. Books for the smallest children are no longer delegated to staff artists or writers and indifferently manufactured. The best is now going into books that will introduce the child to the world, that will, as Eden Lipson has described it, "augment what is happening in their lives and also deal with the purely wonderful."[15] They are books that move the small child comfortably into the world of picturebooks, the world of real books, and a lifetime of new worlds.

Picturebooks

While books for babies and toddlers replicate reality, picturebooks for slightly older children are more complex and are rightly categorized as an art form in themselves. Here the stress is less on function and more on the felicitous combining of story and art, with a focus on the illustrations due to the fact that the intended audience first encounters these books before learning to read.

The illustrator of children's picturebooks is a visual storyteller. He brings the writer's words to life, extending them into the literal world, and, using his imagination and skill, creates the *mise en page* that blends art and text so completely that the reader comes to remember the illustrations as an integral part of the story.

Children's picturebooks in the United States in the nineteenth century were often lost in the deluge of books from other countries, particularly from France and England. American artists were frequently ignored by a public captivated by the creations of Crane, Greenaway, and other British artists, and by the books of Maurice Boutet de Monvel of France. American illustrations were disparaged as primitive or cartoonlike, and American artists often felt that to illustrate a children's book was of no significance. One influential event that drew United States artists into the field of children's book illustration was the publication and subsequent popularity of *St. Nicholas: A Magazine for Boys and Girls,* edited by Mary Mapes Dodge.

When *St. Nicholas* began publication in 1873, Mrs. Dodge outlined her editorial policy, which included the goal of inspiring young people "with a fine appreciation of pictorial art."[16] Just as she sought genius in her authors, so she looked for the best from her illustrators, securing many distinguished artists who in turn led others into the field. One stands out for utilizing the best of romantic naturalism from England and for influencing other illustrators of children's books: Howard Pyle, who has been called the father of modern American illustration.

Dureresque and romantic, Howard Pyle's illustrations capture the mood and mystery of each of his stories yet are carefully accurate as to period clothing and weaponry. He had a flair for delineating character with line and shading and for bringing the action on a page to life. Through the example of his own work and through his teaching, Howard Pyle gave an impetus to book and magazine illustration in America. In establishing a close relationship between text and art, and in demanding an art of fine quality, he set a standard that was, and remains, an inspiration to other artists.

Howard Pyle, followed by others of equal skill, such as his own pupils N. C. Wyeth and Jessie Willcox Smith, set an example in books for older children that was quickly emulated by illustrators of books for younger children. Just as interest in baby books increased in the 1920s, so too did a revolution in picturebooks begin. Suddenly a field shunned by many artists as too limited or insignificant achieved dignity, and this, coupled with improvements in printing technology, led to an influx of artists into children's picturebook illustration and to the diversity of styles that is seen today in the field.

This variety of styles makes classification difficult, but they can be broadly categorized into three general groupings: representational, in the tradition of Greenaway, Crane, and Pyle; abstract expressionist, involving "the use of new shape-line-color-texture patterns to create or express a feeling,"[17] a blending of realism and abstraction in which the poetic and personal combine with the medium to communicate the text; and instructional, the accurate rendering of people, objects, and animals in nonfiction children's books.

The artists who fall within the representational category understandably outnumber those in either of the other two, both because
the category itself is broad and because, in children's picturebooks,
the audience expects to see things represented as they are. Children
respond to people, animals, and things rendered in a realistic manner
tempered by personal style. They often do not yet have the ability
to grasp abstraction in art and will demand a faithful interpretation
of the text. But in addition to putting the right number of fingers
on a hand or correctly colored shoes on a character, the representational artist also creates a sense of mood and dimension, expanding
and opening up the story so the child can participate in it and feel
what both author and artist feel. Representational art is realistic visual
storytelling whether it involves animals, as in the striking work of
Conrad Buff, people, as in the sweet, romantic scenes of Marguerite
de Angeli, or objects, as in the bright, bold illustrations of Virginia
Lee Burton. Whether softening harshness or pointing up the comic,
the representational artist still portrays reality.

One important representationalist who accurately portrayed both
animals and people with sympathetic humor was Kurt Wiese. Born
in Germany, Wiese had journeyed throughout the world before set-
tling in the United States. His experiences as a traveler provided him
with the background to portray distant peoples and places, as in his
Liang and Lo (1930) and his illustrations for Kipling's *Jungle Books*
(1932). Today, however, he is perhaps best known for his illustrations
of *The Story About Ping* (1933) by Marjorie Flack, who was herself an
illustrator in the representational mode. As Barbara Bader points
out, "This was one of the first instances in picturebooks proper of a
story being written by one person to be pictured by another. . . .
Marjorie Flack didn't know China, Kurt Wiese did, that was the
genesis; the ramifications were many."[18] The collaboration between
Wiese and Flack demonstrated that a writer of picturebooks need
not also play the role of artist, nor the artist provide text to illustrate,
as was common before the publication of *Ping*.

The Story About Ping is a memorable book in its own right, however,
as well as being the first modern American collaboration. It is filled
with humor and vitality in both text and pictures. Wiese's lithographs
are rich with colors that capture the feel of the Orient and the gay
innocence of the little duck, Ping. *The Story About Ping* tells the tale
of a little duckling who lives on a boat with his family. One day after
playing about the shore, Ping is left behind. What the little duck does

Kaleidoscope, Eleanor Farjeon, illustrated by Edward Ardizzone

The Story of Ferdinand, Munro Leaf, illustrated by Robert Lawson

and how he is reunited with his family makes a warm and humorous tale. Wiese bleeds his pictures to the upper page edges and, as Ping discovers he has been left behind by his boat, utilizes a two-page spread to capture the feel of distance and the vastness of the river. Wiese puts his knowledge of the Orient to good use while conveying mood, enhancing reality, and bringing the story to life for the reader.

The 1930s abounded with representational artists such as Wiese, able to exploit the newly available technology to create striking and memorable picturebooks. Among them was Wanda Gág, whose *Millions of Cats* (1928) "ushered in what came to be known as 'The Golden Thirties' of picture books."[19] *Millions of Cats,* with its folk tale flavor and cozy, homespun black-and-white pictures, became an instant success with children and a model of the perfect integration of art, text, and format. The hand-lettered text is surrounded by the black-and-white lithographs just as the very old man and very old woman of the story are surrounded by cats: "Cats here, cats there, Cats and kittens everywhere. . . ."

The thirties saw the emergence of picturebook writers and artists whose works are still vivid and whose styles, although portraying life faithfully, are at the same time highly individualistic and recognizable. Among the foremost artist/writers to start publishing during this period was Edward Ardizzone, a master storyteller and a superb illustrator who, like Virginia Burton, thoroughly understood the world of the child. His well-known *Little Tim and the Brave Sea Captain* (1936) was first published with no text at all, and so expressive are the illustrations that the story communicates itself dramatically without the real need for words. Ardizzone used line drawings to which he added soft wash with sweeping brushstrokes to give the dynamic feeling of the sea. He captured every facet of his characters' emotions and personalities and didn't hesitate to experiment with format, often borrowing balloon inserts from the comics for dialogue. His goal was always to delight the child with both story and pictures.

Marguerite de Angeli and Tasha Tudor illustrate in the tradition of Howard Pyle and the romantic naturalist. They are gently expressive, at times almost sentimental in their pictures. Their compositions have a graceful flow to them, and the characters they depict are idealized and lovely. The use of pastel colors and subtle shading, combined with a careful selection of detail, lends a sense of warmth and the romantic to their art.

While de Angeli and Tudor were "gentling down" reality, other artists of the thirties were poking fun at it. James Daugherty, Robert Lawson, and Robert McCloskey took animals and people as their subjects and pointed out how warmly humorous life can be. Indeed, Daugherty's *Andy and the Lion* (1938) borders on caricature in its depiction of Andy's efforts and of the people who encounter the lion. *Andy and the Lion* was Daugherty's first attempt at a picturebook, although he had created art for illustrated books. Much of his art is expressive of the "American spirit" as he conceived it.

Robert Lawson ranged from poking gentle fun at the antics of animals in such books as Munro Leaf's *The Story of Ferdinand* (1936) or his own *Rabbit Hill* (1944) to a satiric portrayal of life and history in such books as *Mr. Popper's Penguins* (1938) and *Ben and Me* (1939). Robert McCloskey's comical ducks and the people who "make way" for them in *Make Way for Ducklings* (1941) share an element of this same satire. The humor in these books is typically American—broad, good-natured, expansive—and each of the aforementioned artists, including McCloskey, has an eye for naturalistic accuracy that enhances and broadens the humor.

While these artists were exploring American themes, other artists were communicating the humor and knowledge of foreign lands. The fictional works of Maud and Miska Petersham are filled with the colors and designs of their native Hungary. *Miki* (1929), written for their son, resonates with Miska's memories of his childhood in Hungary. May Massee, then head of Doubleday's juvenile division, dubbed *Miki* "the first of the international picturebooks," mixing as it does life for a small boy in America and in Hungary. Its popularity at the time reflected the increased emphasis in the schools on a core curriculum centering around social studies, and the lessening of isolationist feeling in the United States.

While *Miki* may have been the first picturebook to interrelate American and foreign life, it was quickly followed by others. Feodor Rojankovsky mixed typically American tales and rhymes with artwork harking back to his native Russia. He used the rich, earthy colors of the land, and his characters have the faces of Russian peasants. Ludwig Bemelmans captured the scenes and wit of France in all of his books but most charmingly in *Madeline* (1939). His sense of humor and ability to express people's moods are especially evident here. His line drawings, with color overlaid, are quick and facile, capturing the fun and exuberance of the moment. Through his *Madeline* books Bemelmans acquaints children with the landmarks of Paris as well as entertaining them with Madeline's uproarious trials and tribulations.

While Bemelmans's art is the quicksilver of the moment, that of Norwegian-born Ingri and Swiss-born Edgar d'Aulaire reflects the hugeness and permanance of the Norse myths even when dealing with such American subjects as *Pocahontas* (1946) or *Abraham Lincoln* (1939). Using stone lithography, which gives unusual strength and solidity to their pictures, they mix folk art and modernist art, playing with perspective and light, to achieve the almost primitive effect seen in the art of children. Their *Ola* (1932), *Ola and Blakken* (1933), and *Children of the Northlights* (1935), according to Barbra Bader, "made the d'Aulaires' reputation as Norwegian emissaries to the United States."[20]

This wave of illustrative and writing talent from both the United States and abroad did not go unrecognized. In 1921 publisher Frederic Melcher had proposed to the American Library Association that a medal be awarded for the most distinguished book for children published during the preceding year—the John Newbery Medal. Later he made a similar suggestion regarding picturebooks, and since 1938 the Caldecott Medal, named for Randolph Caldecott, has been presented to the illustrator of the most distinguished picturebook of the year. (See Appendix B, "Children's Book Awards.")

The golden age of picturebooks came to an end, however, with the outbreak of World War II. "World War II with its restrictions was responsible for changes in the style and mood of book design," writes Diana Klemin in *The Illustrated Book: Its Art and Craft*.[21] Previous to the war, the artist could paint or draw with little editorial direction, shaping the book the way he or she wanted. With World War II, the publisher had to assume greater control over bookmaking, restricting the quantity and quality of paper and the use of color, trying to save materials, labor, and costs. Often the paper was of inferior quality and could not reflect the vibrancy of the colors of an original piece of artwork.

Despite the limitations imposed by World War II, there was no lack of new talent entering the field, nor was there a lack of experimentation in technique. Leonard Weisgard, who first introduced Cubist planes into children's books in Margaret Wise Brown's *The Noisy Book* (1939), was one of the first children's artists to utilize abstract expressionism in picturebooks. *The Noisy Book* is about the noises a little dog, Muffin, hears when he goes out with his eyes bandaged because of an injury. As Barbara Bader points out, Weisgard "had made a picturebook in the McKnight Kauffer-Stuart Davis idiom of the Thirties—'a simplified, formalized and more expressive symbol of the things represented' (Aldous Huxley on Kauffer) employing 'broad generalizations of form and non-imitative use of color' and 'a conceptual instead of an optical perspective' (Davis on Davis)."[22] *The Noisy Book* is bright with solid, unshadowed colors that capture the essence of the text without great detail. Weisgard adapted the techniques of adult art strikingly and effectively for children. The colors and shapes appeal to a child and work brilliantly with the text to evoke a wide variety of sounds.

Another of the first United States artists to experiment with form and medium was Paul Rand, who utilized collage techniques characteristic of Cubism to create visually exciting books for children. His first book (coauthored with his wife, Ann Rand), *I Know a Lot of Things* (1956), fell short of the mark, showing in its coyness a certain lack of awareness of how a child thinks and acts. Their second book, however, *Sparkle and Spin* (1957), demonstrates Rand's eye for graphic design. In the illustrations Rand analyzes figures and landscapes, breaking them down into their essential shapes and unifying them by the use of vividly bright colors. The collage technique emphasizes the shapes of people and objects in the pictures, giving them boldness and strength.

Leo Lionni entered the field of children's book illustration in 1959 after telling a story to his grandchildren. His career as an artist had been distinguished, but he hadn't given any thought to the illustration of children's books previous to this time. The jacket copy to *Little Blue and Little Yellow* tells us Lionni "believes that abstract figures can not only communicate, but can be highly suggestive to a child's creative sense." Using plain colored paper only, Lionni created a charming story for children. While *Little Blue and Little Yellow* is totally abstract, in his later books Lionni combines the abstract with realism to tell his stories more representationally and unite text and art more closely. *The Biggest House in the World* (1968) is perhaps his most harmonious book. In this story of a small snail who tells his father he would like to have "the biggest house in the world," the reader sees the "house"—a snail's shell—grow and grow, becoming ever grander, and learns an unexpected lesson. Lionni used preprinted paper to construct collages, creating illustrations that are bright and complex. Lionni is typical of the abstract expressionist in that he is

Where the Wild Things Are, written and illustrated by Maurice Sendak

The Cat in the Hat, written and illustrated by Dr. Seuss

always experimenting with new mediums and techniques, devising new textures that best tell a particular story.

Ezra Jack Keats was another practitioner of the collage technique. He used oils and collage to create books that are both simple and sophisticated. His first book, *The Snowy Day* (1962), received the Caldecott Medal, as did *Goggles!* (1969). Keats employed textured and patterned materials, cutting with a simplicity of line and broadness of form. In his early books he used only collage, capturing the essence of shapes just as a small child might view things. As his staple character, Peter, grows older, Keats supplements collage with oils to add an element of complexity and lend greater dimension to the scenes in his books. His heavy use of black line and swirling colors reflects the sense of turbulence Peter himself feels in various situations.

Leo Lionni, Paul Rand, and Ezra Jack Keats are only three abstract expressionists among many in the field of children's book illustration. However, because of the limitations the field places upon an artist— the prevalent feeling that the child needs a representation of reality— and because the stories themselves involve description and narration, most books published today tend to be representational in their art.

At the same time that abstract expressionism was making a start, representational artists were seeing new developments within their realm. An offshoot of comic book art, a subgenre of illustrative art, was emerging: the cartoon type of art seen in two major innovators, Walt Disney and Dr. Seuss (Theodor Seuss Geisel). Over the years both the Disney artwork and that of Dr. Seuss have settled into formula. The Walt Disney books and movies, James Steele Smith writes, "are actually very canny compromises; they offer children many unusual, invented creatures like Cinderella's mouse horses, the fearsome witch, and the Disney squirrels, but in a world of quite conventional representation of conventional objects and experiences, all against a background of decorative abstractions."[23] Seuss's world, as seen in *Horton Hatches the Egg* (1940), for example, or his very popular *The Cat in the Hat* (1957), is more fantastic and irrational than Disney's world. Violent colors predominate, and the drawings are a frenzy of activity and movement. The work produced by the Walt Disney Studios and Dr. Seuss is completely predictable, showing little change over the years. This is not to say it lacks appeal for children; children delight in the pastiche of a Disney book or movie and in the ridiculous, mad antics of a Cat in the Hat. But the art of Disney and Seuss is the doggerel of children's book illustration.

At the opposite end of the spectrum, the "fine art" of representational children's books was also influenced by the comic book and by the art of Walt Disney. This is particularly true of one post–World War II artist without mention of whom any discussion of contemporary children's book illustration would be incomplete: Maurice Sendak.

"The good illustrator," according to Edward Ardizzone, "does more than just make a pictorial comment on the written word. He produces a visual counterpart which adds a third dimension to the book, making more vivid and more understandable the author's intention."[24] Perhaps more than any other contemporary artist, Maurice Sendak achieves this extra dimension again and again in both the books he has illustrated and those in which he has been both author and artist. Because of his careful attention to the book as total entity and because of the attention he has drawn to the field of picturebook illustration with his many outstanding books, he has in many ways ushered in a second "golden age" of picturebooks.

Working initially in one color, Sendak first came to the attention of the children's book world with his pictures for Ruth Krauss's *A Hole Is to Dig* (1952). His whimsical line drawings charmed and captivated children everywhere, opened up the field of children's book illustration to him, and were followed by a plethora of other books for children. In Ruth Krauss's *Charlotte and the White Horse* (1955), Sendak began to work in color. Using an impressionistic technique, with line and color reminiscent of William Blake, Sendak gave a sense of the ethereal to this delicate story.

Charlotte and the White Horse is but one example of how skillfully Sendak adapts technique to subject matter, integrating text and art. Krauss's story calls for the fragile luminescence of Sendak's softened, glowing colors and gentle lines. Similarly, in Janice May Udry's *The Moon Jumpers* (1959), Sendak employs pointillism and plays with light and shadow to capture the moon's haunting qualities. With *The Griffin and the Minor Canon* (1963) by Frank R. Stockton, Sendak turns to caricature to interpret character and atmosphere for full comic effect.

Another way in which Sendak achieves a harmony between text and pictures is through his concern for design and format. He is as excited by the *mise en page* as he is by story interpretation. This is best seen in his own *Where the Wild Things Are* (1963), for which he received the Caldecott Medal in 1964. In this interpretation of a child's dream, Sendak arranges the text and pictures carefully, slowly drawing the reader into the world of his character, Max, and then safely bringing both Max and reader back to reality. He does this by increasing, and then decreasing, the size of the pictures on each page and by running the text continuously from one page to the next, except in the middle, where both reader and Max are so involved in the dream that text is not even necessary. Sendak combines the luminescence of color in *The Moon Jumpers* with the cartoonlike caricature of figures in *The Griffin and the Minor Canon* to create illustrations in *Where the Wild Things Are* that are both stunning and comical. All of Sendak's work reflects this concern for the *total* book: design, format, typography, and illustrative technique combine with the text to make each book something special, a work of art.

While Sendak's is perhaps the best-known name in children's book illustration today, other representationalist artists show equal regard for the book as a unity of text and art. Uri Shulevitz achieves a similar adaptation of technique to subject. His *Dawn* (1974), the story of a boy and his grandfather awakening in early morning by a lake, combines abstract forms with an impressionistic use of color to produce a strong, richly emotional book that is visually stunning. On the other hand, *The Fool of the World and the Flying Ship* (1968) by Arthur Ransome, for which Shulevitz received the 1969 Caldecott Medal, is brilliant with color, while its style captures the Russian background of the book.

Yet another artist who uses color to its best effect to interpret mood and expand the text is Barbara Cooney. In her first color book, Lee Kingman's *Peter's Long Walk* (1953), she employs muted colors to portray the New England countryside and a child's long journey through it. In *A White Heron* (1963) by Sarah Orne Jewett, she captures with beauty and intensity of detail the quiet setting of Maine.

At the other end of the spectrum is James Marshall, who, rather than capturing quiet moods and landscapes, explores the rollicking world of habit and humor. His George and Martha books, published during the 1970s, comment on human behavior and foibles—this despite the fact that his characters are two hippopotami. His line drawings with a color wash, cartoonlike yet not stereotypic, abound with fun and wit and are immediately recognizable wherever they appear.

Today there are so many notable artists with distinct personal styles—Steven Kellogg, Trina Schart Hyman, William Steig, Richard Scarry—that it is impossible in a short space to cover all of them. In discussions of children's books, however, one group of artists is often overlooked: illustrators of informational and instructional books. They are often slighted because of the requirements of their field, which demands that they reflect the world as it is to a greater degree than illustrators of fiction or fantasy. They cannot use total abstraction, as did Lionni in *Little Blue and Little Yellow,* because the object, person, or animal must be highly recognizable. In some ways illustrators of informational books face a more difficult task than illustrators of fictional books. Their primary purpose is to convey information; art is secondary. They must follow the text closely and are often restricted by the text. With talent and insight, however, they can achieve the same harmony of text and pictures that the fictonal book illustrator strives for, and can produce books that delight the eye while filling the mind.

Although almost all of the illustrators previously mentioned have worked on informational books at one time or another, a few artists have made this area their specialty. Dorothy Waugh, who started in the thirties, has produced a number of informational books of very high quality. Her *Warm Earth* (1943), for example, explains how the earth supports various life forms. Her shaded pencil drawings of the earth and of fruits and flowers are marvels of texture and pattern. She demonstrates how effectively the informational illustrator can "take advantage of the artist's freedom to select and emphasize, to interpret and compose."[25]

During the 1940s and 1950s, illustrators of informational books experimented with style and technique just as fictional artists did. The 1950s saw the publication of the stylized, childlike illustrations of Leonard Kessler in such books as his *What's in a Line?* (1951) and John Lewellen's *Tommy Learns to Fly!* (1956). In Kessler's illustrations, detail and humor combine with realism to communicate information effectively.

Just as the 1960s was the start of a second golden age for fictional picturebooks, so was it a golden age for informational books, a decade of experimentation in style and technique in both fields. Helen Borten's *The Moon Seems to Change* (1960) by Franklyn M. Branley was one of many books published during the sixties that demonstrated that informational books didn't have to employ total realism to teach or inform. Borten's almost abstractionist woodcuts are strong and vivid. Employing startling colors, she uses the illustrations, as Barbara Bader points out, "less to clarify than to conjure up, to present images

Doctor De Soto, written and illustrated by William Steig

One Monday Morning, written and illustrated by Uri Shulevitz

of glaring heat and deepest cold, of size and distance and want of life."[26]

Superior storytelling, whether of a fictional or nonfictional nature, has always been the goal of the children's picturebook. "By telling a story visually instead of through verbal description, a picture book becomes a dramatic experience: immediate, vivid, moving," says Uri Shulevitz in his *Writing with Pictures*.[27] The superior children's book is one that creates a memorable moment visually and verbally in the life of a child. Children's book illustration is the most challenging task an illustrator can face, and when the intended audience is considered, as well as the effect an exceptional book can have upon that audience, it is also perhaps the most rewarding.

Notes

1. Barbara Bader, *American Picturebooks from Noah's Ark to the Beast Within* (New York: Macmillan, 1976), p. 3.

2. Bader, *American Picturebooks*, p. 73. For further discussion of Ellen Key, see the introduction to this volume.

3. Anne Carroll Moore, *The Three Owls: Third Book* (New York: Coward-McCann, 1931), p. xv.

4. Bader, *American Picturebooks*, p. 240.

5. Ibid., p. 288.

6. "Bringing Up Superbaby," *Newsweek*, March 28, 1983, p. 62.

7. Telephone interview with Eden Ross Lipson, August 1985.

8. Response to a 1983 survey questionnaire sent to Margaret Firth, editor in chief, Putnam Books.

9. Dorothy Butler, *Babies Need Books* (New York: Atheneum, 1980), pp. 37–38.

10. Quoted in Anne Devereaux Jordan and Jean Mercier, "Baby Lit," *Publishers Weekly*, April 20, 1984, p. 30.

11. Butler, *Babies Need Books*, p. 18.

12. Jordan and Mercier, "Baby Lit," p. 30.

13. Ibid.

14. Ibid.

15. Lipson interview.

16. Quoted in Cornelia Meigs et al., *A Critical History of Children's Literature* (New York: Macmillan, 1953), p. 280.

17. James Steele Smith, *A Critical Approach to Children's Literature* (New York: McGraw-Hill, 1967), p. 310.

18. Bader, *American Picturebooks*, p. 66.

19. Zena Sutherland et al., *Children and Books* (Glenview, Ill.: Scott, Foresman, 1981), p. 135.

20. Bader, *American Picturebooks*, p. 44.

21. Diana Klemin, *The Illustrated Book: Its Art and Craft* (New York: Clarkson N. Potter, 1970), p. 26.

22. Bader, *American Picturebooks*, p. 224.

23. Smith, *A Critical Approach*, p. 313.

24. Edward Ardizzone, "The Born Illustrator," *Motif*, November 1958, p. 38.

25. Bader, *American Picturebooks*, p. 383.

26. Ibid., p. 403.

27. Uri Shulevitz, *Writing with Pictures: How to Write and Illustrate Children's Books* (New York: Watson-Guptill, 1985), p. 16.

Appendix A

Masterworks of Children's Literature
Contents, Volumes 1–7

Volume 1: The Early Years (1550–1739)

Volume 2: The Early Years (1550–1739)

Volume 3: Middle Period (1740–1836)

Volume 4: Middle Period (1740–1836)

Volume 5, Part 1: The Victorian Age (1837–1900)

Volume 5, Part 2: The Victorian Age (1837–1900)

Volume 6: The Victorian Age (1837–1900)

Volume 7: Victorian Color Picture Books

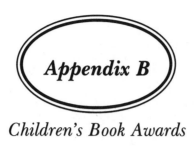

Appendix B

Children's Book Awards

This appendix includes the major English-language children's book awards as well as the two most prestigious international awards, the Hans Christian Andersen Medal and the related International Board on Books for Young People Honor List. Unless otherwise indicated, year of publication is as stated in the headnote to each award (year of award or year preceding award). For illustrated books, as indicated either by category of award or in the bibliographical data, where no separate illustrator is named, the author is the illustrator.

For a full listing of children's book awards, consult *Children's Literature Awards and Prizes: A Directory of Prizes, Authors, and Illustrators,* 1st ed., comp. Dolores Blythe Jones (Detroit: Neal-Schumann Publishers in Association with Gale Research Co., 1983; 1st supplement, 1985), and the 1985 edition of *Children's Books Awards and Prizes,* comp. and ed. Children's Book Council (New York: Children's Book Council, 1986).

JOHN NEWBERY MEDAL

The Newbery Medal is administered by the Association for Library Service to Children of the American Library Association and awarded annually to the "author [U.S. citizen or resident] of the most distinguished contribution to American literature for children published in the U.S. during the preceding year." It was established in 1922 at the suggestion of editor Frederic G. Melcher in honor of John Newbery, the first English publisher of books for children. The medal is donated each year by the Melcher family. The following list includes medal winners and honor books (except for years where there is no record for honor books).

1922   *The Story of Mankind,* Hendrik Willem Van Loon, ill. (Boni & Liveright)

HONOR BOOKS
Cedric the Forester, Bernard G. Marshall (Appleton)
The Golden Fleece and the Heroes Who Lived Before Achilles, Padraic Colum, ill. Willy Pogany (Macmillan)
The Great Quest: A Romance of 1826, Charles Boardman Hawes, ill. George Varian (Little)
The Old Tobacco Shop: A True Account of What Befell a Little Boy in Search of Adventure, William Bowen, ill. Reginald Birch (Macmillan)
The Windy Hill, Cornelia Meigs (Macmillan)

1923   *The Voyages of Doctor Dolittle,* Hugh Lofting, ill. (Stokes)

1924   *The Dark Frigate,* Charles Boardman Hawes, ill. A. L. Ripley (Atlantic Monthly)

1925   *Tales from Silver Lands,* Charles J. Finger, ill. Paul Honoré (Doubleday)

HONOR BOOKS
The Dream Coach, Anne and Dillwyn Parrish, ill. (Macmillan)
Nicholas: A Manhattan Christmas Story, Anne Carroll Moore, ill. J. Van Everen (Putnam)

1926   *Shen of the Sea: A Book for Children,* Arthur Bowie Chrisman, ill. Else Hasselriis (Dutton)

HONOR BOOKS
The Voyagers: Being Legends and Romances of Atlantic Discovery, Padraic Colum, ill. Wilfred Jones (Macmillan)

1927   *Smoky the Cowhorse,* Will James, ill. (Scribner)

1928   *Gay-Neck: The Story of a Pigeon,* Dhan Gopal Mukerji, ill. Boris Artzybasheff (Dutton)

HONOR BOOKS
Downright Dencey, Caroline Dale Snedeker, ill. Maginel W. Barney (Doubleday)
The Wonder-Smith and His Son: A Tale from the Golden Childhood of the World, Ella Young, ill. Boris Artzybasheff (Longmans)

1929   *The Trumpeter of Krakow,* Eric P. Kelly, ill. Angela Pruszynska (Macmillan)

HONOR BOOKS
The Boy Who Was, Grace T. Hallock, ill. Harrie Wood (Dutton)
Clearing Weather, Cornelia Meigs, ill. Frank Dobias (Little)

Millions of Cats, Wanda Gág, ill. (Coward)
The Pigtail of Ah Lee Ben Loo with Seventeen Other Laughable Tales and 200 Comical Silhouettes, John Bennett, ill. (Longmans)
The Runaway Papoose, Grace P. Moon, ill. Carl Moon (Doubleday)
Tod of the Fens, Elinor Whitney, ill. (Macmillan)

1930   *Hitty, Her First Hundred Years*, Rachel Field, ill. Dorothy P. Lathrop (Macmillan)

HONOR BOOKS
A Daughter of the Seine: The Life of Madame Roland, Jeanette Eaton (Harper)
Jumping-Off Place, Marian Hurd McNeely, ill. William Siegel (Longmans)
Little Blacknose: The Story of a Pioneer, Hildegarde Swift, ill. Lynd Ward (Harcourt)
Pran of Albania, Elizabeth C. Miller, ill. Maud and Miska Petersham (Doubleday)
Tangle-Coated Horse and Other Tales: Episodes from the Fionn Saga, Ella Young, ill. Vera Bock (Longmans)
Vaino, a Boy of New Finland, Julia Davis Adams, ill. Lempi Ostman (Dutton)

1931   *The Cat Who Went to Heaven*, Elizabeth Coatsworth, ill. Lynd Ward (Macmillan)

HONOR BOOKS
The Dark Star of Itza, Alida Malkus, ill. Lowell Houser (Harcourt)
Floating Island, Anne Parrish, ill. (Harper)
Garram the Hunter: A Boy of the Hill Tribes, Herbert Best, ill. Erick Berry (Doubleday)
Meggy MacIntosh, Elizabeth Janet Gray, ill. Marguerite de Angeli (Doubleday)
Mountains Are Free, Julia Davis Adams, ill. Theodore Nadejen (Dutton)
Ood-Le-Uk the Wanderer, Alice Lide and Margaret Johansen, ill. Raymond Lufkin (Little)
Queer Person, Ralph Hubbard, ill. Harold Von Schmidt (Doubleday)
Spice and the Devil's Cave, Agnes D. Hewes, ill. Lynd Ward (Knopf)

1932   *Waterless Mountain*, Laura Adams Armer, ill. Sidney and Laura Armer (Longmans)

HONOR BOOKS
Boy of the South Seas, Eunice Tietjens, ill. Myrtle Sheldon (Coward)
Calico Bush, Rachel Field, ill. Allen Lewis (Macmillan)
The Fairy Circus, Dorothy P. Lathrop, ill. (Macmillan)
Jane's Island, Marjorie Hill Allee, ill. Maitland de Gogorza (Houghton)

Out of the Flame, Eloise Lownsbery, ill. Elizabeth T. Wolcott (Longmans)
Truce of the Wolf and Other Tales of Old Italy, Mary Gould Davis, ill. J. Van Everen (Harcourt)

1933   *Young Fu of the Upper Yangtze,* Elizabeth Foreman Lewis, ill. Kurt Wiese (Winston)

HONOR BOOKS
Children of the Soil: A Story of Scandinavia, Nora Burglon, ill. E. Parin d'Aulaire (Doubleday)
The Railroad to Freedom: A Story of the Civil War, Hildegarde Swift, ill. James Daugherty (Harcourt)
Swift Rivers, Cornelia Meigs, ill. Peter Hurd (Little)

1934   *Invincible Louisa: The Story of the Author of "Little Women"* Cornelia Meigs, ill. with photos (Little)

HONOR BOOKS
ABC Bunny, Wanda Gág, ill. (Coward)
Apprentices of Florence, Anne Kyle, ill. Erick Berry (Houghton)
Big Tree of Bunlahy: Stories of My Own Countryside, Padraic Colum, ill. Jack Yeats (Macmillan)
Forgotten Daughter, Caroline Dale Snedeker, ill. Dorothy P. Lathrop (Doubleday)
Glory of the Seas, Agnes Hewes, ill. N. C. Wyeth (Knopf)
New Land, Sarah L. Schmidt, ill. Frank Dobias (McBride)
Swords of Steel: The Story of a Gettysburg Boy, Elsie Singmaster, ill. David Hendrickson (Houghton)
Winged Girl of Knossos, Erick Berry, ill. (Appleton)

1935   *Dobry,* Monica Shannon, ill. Atanas Katchamakoff (Viking)

HONOR BOOKS
Davy Crockett, Constance Rourke, ill. James MacDonald (Harcourt)
A Day on Skates: The Story of a Dutch Picnic, Hilda Van Stockum, ill. (Harper)
The Pageant of Chinese History, Elizabeth Seeger, ill. Bernard Watkins (Longmans)

1936   *Caddie Woodlawn,* Carol Ryrie Brink, ill. Kate Seredy (Macmillan)

HONOR BOOKS
All Sail Set: A Romance of the "Flying Cloud," Armstrong Sperry, ill. (Winston)
The Good Master, Kate Seredy, ill. (Viking)
Honk the Moose, Phil Strong, ill. Kurt Wiese (Dodd)
Young Walter Scott, Elizabeth Janet Gray, ill. Kate Seredy (Viking)

1937   *Roller Skates*, Ruth Sawyer, ill. Valenti Angelo (Viking)

HONOR BOOKS
Audubon, Constance M. Rourke, ill. James MacDonald (Harcourt)
The Codfish Musket, Agnes D. Hewes, ill. Armstrong Sperry (Doubleday)
The Golden Basket, Ludwig Bemelmans, ill. (Viking)
Phebe Fairchild: Her Book, Lois Lenski, ill. (Lippincott)
Whistler's Van, Idwal Jones, ill. Zhenya Gay (Viking)
Winterbound, Margery Bianco, ill. Kate Seredy (Viking)

1938   *The White Stag*, Kate Seredy, ill. (Viking)

HONOR BOOKS
Bright Island, Mabel L. Robinson, ill. Lynd Ward (Random House)
On the Banks of Plum Creek, Laura Ingalls Wilder, ill. Mildred Boyle
    and Helen Sewell (Harper)
Pecos Bill: The Greatest Cowboy of All Time, James Cloyd Bowman, ill.
    Laura Bannon (Whitman)

1939   *Thimble Summer*, Elizabeth Enright, ill. (Farrar)

HONOR BOOKS
Leader by Destiny: George Washington, Man and Patriot, Jeanette Eaton,
    ill. J. M. Rose (Harcourt)
Mr. Popper's Penguins, Richard and Florence Atwater, ill. Robert Law-
    son (Little)
Nino, Valenti Angelo, ill. (Viking)
Penn, Elizabeth Janet Gray, ill. George G. Whitney (Viking)

1940   *Daniel Boone*, James H. Daugherty, ill. (Viking)

HONOR BOOKS
Boy with a Pack, Stephen W. Meader, ill. Edward Shenton (Harcourt)
By the Shores of Silver Lake, Laura Ingalls Wilder, ill. Helen Sewell and
    Mildred Boyle (Harper)
Runners of the Mountain Tops: The Life of Louis Agassiz, Mabel L. Rob-
    inson, ill. Lynd Ward (Random)
The Singing Tree, Kate Seredy, ill. (Viking)

1941   *Call It Courage*, Armstrong Sperry, ill. (Macmillan)

HONOR BOOKS
Blue Willow, Doris Gates, ill. Paul Lantz (Viking)
The Long Winter, Laura Ingalls Wilder, ill. Helen Sewell and Mildred
    Boyle (Harper)
Nansen, Anna Gertrude Hall, ill. Boris Artzybasheff (Viking)
Young Mac of Fort Vancouver, Mary Jane Carr, ill. Richard Holberg
    (Crowell)

1942   *The Matchlock Gun,* Walter D. Edmonds, ill. Paul Lantz (Dodd)

HONOR BOOKS
Down Ryton Water, Eva Roe Gaggin, ill. Elmer Hader (Viking)
George Washington's World, Genevieve Foster, ill. (Scribner)
Indian Captive: The Story of Mary Jemison, Lois Lenski, ill. (Stokes)
Little Town on the Prairie, Laura Ingalls Wilder, ill. Mildred Boyle and
   Helen Sewell (Harper)

1943   *Adam of the Road,* Elizabeth Janet Gray, ill. Robert Lawson (Viking)

HONOR BOOKS
Have You Seen Tom Thumb? Mabel Leigh Hunt, ill. Fritz Eichenberg
   (Stokes)
The Middle Moffat, Eleanor Estes, ill. Louis Slobodkin (Harcourt)

1944   *Johnny Tremain,* Esther Forbes, ill. Lynd Ward (Houghton)

HONOR BOOKS
Fog Magic, Julia L. Sauer, ill. Lynd Ward (Viking)
Mountain Born, Elizabeth Yates, ill. Nora S. Unwin (Coward)
Rufus M., Eleanor Estes, ill. Louis Slobodkin (Harcourt)
These Happy Golden Years, Laura Ingalls Wilder, ill. Mildred Boyle and
   Helen Sewell (Harper)

1945   *Rabbit Hill,* Robert Lawson, ill. (Viking)

HONOR BOOKS
Abraham Lincoln's World, Genevieve Foster, ill. (Scribner)
The Hundred Dresses, Eleanor Estes, ill. Louis Slobodkin (Harcourt)
Lone Journey: The Life of Roger Williams, Jeanette Eaton, ill. Woodi
   Ishmael (Harcourt)
The Silver Pencil, Alice Dalgliesh, ill. Katherine Milhous (Scribner)

1946   *Strawberry Girl,* Lois Lenski, ill. (Lippincott)

HONOR BOOKS
Bhimsa, the Dancing Bear, Christine Weston, ill. Roger Duvoisin (Scrib-
   ner)
Justin Morgan Had a Horse, Marguerite Henry, ill. Wesley Dennis (Wil-
   cox & Follett)
The Moved-Outers, Florence Crannell Means, ill. Helen Blair (Hough-
   ton)
New Found World, Katherine B. Shippen, ill. C. B. Falls (Viking)

1947   *Miss Hickory,* Carolyn Sherwin Bailey, ill. Ruth Chrisman Gannett (Viking)

HONOR BOOKS
The Avion My Uncle Flew, Cyrus Fisher, ill. Richard Floethe (Appleton)
Big Tree, Mary and Conrad Buff, ill. (Viking)
The Heavenly Tenants, William Maxwell, ill. Ilonka Karasz (Harper)
The Hidden Treasure of Glaston, Eleanore Myers Jewett, ill. Frederick
    T. Chapman (Viking)
The Wonderful Year, Nancy Barnes, ill. Kate Seredy (Messner)

1948   *The Twenty-One Balloons,* William Pène du Bois, ill. (Viking)

HONOR BOOKS
Cow-Tail Switch and Other West African Stories, George Herzog and
    Harold Courlander, ill. Madye Lee Chastain (Holt)
Li Lun, Lad of Courage, Carolyn Treffinger, ill. Kurt Wiese (Abingdon)
Misty of Chincoteague, Marguerite Henry, ill. Wesley Dennis (Rand
    McNally)
Pancakes-Paris, Claire Huchet Bishop, ill. Georges Schreiber (Viking)
The Quaint and Curious Quest of Johnny Longfoot, the Shoe King's Son,
    Catherine Besterman, ill. Warren Chappell (Bobbs-Merrill)

1949   *King of the Wind,* Marguerite Henry, ill. Wesley Dennis (Rand McNally)

HONOR BOOKS
Daughter of the Mountains, Louise S. Rankin, ill. Kurt Wiese (Viking)
My Father's Dragon, Ruth Stiles Gannett, ill. Ruth Chrisman Gannett
    (Random)
Seabird, Holling Clancy Holling, ill. (Houghton)
Story of the Negro, Arna W. Bontemps, ill. Raymond Lufkin (Knopf)

1950   *The Door in the Wall: Story of Medieval London,* Marguerite de Angeli,
        ill. (Doubleday)

HONOR BOOKS
The Blue Cat of Castle Town, Catherine C. Coblentz, ill. Janice Holland
    (Longmans)
George Washington: An Initial Biography, Genevieve Foster, ill. (Scrib-
    ner)
Kildee House, Rutherford Montgomery, ill. Barbara Cooney (Double-
    day)
Song of the Pines: A Story of Norwegian Lumbering in Wisconsin, Walter
    and Marion Havighurst, ill. Richard Floethe (Winston)
Tree of Freedom, Rebecca Caudill, ill. Dorothy Bayley Morse (Viking)

1951   *Amos Fortune, Free Man,* Elizabeth Yates, ill. Nora S. Unwin (Aladdin)

HONOR BOOKS
Abraham Lincoln, Friend of the People, Clara I. Judson, ill. Robert Fran-
    kenberg (Wilcox & Follett)

Better Known as Johnny Appleseed, Mabel Leigh Hunt, ill. James Daugherty (Lippincott)
Gandhi, Fighter Without a Sword, Jeannette Eaton, ill. Ralph Ray (Morrow)
The Story of Appleby Capple, Anne Parrish, ill. (Harper)

1952   *Ginger Pye*, Eleanor Estes, ill. (Harcourt)

HONOR BOOKS
Americans Before Columbus, Elizabeth Chesley Baity, ill. C. B. Falls (Viking)
The Apple and the Arrow, Conrad and Mary Buff, ill. (Houghton) 1951.
The Defender, Nicholas Kalashnikoff, ill. Claire and George Louden (Scribner)
The Light at Tern Rock, Julia L. Sauer, ill. Georges Schreiber (Viking)
Minn of the Mississippi Holling Clancy Holling, ill. (Houghton)

1953   *Secret of the Andes*, Ann Nolan Clark, ill. Jean Charlot (Viking)

HONOR BOOKS
The Bears on Hemlock Mountain, Alice Dalgliesh, ill. Helen Sewell (Scribner)
Birthdays of Freedom: America's Heritage from the Ancient World, Genevieve Foster, ill. (Scribner)
Charlotte's Web, E. B. White, ill. Garth Williams (Harper)
Moccasin Trail, Eloise J. McGraw, ill. Paul Galdone (Coward)
Red Sails to Capri, Ann Weil, ill. C. B. Falls (Viking)

1954   *And Now Miguel*, Joseph Krumgold, ill. Jean Charlot (Crowell)

HONOR BOOKS
All Alone, Claire Huchet Bishop, ill. Feodor Rojankovsky (Viking)
Hurry Home, Candy, Meindert DeJong, ill. Maurice Sendak (Harper)
Magic Maize, Conrad and Mary Buff, ill. (Houghton)
Shadrach, Meindert DeJong, ill. Maurice Sendak (Harper)
Theodore Roosevelt, Fighting Patriot, Clara I. Judson, ill. Lorence F. Bjorklund (Follett)

1955   *The Wheel on the School*, Meindert DeJong, ill. Maurice Sendak (Harper)

HONOR BOOKS
Banner in the Sky: The Story of a Boy and a Mountain, James Ramsey Ullman (Lippincott)
The Courage of Sarah Noble, Alice Dalgliesh, ill. Leonard Weisgard (Scribner)

1956   *Carry On, Mr. Bowditch*, Jean Lee Latham, ill. J. O. Cosgrove (Houghton)

HONOR BOOKS
The Golden Name Day, Jennie D. Lindquist, ill. Garth Williams (Harper)
Men, Microscopes and Living Things, Katherine B. Shippen, ill. Anthony Ravielli (Viking)
The Secret River, Marjorie Kinnan Rawlings, ill. Leonard Weisgard (Scribner)

1957   *Miracles on Maple Hill*, Virginia Sorensen, ill. Beth and Joe Krush (Harcourt)

HONOR BOOKS
The Black Fox of Lorne, Marguerite de Angeli, ill. (Doubleday)
The Corn Grows Ripe, Dorothy Rhoads, ill. Jean Charlot (Viking)
The House of Sixty Fathers, Meindert DeJong, ill. Maurice Sendak (Harper)
Mr. Justice Holmes, Clara I. Judson, ill. Robert Todd (Follett)
Old Yeller, Fred Gipson, ill. Carl Burger (Harper)

1958   *Rifles for Watie*, Harold Keith, ill. Peter Burchard (Crowell)

HONOR BOOKS
Gone-Away Lake, Elizabeth Enright, ill. Beth and Joe Krush (Harcourt)
The Great Wheel, Robert Lawson, ill. (Viking)
The Horsecatcher, Mari Sandoz (Westminster)
Tom Paine, Freedom's Apostle, Leo Gurko, ill. Fritz Kredel (Crowell)

1959   *The Witch of Blackbird Pond*, Elizabeth George Speare (Houghton)

HONOR BOOKS
Along Came a Dog, Meindert DeJong, ill. Maurice Sendak (Harper)
Chucaro: Wild Pony of the Pampa, Francis Kalnay, ill. Julian DeMiskey (Harcourt)
The Family Under the Bridge, Natalie Savage Carlson, ill. Garth Williams (Harper)
The Perilous Road, William O. Steele, ill. Paul Galdone (Harcourt)

1960   *Onion John*, Joseph Krumgold, ill. Symeon Shimin (Crowell)

HONOR BOOKS
America Is Born: A History for Peter, Gerald W. Johnson, ill. Leonard E. Fisher (Morrow)
The Gammage Cup, Carol Kendall, ill. Erik Blegvad (Harcourt)
My Side of the Mountain, Jean Craighead George, ill. (Dutton)

1961   *Island of the Blue Dolphins*, Scott O'Dell, ill. Evaline Ness (Houghton)

HONOR BOOKS
America Moves Forward: A History for Peter, Gerald W. Johnson, ill. Leonard E. Fisher (Morrow)
The Cricket in Times Square, George Selden, ill. Garth Williams (Farrar)
Old Ramon, Jack Schaefer, ill. Harold West (Houghton)

1962   *The Bronze Bow*, Elizabeth George Speare (Houghton)

HONOR BOOKS
Belling the Tiger, Mary Stolz, ill. Beni Montresor (Harper)
Frontier Living, Edwin Tunis, ill. (World)
The Golden Goblet, Eloise Jarvis McGraw (Coward)

1963   *A Wrinkle in Time*, Madeleine L'Engle (Farrar)

HONOR BOOKS
Men of Athens, Olivia Coolidge, ill. Milton Johnson (Houghton)
Thistle and Thyme: Tales and Legends from Scotland, Sorche Nic Leodhas, ill. Evaline Ness (Holt)

1964   *It's Like This, Cat*, Emily Cheney Neville, ill. Emil Weiss (Harper)

HONOR BOOKS
The Loner, Ester Weir, ill. Christine Price (McKay)
Rascal: A Memoir of a Better Era, Sterling North, ill. John Schoenherr (Dutton)

1965   *Shadow of a Bull*, Maia Wojciechowska, ill. Alvin Smith (Atheneum)

HONOR BOOKS
Across Five Aprils, Irene Hunt, ill. Albert J. Pucci (Follett)

1966   *I, Juan de Pareja*, Elizabeth Borton de Treviño (Farrar)

HONOR BOOKS
The Animal Family, Randall Jarrell, ill. Maurice Sendak (Pantheon)
The Black Cauldron, Lloyd Alexander (Holt)
The Noonday Friends, Mary Stolz, ill. Louis S. Glanzman (Harper)

1967   *Up a Road Slowly*, Irene Hunt (Follett)

HONOR BOOKS
The Jazz Man, Mary Hays Weik, ill. Ann Grifalconi (Atheneum)
The King's Fifth, Scott O'Dell, ill. Samuel Bryant (Houghton)
Zlateh the Goat and Other Stories, Isaac Bashevis Singer, ill. Maurice Sendak (Harper)

1968 *From the Mixed-Up Files of Mrs. Basil E. Frankweiler,* E. L. Konigsburg, ill. (Atheneum)

HONOR BOOKS
The Black Pearl, Scott O'Dell, ill. Milton Johnson (Houghton)
The Egypt Game, Zilpha Keatley Snyder, ill. Alton Raible (Atheneum)
The Fearsome Inn, Isaac Bashevis Singer, ill. Nonny Hogrogian (Scribner)
Jennifer, Hecate, Macbeth, William McKinley, and Me, Elizabeth, E. L. Konigsburg, ill. (Atheneum)

1969 *The High King,* Lloyd Alexander (Holt)

HONOR BOOKS
To Be a Slave, Julius Lester, ill. Tom Feelings (Dial)
When Schlemiel Went to Warsaw and Other Stories, Isaac Bashevis Singer, ill. Margot Zemach (Farrar)

1970 *Sounder,* William H. Armstrong, ill. James Barkley (Harper)

HONOR BOOKS
Journey Outside, Mary Q. Steele, ill. Rocco Negri (Viking)
The Many Ways of Seeing: An Introduction to the Pleasures of Art, Janet Gaylord Moore, ill. (Collins)
Our Eddie, Sulamith Ish-Kishor (Pantheon)

1971 *Summer of the Swans,* Betsy Byars, ill. Ted CoConis (Viking)

HONOR BOOKS
Enchantress from the Stars, Sylvia Louise Engdahl, ill. Rodney Shackell (Atheneum)
Knee-Knock Rise, Natalie Babbitt, ill. (Farrar)
Sing Down the Moon, Scott O'Dell (Houghton)

1972 *Mrs. Frisby and the Rats of NIMH,* Robert C. O'Brien, ill. Zena Bernstein (Atheneum)

HONOR BOOKS
Anne and the Old One, Miska Miles, ill. Peter Parnall (Atlantic-Little)
The Headless Cupid, Zilpha Keatley Snyder, ill. Alton Raible (Atheneum)
Incident at Hawk's Hill, Allan W. Eckert, ill. John Schoenherr (Little)
The Planet of Junior Brown, Virginia Hamilton (Macmillan)
The Tombs of Atuan, Ursula K. Le Guin, ill. Gail Garraty (Atheneum)

1973 *Julie of the Wolves,* Jean Craighead George, ill. John Schoenherr (Harper)

HONOR BOOKS
Frog and Toad Together, Arnold Lobel, ill. (Harper)
The Upstairs Room, Johanna Reiss (Crowell)

The Witches of Worm, Zilpha Keatley Snyder, ill. Alton Raible (Atheneum)

1974   *The Slave Dancer,* Paula Fox, ill. Eros Keith (Bradbury)

HONOR BOOKS
The Dark Is Rising, Susan Cooper, ill. Alan Cober (Atheneum/Mc-Elderry)

1975   *M. C. Higgins, the Great,* Virginia Hamilton (Macmillan)

HONOR BOOKS
Figgs and Phantoms, Ellen Raskin, ill. (Dutton)
My Brother Sam Is Dead, James Lincoln Collier and Christopher Collier (Four Winds/Scholastic)
The Perilous Gard, Elizabeth M. Pope, ill. Richard Cuffari (Houghton)
Philip Hall Likes Me, I Reckon Maybe, Bette Greene, ill. Charles Lilly (Dial)

1976   *The Grey King,* Susan Cooper, ill. Michael Heslop (Atheneum)

HONOR BOOKS
Dragonwings, Laurence Yep (Harper)
Hundred Penny Box, Sharon Bell Mathis, ill. Leo and Diane Dillon (Viking)

1977   *Roll of Thunder, Hear My Cry,* Mildred D. Taylor, ill. Jerry Pinkney (Dial)

HONOR BOOKS
Abel's Island, William Steig, ill. (Farrar)
A String in the Harp, Nancy Bond, ill. Allen Davis (Atheneum/Mc-Elderry)

1978   *Bridge to Terabithia,* Katherine Paterson, ill. Donna Diamond (Crowell)

HONOR BOOKS
Anpao: An American Indian Odyssey, Jamake Highwater, ill. Fritz Scholder (Lippincott)
Ramona and Her Father, Beverly Cleary, ill. Alan Tiegreen (Morrow)

1979   *The Westing Game,* Ellen Raskin (Dutton)

HONOR BOOKS
The Great Gilly Hopkins, Katherine Paterson (Crowell)

1980   *A Gathering of Days: A New England Girl's Journal, 1830–32—A Novel,* Joan W. Blos (Scribner)

HONOR BOOKS
The Road from Home: The Story of an Armenian Girl, David Kherdian (Greenwillow)

1981   *Jacob Have I Loved,* Katherine Paterson (Crowell)

HONOR BOOKS
The Fledgling, Jane Langton, ill. Erik Blegvad (Harper)
A Ring of Endless Light, Madeleine L'Engle (Farrar)

1982   *A Visit to William Blake's Inn: Poems for Innocent and Experienced Travelers,* Nancy Willard, ill. Alice and Martin Provensen (Harcourt)

HONOR BOOKS
Ramona Quimby, Age 8, Beverly Cleary, ill. Alan Tiegreen (Morrow)
Upon the Head of a Goat: A Childhood in Hungary, 1939–1944, Aranka Siegal (Farrar)

1983   *Dicey's Song,* Cynthia Voigt (Atheneum)

HONOR BOOKS
The Blue Sword, Robin McKinley (Greenwillow)
Doctor De Soto, William Steig, ill. (Farrar)
Graven Images: Three Stories, Paul Fleishman, ill. Andrew Glass (Harper)
Homesick: My Own Story, Jean Fritz, ill. with drawings by Margot Tomes and photos (Putnam)
Sweet Whispers, Brother Rush, Virginia Hamilton (Philomel)

1984   *Dear Mr. Henshaw,* Beverly Cleary, ill. Paul O. Zelinsky, (Morrow)

HONOR BOOKS
The Sign of the Beaver, Elizabeth George Speare (Houghton)
A Solitary Blue, Cynthia Voigt (Atheneum)
Sugaring Time, Kathryn Lasky, photos Christopher G. Knight (Macmillan)
The Wish Giver: Three Tales of Coven Tree, William Brittain, ill. Andrew Glass (Harper)

1985   *The Hero and the Crown,* Robin McKinley (Greenwillow)

HONOR BOOKS
Like Jake and Me, Mavis Jukes, ill. Lloyd Bloom (Knopf)
The Moves Make the Man, Bruce Brooks (Harper)
One-Eyed Cat, Paula Fox (Bradbury)

1986   *Sarah, Plain and Tall*, Patricia MacLachlan (Harper)

HONOR BOOKS
Commodore Perry in the Land of the Shogun, Rhoda Blumberg, ill. with
   photos (Lothrop)
Dogsong, Gary Paulsen (Bradbury)

RANDOLPH CALDECOTT MEDAL

In 1937 Frederic G. Melcher, originator of the Newbery Medal, proposed a
similar award for illustrated books, to be named for Randolph Caldecott, the
noted nineteenth-century British illustrator. The award has been given annually
since 1938 to "the artist [U.S. citizen or resident] of the most distinguished
American picture book for children published in the U.S. during the preceding
year." Like the Newbery Medal, it is administered by the Association for Library
Service to Children of the American Library Association and donated by the
Melcher family.

1938   *Animals of the Bible: A Picture Book*, Helen Dean Fish, ill. Dorothy P.
   Lathrop (Stokes)

HONOR BOOKS
*Four and Twenty Blackbirds: Nursery Rhymes of Yesterday Recalled for
   Children of Today*, Helen Dean Fish, ill. Robert Lawson (Lippincott)
Seven Simeons: A Russian Tale, Boris Artzybasheff (Viking)

1939   *Mei Li*, Thomas Handforth (Doubleday)

HONOR BOOKS
Andy and the Lion, James Daugherty (Viking)
Barkis, Clare Turlay Newberry (Harper)
The Forest Pool, Laura Adams Armer (Longmans)
Snow White and the Seven Dwarfs, trans. and ill. Wanda Gág (Coward)
Wee Gillis, Munro Leaf, ill. Robert Lawson (Viking)

1940   *Abraham Lincoln*, Edgar and Ingri d'Aulaire (Doubleday)

HONOR BOOKS
The Ageless Story with Its Antiphons, Lauren Ford (Dodd)
Cock-A-Doodle Doo, Berta and Elmer Hader (Macmillan)
Madeline, Ludwig Bemelmans (Simon & Schuster)

1941   *They Were Strong and Good,* Robert Lawson (Viking)

HONOR BOOKS
April's Kittens, Clare Turlay Newberry (Harper)

1942   *Make Way for Ducklings,* Robert McCloskey (Viking)

HONOR BOOKS
An American ABC, Miska and Maud Petersham (Macmillan)
In My Mother's House, Ann Nolan Clark, ill. Velino Herrera (Viking)
Nothing at All, Wanda Gág (Coward)
Paddle-to-the-Sea, Holling Clancy Holling (Houghton)

1943   *The Little House,* Virginia Lee Burton (Houghton)

HONOR BOOKS
Dash and Dart, Conrad and Mary Buff (Viking)
Marshmallow, Clare Turlay Newberry (Harper)

1944   *Many Moons,* James Thurber, ill. Louis Slobodkin (Harcourt)

HONOR BOOKS
A Child's Good Night Book, Margaret Wise Brown, ill. Jean Charlot (Scott)
Good Luck Horse, Chih-Yi Chan, ill. Plato Chan (Whittlesey)
Mighty Hunter, Elmer and Berta Hader (Macmillan)
Pierre Pidgeon, Lee Kingman, ill. Arnold Edwin Bare (Houghton)
Small Rain: Verses from the Bible, Jessie Orton Jones, ill. Elizabeth Orton Jones (Viking)

1945   *Prayer for a Child,* Rachel Field, ill. Elizabeth Orton Jones (Macmillan)

HONOR BOOKS
The Christmas Anna Angel, Ruth Sawyer, ill. Kate Seredy (Viking)
In the Forest, Marie Hall Ets (Viking)
Mother Goose, comp. and ill. Tasha Tudor (Oxford)
Yonie Wondernose, Marguerite de Angeli (Doubleday)

1946   *The Rooster Crows,* Maud and Miska Petersham (Macmillan)

HONOR BOOKS
Little Lost Lamb, Golden MacDonald, ill. Leonard Weisgard (Doubleday)
My Mother Is the Most Beautiful Woman in the World, Becky Reyher, ill. Ruth C. Gannett (Lothrop)
Sing Mother Goose, music Opal Wheeler, ill. Marjorie Torrey (Dutton)
You Can Write Chinese, Kurt Wiese (Viking)

1947   *The Little Island,* Golden MacDonald, ill. Leonard Weisgard (Double-
        day)

        HONOR BOOKS
        Boats on the River, Marjorie Flack, ill. Jay Hyde Barnum (Viking)
        Pedro, the Angel of Olvera Street, Leo Politi (Scribner)
        Rain Drop Splash, Alvin R. Tresselt, ill. Leonard Weisgard (Lothrop)
        Sing in Praise: A Collection of Best Loved Hymns, Opal Wheeler, ill.
            Marjorie Torrey (Dutton)
        Timothy Turtle, Al Graham, ill. Tony Palazzo (Robert Welch)

1948   *White Snow, Bright Snow,* Alvin Tresselt, ill. Roger Duvoisin (Lothrop)

        HONOR BOOKS
        Bambino the Clown, Georges Schreiber (Viking)
        McElligot's Pool, Dr. Seuss (Random)
        Roger and the Fox, Lavinia R. Davis, ill. Hildegard Woodward (Dou-
            bleday)
        Song of Robin Hood, ed. Anne B. Malcolmson, ill. Virginia Lee Burton
            (Houghton)
        Stone Soup, Marcia Brown (Scribner)

1949   *The Big Snow,* Elmer and Berta Hader (Macmillan)

        HONOR BOOKS
        All Around the Town, Phyllis McGinley, ill. Helen Stone (Lippincott)
        Blueberries for Sal, Robert McCloskey (Viking)
        Fish in the Air, Kurt Wiese (Viking)
        Juanita, Leo Politi (Scribner)

1950   *Song of the Swallows,* Leo Politi (Scribner)

        HONOR BOOKS
        America's Ethan Allen, Stewart Holbrook, ill. Lynd Ward (Houghton)
        Bartholomew and the Oobleck, Dr. Seuss (Random)
        The Happy Day, Ruth Krauss, ill. Marc Simont (Harper)
        Henry-Fisherman, Marcia Brown (Scribner)
        The Wild Birthday Cake, Lavinia R. Davis, ill. Hildegard Woodward
            (Doubleday)

1951   *The Egg Tree,* Katherine Milhous (Scribner)

        HONOR BOOKS
        Dick Whittington and His Cat, Marcia Brown (Scribner)
        If I Ran the Zoo, Dr. Seuss (Random)
        The Most Wonderful Doll in the World, Phyllis McGinley, ill. Helen Stone
            (Lippincott)

T-Bone, the Baby Sitter, Clare Turlay Newberry (Harper)
The Two Reds, William Lipkind, ill. Nicolas Mordvinoff (Harcourt)

1952 *Finders Keepers,* William Lipkind, ill. Nicolas Mordvinoff (Harcourt)

HONOR BOOKS
All Falling Down, Gene Zion, ill. Margaret Bloy Graham (Harper)
Bear Party, William Pène du Bois (Viking)
Feather Mountain, Elizabeth Olds (Houghton)
Mr. T. W. Anthony Woo: The Story of a Cat and a Dog and a Mouse, Marie Hall Ets (Viking)
Skipper John's Cook, Marcia Brown (Scribner)

1953 *The Biggest Bear,* Lynd Ward (Houghton)

HONOR BOOKS
Ape in a Cape: An Alphabet of Odd Animals, Fritz Eichenberg (Harcourt)
Five Little Monkeys, Juliet Kepes (Houghton)
One Morning in Maine, Robert McCloskey (Viking)
Puss in Boots, Charles Perrault, ill. Marcia Brown (Scribner)
The Storm Book, Charlotte Zolotow, ill. Margaret Bloy Graham (Harper)

1954 *Madeline's Rescue,* Ludwig Bemelmans (Viking)

HONOR BOOKS
Green Eyes, Abe Birnbaum (Capitol)
Journey Cake, Ho!, Ruth Sawyer, ill. Robert McCloskey (Viking)
The Steadfast Tin Soldier, Hans Christian Andersen, ill. Marcia Brown (Scribner)
A Very Special House, Ruth Krauss, ill. Maurice Sendak (Harper)
When Will the World Be Mine? The Story of a Snowshoe Rabbit, Miriam Schlein, ill. Jean Charlot (Scott)

1955 *Cinderella; or, The Little Glass Slipper,* Charles Perrault, ill. Marcia Brown (Scribner)

HONOR BOOKS
Marguerite de Angeli's Book of Nursery and Mother Goose Rhymes, comp. and ill. Marguerite de Angeli (Doubleday)
The Thanksgiving Story, Alice Dalgliesh, ill. Helen Sewell (Scribner)
Wheel on the Chimney, Margaret Wise Brown, ill. Tibor Gergely (Lippincott)

1956 *Frog Went a-Courtin',* John Langstaff, ill. Feodor Rojankovsky (Harcourt)

HONOR BOOKS
Crow Boy, Taro Yashima (Viking)
Play with Me, Marie Hall Ets (Viking)

1957   *A Tree Is Nice*, Janice May Udry, ill. Marc Simont (Harper)

HONOR BOOKS
Anatole, Eve Titus, ill. Paul Galdone (Whittlesey)
Gillespie and the Guards, Benjamin Elkin, ill. James Daugherty (Viking)
Lion, William Pène du Bois (Viking)
Mr. Penny's Race Horse, Marie Hall Ets (Viking)
One Is One, Tasha Tudor (Oxford)

1958   *Time of Wonder*, Robert McCloskey (Viking)

HONOR BOOKS
Anatole and the Cat, Eve Titus, ill. Paul Galdone (Whittlesey)
Fly High, Fly Low, Don Freeman (Viking)

1959   *Chanticleer and the Fox*, Barbara Cooney (Crowell)

HONOR BOOKS
The House That Jack Built: A Picture Book in Two Languages, Antonio
    Frasconi (Harcourt)
Umbrella, Taro Yashima (Viking)
What Do You Say, Dear?, Sesyle Joslin, ill. Maurice Sendak (Scott)

1960   *Nine Days to Christmas*, Aurora Labastida and Marie Hall Ets, ill. Marie
    Hall Ets (Viking)

HONOR BOOKS
Houses from the Sea, Alice E. Goudey, ill. Adrienne Adams (Scribner)
The Moon Jumpers, Janice May Udry, ill. Maurice Sendak (Harper)

1961   *Baboushka and the Three Kings*, Ruth Robbins, ill. Nicolas Sidjakov (Par-
    nassus)

HONOR BOOKS
Inch by Inch, Leo Lionni (Obolensky)

1962   *Once a Mouse*, Marcia Brown (Scribner)

HONOR BOOKS
The Day We Saw the Sun Come Up, Alice E. Goudey, ill. Adrienne Adams
    (Scribner)
The Fox Went out on a Chilly Night, Peter Spier (Doubleday)
Little Bear's Visit, Else Holmelund Minarik, ill. Maurice Sendak (Har-
    per)

1963   *The Snowy Day*, Ezra Jack Keats (Viking)

HONOR BOOKS
Mr. Rabbit and the Lovely Present, Charlotte Zolotow, ill. Maurice Sendak
    (Harper)

The Sun Is a Golden Earring, Natalia M. Belting, ill. Bernarda Bryson (Holt)

1964   *Where the Wild Things Are*, Maurice Sendak (Harper)

HONOR BOOKS
All in the Morning Early, Sorche Nic Leodhas, ill. Evaline Ness (Holt)
Mother Goose and Nursery Rhymes, Philip Reed (Atheneum)
Swimmy, Leo Lionni (Pantheon)

1965   *May I Bring a Friend?*, Beatrice Schenk de Regniers, ill. Beni Montresor (Atheneum)

HONOR BOOKS
A Pocketful of Cricket, Rebecca Caudill, ill. Evaline Ness (Holt)
Rain Makes Applesauce, Julian Scheer, ill. Marvin Bileck (Holiday)
The Wave, Margaret Hodges, ill. Blair Lent (Houghton)

1966   *Always Room for One More*, Sorche Nic Leodhas, ill. Nonny Hogrogian (Holt)

HONOR BOOKS
Hide and Seek Fog, Alvin Tresselt, ill. Roger Duvoisin (Lothrop)
Just Me, Marie Hall Ets (Viking)
Tom Tit Tot, Joseph Jacobs, ill. Evaline Ness (Schribner)

1967   *Sam, Bangs, and Moonshine*, Evaline Ness (Holt)

HONOR BOOKS
One Wide River to Cross, Barbara Emberley, ill. Ed Emberley (Prentice)

1968   *Drummer Hoff*, adapt. Barbara Emberley, ill. Ed Emberley (Prentice)

HONOR BOOKS
The Emperor and the Kite, Jane Yolen, ill. Ed Young (Collins)
Frederick, Leo Lionni (Pantheon)
Seashore Story, Taro Yashima (Viking)

1969   *The Fool of the World and the Flying Ship*, Arthur Ransome, ill. Uri Shulevitz (Farrar)

HONOR BOOKS
Why the Sun and the Moon Live in the Sky: An African Folktale, Elphinstone Dayrell, ill. Blair Lent (Houghton)

1970   *Sylvester and the Magic Pebble*, William Steig (Windmill/Simon & Schuster)

HONOR BOOKS
Alexander and the Wind-Up Mouse, Leo Lionni (Pantheon)
Goggles, Ezra Jack Keats (Macmillan)

The Judge, Harve Zemach, ill. Margot Zemach (Farrar)
Pop Corn and Ma Goodness, Edna Mitchell Preston, ill. Robert Andrew Parker (Viking)
Thy Friend, Obadiah, Brinton Turkle (Viking)

1971   *A Story, a Story,* Gail E. Haley (Atheneum)

HONOR BOOKS
The Angry Moon, William Sleator, ill. Blair Lent (Atlantic-Little)
Frog and Toad Are Friends, Arnold Lobel (Harper)
In the Night Kitchen, Maurice Sendak (Harper)

1972   *One Fine Day,* Nonny Hogrogian (Macmillan)

HONOR BOOKS
Hildilid's Night, Cheli Duran Ryan, ill. Arnold Lobel (Macmillan)
If All the Seas Were One Sea, Janina Domanska (Macmillan)
Moja Means One: Swahili Counting Book, Muriel Feelings, ill. Tom Feelings (Dial)

1973   *The Funny Little Woman,* Arlene Mosel, ill. Blair Lent (Dutton)

HONOR BOOKS
Anansi the Spider: A Tale from the Ashanti, Gerald McDermott (Holt)
Hosie's Alphabet, Hosea, Tobias and Lisa Baskin, ill. Leonard Baskin (Viking)
Snow White and the Seven Dwarfs, Jacob and Wilhelm Grimm, trans. Randall Jarrell, ill. Nancy Ekholm Burkert (Farrar)
When Clay Sings, Byrd Baylor, ill. Tom Bahti (Scribner)

1974   *Duffy and the Devil,* Harve Zemach, ill. Margot Zemach (Farrar)

HONOR BOOKS
Cathedral: The Story of Its Construction, David Macaulay (Houghton)
The Three Jovial Huntsmen: A Mother Goose Rhyme, Susan Jeffers (Bradbury)

1975   *Arrow to the Sun: A Pueblo Indian Tale,* Gerald McDermott (Viking)

HONOR BOOKS
Jambo Means Hello: Swahili Alphabet Book, Muriel Feelings, ill. Tom Feelings (Dial)

1976   *Why Mosquitoes Buzz in People's Ears: A West African Tale,* Verna Aardema, ill. Leo and Diane Dillon (Dial)

HONOR BOOKS
The Desert Is Theirs, Byrd Baylor, ill. Peter Parnall (Scribner)
Strega Nona, Tomie de Paola (Prentice)

1977   *Ashanti to Zulu: African Traditions,* Margaret Musgrove, ill. Leo and Diane Dillon (Dial)

HONOR BOOKS
The Amazing Bone, William Steig (Farrar)
The Contest, Nonny Hogrogian (Greenwillow)
Fish for Supper, M. B. Goffstein (Dial)
The Golem: A Jewish Legend, Beverly Brodsky McDermott (Lippincott, 1975)
Hawk, I'm Your Brother, Byrd Baylor, ill. Peter Parnall (Scribner)

1978   *Noah's Ark,* Peter Spier (Doubleday)

HONOR BOOKS
Castle, David Macaulay (Houghton)
It Could Always Be Worse: A Yiddish Folktale, Margot Zemach (Farrar)

1979   *The Girl Who Loved Wild Horses,* Paul Goble (Bradbury)

HONOR BOOKS
Freight Train, Donald Crews (Greenwillow)
The Way to Start a Day, Byrd Baylor, ill. Peter Parnall (Scribner)

1980   *Ox-Cart Man,* Donald Hall, ill. Barbara Cooney (Viking)

HONOR BOOKS
Ben's Trumpet, Rachel Isadora (Greenwillow)
The Garden of Abdul Gasazi, Chris Van Allsburg (Houghton)
The Treasure, Uri Shulevitz (Farrar)

1981   *Fables,* Arnold Lobel (Harper)

HONOR BOOKS
The Bremen-Town Musicians, Ilse Plume (Doubleday)
The Grey Lady and the Strawberry Snatcher, Molly Bang (Four Winds)
Mice Twice, Joseph Low (Atheneum)
Truck, Donald Crews (Greenwillow)

1982   *Jumanji,* Chris Van Allsburg (Houghton)

HONOR BOOKS
On Market Street, Arnold Lobel, ill. Anita Lobel (Greenwillow)
Outside Over There, Maurice Sendak (Harper)
A Visit to William Blake's Inn: Poems for Innocent and Experienced Travelers, Nancy Willard, ill. Alice and Martin Provensen (Harcourt)
Where the Buffaloes Begin, Olaf Baker, ill. Steven Gammell (Warne)

1983   *Shadow,* trans. and ill. Marcia Brown, from the French of Blaise Cendrars (Scribner)

HONOR BOOKS
A Chair for My Mother, Vera B. Williams (Greenwillow)
When I Was Young in the Mountains, Cynthia Rylant, ill. Diane Goode (Dutton)

1984   *The Glorious Flight: Across the Channel with Louis Bleriot,* Alice and Martin Provensen (Viking)

HONOR BOOKS
Little Red Riding Hood, Jacob and Wilhelm Grimm, retold and ill. Trina Schart Hyman (Holiday)
Ten, Nine, Eight, Molly Bang (Greenwillow)

1985   *Saint George and the Dragon: A Golden Legend,* Margaret Hodges, ill. Trina Schart Hyman (Little)

HONOR BOOKS
Hansel and Gretel, Rika Lesser, ill. Paul Zelinsky (Dodd)
Have You Seen My Duckling?, Nancy Tafuri (Greenwillow)
The Story of Jumping Mouse, John Steptoe (Lothrop)

1986   *The Polar Express,* Chris Van Allsburg (Houghton)

HONOR BOOKS
King Bidgood's in the Bathtub, Audrey Wood, ill. Don Wood (Harcourt)
The Relatives Game, Cynthia Rylant, ill. Stephen Gammell (Bradbury)

LAURA INGALLS WILDER AWARD

The Association for Library Service to Children of the American Library Association presents this award every three years (initially every five years) to a U.S. author or illustrator who has made "a substantial and lasting contribution to literature for children." It was established to honor the creator of the Little House series, who was its first recipient.

1954   Laura Ingalls Wilder

1960   Clara Ingram Judson

1965   Ruth Sawyer

1970   E. B. White

1975   Beverly Cleary

1980   Theodor Seuss Geisel (Dr. Seuss)

1983   Maurice Sendak

1986   Jean Fritz

NATIONAL BOOK AWARDS

Established in 1950 by the Association of American Publishers, the National
Book Awards added a children's category in 1969 to recognize the most distinguished contribution to children's literature by an American citizen published
in the U.S. during the preceding year. The awards were given annually until
1979, when they were replaced by the American Book Awards (see next listing).

1969   *Journey from Peppermint Street*, Meindert DeJong, ill. Emily McCully
        (Harper)

        FINALISTS
        Constance: A Story of Early Plymouth, Patricia Clapp (Lothrop)
        The Endless Steppe: Growing Up in Siberia, Esther Hautzig (Crowell)
        The High King, Lloyd Alexander (Holt)
        Langston Hughes: A Biography, Milton Meltzer (Crowell)

1970   *A Day of Pleasure: Stories of a Boy Growing Up in Warsaw*, Isaac Bashevis
        Singer, ill. Roman Vishniac (Farrar)

        FINALISTS
        Pop Corn and Ma Goodness, Edna Mitchell Preston, ill. Robert Andrew
           Parker (Viking)
        Sylvester and the Magic Pebble, William Steig, ill. (Windmill/Simon &
           Schuster)
        Where the Lilies Bloom, Bill and Vera Cleaver, ill. Jim Spanfeller (Lip-
           pincott)
        The Young United States: 1783–1830, Edwin Tunis, ill. (World)

1971   *The Marvelous Misadventures of Sebastian: Grand Extravaganza, Including a Performance by the Entire Cast of the Gallimaufry-Theatricus,* Lloyd Alexander (Dutton)

FINALISTS
Blowfish Live in the Sea, Paula Fox (Bradbury)
Frog and Toad Are Friends, Arnold Lobel, ill. (Harper)
Grover, Bill and Vera Cleaver, ill. Frederic Marvin (Lippincott)
Trumpet of the Swan, E. B. White, ill. Edward Frascino (Harper)

1972   *The Slightly Irregular Fire Engine, or, The Hithering, Thithering Djinn,* Donald Barthelme, ill. (Farrar)

FINALISTS
Amos and Boris, William Steig, ill. (Farrar)
The Art and Industry of Sandcastles, Jan Adkins, ill. (Walker)
The Bears' House, Marilyn Sachs, ill. Louis Glanzman (Doubleday)
Father Fox's Pennyrhymes, Clyde Watson, ill. Wendy Watson (Crowell)
Hildilid's Night, Cheli Duran Ryan, ill. Arnold Lobel (Macmillan)
His Own Where, June Jordan (Crowell)
Mrs. Frisby and the Rats of NIMH, Robert C. O'Brien, ill. Zena Bernstein (Atheneum)
The Planet of Junior Brown, Virginia Hamilton (Macmillan)
The Tombs of Atuan, Ursula K. Le Guin, ill. Gail Garraty (Atheneum)
Wild in the World, John Donovan (Harper)

1973   *The Farthest Shore,* Ursula K. Le Guin, ill. Gail Garraty (Atheneum)

FINALISTS
Children of Vietnam, Betty Jean Lifton and Thomas C. Fox, ill. Thomas C. Fox (Atheneum)
D'Aulaires' Trolls, Edgar and Ingri d'Aulaire, ill. (Doubleday)
Dominic, William Steig, ill. (Farrar)
The House of Wings, Betsy Byars, ill. Daniel Schwartz (Viking)
The Impossible People: A History Natural and Unnatural of Beings Terrible and Wonderful, Georgess McHargue, ill. Frank Bozzo (Holt)
Julie of the Wolves, Jean Craighead George, ill. John Schoenherr (Harper)
Long Journey Home: Stories from Black History, Julius Lester (Dial)
The Witches of Worm, Zilpha Keatley Snyder, ill. Alton Raible (Atheneum)

1974   *The Court of the Stone Children,* Eleanor Cameron (Dutton)

FINALISTS
Duffy and the Devil, Harve Zemach, ill. Margot Zemach (Farrar)
A Figure of Speech, Norma Fox Mazer (Delacorte)

Guests in the Promised Land: Stories, Kristin Hunter (Scribner)
A Hero Ain't Nothin' But a Sandwich, Alice Childress (Coward)
Poor Richard in France, F. N. Monjo, ill. Brinton Turkle (Holt)
A Proud Taste for Scarlet and Miniver, E. L. Konigsburg, ill. (Atheneum)
Summer of My German Soldier, Bette Greene (Dial)
The Treasure Is the Rose, Julia Cunningham, ill. Judy Graese (Pantheon)
The Whys and Wherefores of Littabelle Lee, Bill and Vera Cleaver (Atheneum)

1975   *M. C. Higgins, the Great,* Virginia Hamilton (Macmillan)

FINALISTS
The Devil's Storybook, Natalie Babbitt, ill. (Farrar)
Doctor in the Zoo, Bruce Buchenholz, ill. with drawings and photos (Studio/Viking)
The Edge of Next Year, Mary Stolz (Harper)
The Girl Who Cried Flowers and Other Tales, Jane Yolen, ill. David Palladini (Crowell)
I Tell a Lie Every So Often, Bruce Clements (Farrar)
Joi Bangla! The Children of Bangladesh, Ettagale and Jason Laure, ill. Jason Laure (Farrar)
My Brother Sam Is Dead, James Lincoln Collier and Christopher Collier (Four Winds/Scholastic)
Remember the Days: A Short History of the Jewish American, Milton Meltzer, ill. Harvey Dinnerstein (Zenith/Doubleday)
Wings, Adrienne Richard (Atlantic-Little)
World of Our Fathers: The Jews of Eastern Europe, Milton Meltzer, ill. with photos (Farrar)

1976   *Bert Breen's Barn,* Walter D. Edmonds (Little)

FINALISTS
As I Was Crossing Boston Common, Norma Farber, ill. Arnold Lobel (Dutton)
El Bronx Remembered: A Novella and Stories, Nicholasa Mohr (Harper)
Ludell, Brenda Wilkinson (Harper)
Of Love and Death and Other Journeys, Isabelle Holland (Lippincott)
The Star in the Pail, David McCord, ill. Marc Simont (Little)
To the Green Mountains, Eleanor Cameron (Dutton)

1977   *The Master Puppeteer,* Katherine Paterson, ill. Haru Wells (Crowell)

FINALISTS
Never to Forget: The Jews of the Holocaust, Milton Meltzer (Harper)
Ox Under Pressure, John Ney (Lippincott)

Roll of Thunder, Hear My Cry, Mildred D. Taylor, ill. Jerry Pinkney (Dial)

Tunes for a Small Harmonica, Barbara Wersba (Harper)

1978   *The View from the Oak,* Herbert and Judith Kohl, ill. Roger Bayless (Sierra Club/Scribner)

FINALISTS

Caleb and Kate, William Steig, ill. (Farrar)

Hew Against the Grain, Betty Sue Cummings (Atheneum)

Mischling, Second Degree: My Childhood in Nazi Germany, Ilse Koehn (Greenwillow)

One at a Time: His Collected Poems for the Young, David McCord, ill. Henry B. Kane (Little)

1979   *The Great Gilly Hopkins,* Katherine Paterson (Crowell)

FINALISTS

The First Two Lives of Lukas-Kasha, Lloyd Alexander (Dutton)

Humbug Mountain, Sid Fleischman, ill. Eric von Schmidt (Atlantic-Little)

The Little Swineherd and Other Tales, Paula Fox, ill. Leonard Lubin (Dutton)

Queen of Hearts, Bill and Vera Cleaver (Lippincott)

AMERICAN BOOK AWARDS

This annual award, inaugurated in 1980 by the Association of American Publishers, replaces the National Book Awards. It is restricted to American citizens and to books published during the preceding year in the U.S. The categories of recognition pertaining to children's literature, discontinued in 1983, were fiction, nonfiction, and graphics, in hardback and paperback.

1980   Fiction (hardback): *A Gathering of Days: A New England Girl's Journal, 1830–32—A Novel* Joan W. Blos (Scribner)

Fiction (paperback): *A Swiftly Tilting Planet,* Madeleine L'Engle (Dell)

1981   Fiction (hardback): *Night Swimmers,* Betsy Byars, ill. Troy Howell (Delacorte)

Fiction (paperback): *Ramona and Her Mother,* Beverly Cleary, ill. Alan Tiegreen (Dell/Yearling)

Nonfiction (hardback): *Oh, Boy! Babies!,* Jane Lawrence Mali and Alison Cragin Herzig, ill. Katrina Thomas (Little)

1982   Fiction (hardback): *Westmark,* Lloyd Alexander (Dutton)
Fiction (paperback): *Words by Heart,* Ouida Sebestyen (Bantam)
Nonfiction: *A Penguin Year,* Susan Bonners, ill. (Delacorte)
Picturebook (hardback): *Outside Over There,* Maurice Sendak (Harper)
Picturebook (paperback): *Noah's Ark,* Peter Spier (Doubleday)
Book illustration (original art): *Jumanji,* Chris Van Allsburg (Houghton)

1983   Fiction (hardback): *Homesick: My Own Story,* Jean Fritz, ill. with drawings by Margot Tomes and photos (Putnam)
Fiction (paperback): *A Place Apart,* Paula Fox (NAL, 1982)
Fiction (paperback): *Marked by Fire,* Joyce Carol Thomas (Avon)
Nonfiction: *Chimney Sweeps, Yesterday and Today,* James C. Giblin, ill. Margot Tomes (Crowell)
Picturebook (hardback): *Doctor De Soto,* William Steig (Farrar)
Picturebook (hardback): *Miss Rumphius,* Barbara Cooney (Viking)
Picturebook (paperback): *A House Is a House for Me,* Mary Ann Hoberman, ill. Betty Fraser (Puffin, 1982)
Pictorial design: *Lewis Carroll's Alice's Adventures in Wonderland,* ill. Barry Moser, ed. Selwyn H. Goodacre, pref. and notes James R. Kincaid (University of California, 1982)

BOSTON GLOBE–HORN BOOK AWARDS

This annual award, established in 1967, is sponsored jointly by the *Boston Globe* newspaper and the *Horn Book* magazine. From 1967 to 1975 the award categories were for outstanding text and illustration; since 1976 three categories of achievement have been recognized: fiction, nonfiction, and illustration. Any book published in the United States during the award period (July 1–June 30) is eligible.

1967   Text: *The Little Fishes,* Erik Christian Haugaard, ill. Milton Johnson (Houghton, 1967)
Illustration: *London Bridge Is Falling Down!,* Peter Spier (Doubleday, 1967)

1968   Text: *The Spring Rider,* John Lawson (Crowell, 1968)
Illustration: *Tikki Tikki Tembo,* Arlene Mosel, ill. Blair Lent (Holt, 1968)

1969   Text: *The Wizard of Earthsea*, Ursula K. Le Guin, ill. Ruth Robbins (Parnassus, 1968)
        Illustration: *The Adventures of Paddy Pork*, John S. Goodall (Harcourt, 1968)

1970   Text: *The Intruder*, John Rowe Townsend, ill. Joseph A. Phelan (Lippincott, 1970)
        Illustration: *Hi, Cat!*, Ezra Jack Keats (Macmillan, 1970)

1971   Text: *A Room Made of Windows*, Eleanor Cameron, ill. Trina Schart Hyman (Atlantic-Little, 1971)
        Illustration: *If I Built a Village*, Kazue Mizumura (Crowell, 1971)

1972   Text: *Tristan and Iseult*, Rosemary Sutcliff (Dutton, 1971)
        Illustration: *Mr. Gumpy's Outing*, John Burningham (Holt, 1970)

1973   Text: *The Dark Is Rising*, Susan Cooper, ill. Alan Cober (Atheneum/McElderry, 1973)
        Illustration: *King Stork*, Howard Pyle, ill. Trina Schart Hyman (Little, 1973)

1974   Text: *M. C. Higgins, the Great*, Virginia Hamilton (Macmillan, 1974)
        Illustration: *Jambo Means Hello: Swahili Alphabet Book*, Muriel Feelings, ill. Tom Feelings (Dial, 1974)

1975   Text: *Transport 7-41-R*, T. Degens (Viking, 1974)
        Illustration: *Anno's Alphabet: An Adventure in Imagination*, Mitsumasa Anno (Crowell, 1975)

1976   Fiction: *Unleaving*, Jill Paton Walsh (Farrar, 1976)
        Nonfiction: *Voyaging to Cathay: Americans in the China Trade*, Shirley Glubok and Alfred Tamarin, ill. with photos (Viking, 1976)
        Illustration: *Thirteen*, Jerry Joyner and Remy Charlip (Parents, 1975)

1977   Fiction: *Child of the Owl*, Laurence Yep (Harper, 1977)
        Nonfiction: *Chance, Luck and Destiny*, Peter Dickinson, ill. Victor Ambrus and David Smee (Atlantic-Little, 1976)
        Illustration: *Granfa' Grig Had a Pig and Other Rhymes Without Reason from Mother Goose*, Wallace Tripp (Little, 1976)

1978   Fiction: *The Westing Game*, Ellen Raskin (Dutton, 1978)
        Nonfiction: *Mischling, Second Degree: My Childhood in Nazi Germany*, Ilse Koehn (Greenwillow, 1977)
        Illustration: *Anno's Journey*, Mitsumasa Anno (Collins-World, 1978)

1979   Fiction: *Humbug Mountain*, Sid Fleischman, ill. Eric Von Schmidt (Atlantic-Little, 1978)
        Nonfiction: *The Road from Home: The Story of an Armenian Girl*, David Kherdian (Greenwillow, 1979)
        Illustration: *The Snowman*, Raymond Briggs (Random, 1978)

1980   Fiction: *Conrad's War*, Andrew Davies (Crown, 1980)
        Nonfiction: *Building: The Fight Against Gravity*, Mario Salvadori, ill. Saralinda Hooker and Christopher Ragus (Atheneum/McElderry, 1979)
        Illustration: *The Garden of Abdul Gasazi*, Chris Van Allsburg (Houghton, 1979)

1981   Fiction: *The Leaving*, Lynn Hall (Scribner, 1980)
        Nonfiction: *The Weaver's Gift*, Kathryn Lasky, ill. with photos by Christopher G. Knight (Warne, 1981)
        Illustration: *Outside Over There*, Maurice Sendak (Harper, 1981)

1982   Fiction: *Playing Beatie Bow*, Ruth Park (Kestrel Atheneum, 1982)
        Nonfiction: *Upon the Head of a Goat: A Childhood in Hungary, 1939–1944*, Aranka Siegal (Farrar, 1981)
        Illustration: *A Visit to William Blake's Inn: Poems for Innocent and Experienced Travelers*, Nancy Willard, ill. Alice and Martin Provensen (Harcourt, 1981)

1983   Fiction: *Sweet Whispers, Brother Rush*, Virginia Hamilton (Philomel, 1982)
        Nonfiction: *Behind Barbed Wire: The Imprisonment of Japanese Americans During World War II*, Daniel S. Davis, ill. with photos (Dutton, 1982)
        Illustration: *A Chair for My Mother*, Vera B. Williams (Greenwillow, 1982)

1984   Fiction: *A Little Fear*, Patricia Wrightson (Atheneum/McElderry, 1983)
        Nonfiction: *The Double Life of Pocahontas*, Jean Fritz, ill. Ed Young (Putnam, 1983)
        Illustration: *Jonah and the Great Fish*, retold and ill. Warwick Hutton (Atheneum/McElderry, 1983)

1985   Fiction: *The Moves Make the Man*, Bruce Brooks (Harper, 1984)
        Nonfiction: *Commodore Perry in the Land of the Shogun*, Rhoda Blumberg, ill. with photos (Lothrop, 1985)
        Illustration: *Mama Don't Allow*, Thatcher Hurd (Harper, 1984)
        Special award for board books: *1, 2, 3*, Tana Hoban (Greenwillow, 1985)

NEW YORK TIMES CHOICE OF
BEST ILLUSTRATED CHILDREN'S BOOKS OF THE YEAR

Begun in 1952, this listing appears annually in the children's supplement of the *New York Times Book Review* in mid-November. The selection, usually of ten books, is made by the children's book editor, an artist, and a critic, from all the illustrated children's books published in the U.S. during the year.

1952   *The Animal Farm*, Alice and Martin Provensen (Simon & Schuster)
Beasts and Nonsense, Marie Hall Ets (Viking)
The Dogcatcher's Dog, André Dugo (Holt)
Five Little Monkeys, Juliet Kepes (Houghton)
The Happy Place, Ludwig Bemelmans (Little)
A Hole Is To Dig, Ruth Krauss, ill. Maurice Sendak (Harper)
The Magic Currant Bun, John Symonds, ill. André François (Lippincott)

1953   *Fast Is Not a Ladybug: A Book About Fast and Slow Things*, Miriam Schlein, ill. Leonard Kessler (Scott)
Florinda and the Wild Bird, Selina Chönz, trans. Anne and Ian Serraillier, ill. Alois Carigiet (Oxford)
The Golden Bible for Children: The New Testament, ill. Alice and Martin Provensen, ed. Elsa Jane Werner (Golden)
Green Eyes, Abe Birnbaum (Capitol)
A Hero by Mistake, Anita Brenner, ill. Jean Charlot (Scott)
Lucky Blacky, Eunice Lackey, ill. Winifred Greene (Watts)
Madeline's Rescue, Ludwig Bemelmans (Viking)
Mother Goose Riddle Rhymes, Ruth and Joseph Low, ill. Joseph Low (Harcourt)
Pitschi: The Kitten Who Always Wanted to Be Something Else, Hans Fischer (Harcourt)
Who Gave Us . . . Peacocks? Planes? and Ferris Wheels?, Madeleine Gekiere (Pantheon)

1954   *Andy Says . . . Bonjour!*, Pat Diska, ill. Chris Jenkyns (Vanguard)
The Animal Frolic, ill. Toba Sojo, adapt. Velma Varner (Putnam)
Circus Ruckus, William Lipkind, ill. Nicolas Mordvinoff (Harcourt)
The Happy Lion, Louise Fatio, ill. Roger Duvoisin (McGraw)
Heavy Is a Hippopotamus, Miriam Schlein, ill. Leonard Kessler, (Scott)
I'll Be You and You Be Me, Ruth Krauss, ill. Maurice Sendak, (Harper)
Jenny's Birthday Book, Esther Averill (Harper)
A Kiss Is Round: Verses, Blossom Budney, ill. Vladimir Bobri (Lothrop)

The Sun Looks Down, Miriam Schlein, ill. Abner Graboff (Abelard-Schuman)

The Wet World, Norma Simon, ill. Jane Miller (Lippincott)

1955 *Beasts from a Brush,* Juliet Kepes (Pantheon)
Chaga, William Lipkind, ill. Nicolas Mordvinoff (Harcourt)
The Happy Lion in Africa, Louise Fatio, ill. Roger Duvoisin (McGraw)
A Little House of Your Own, Beatrice Schenk de Regniers, ill. Irene Hunt (Harcourt)
Parsley, Ludwig Bemelmans (Harper)
Rumpelstiltskin, Jacob and Wilhelm Grimm, adapt. Patricia Jones, ill. Jan B. Balet (Rand McNally)
See and Say: A Picture Book in Four Languages, Antonio Frasconi (Harcourt)
Switch on the Night, Ray Bradbury, ill. Madeleine Gekiere (Pantheon)
The Three Kings of Saba, Alf Evers, ill. Helen Sewell (Lippincott)
Uncle Ben's Whale, Walter D. Edmonds, ill. William Gropper (Dodd)

1956 *Babar's Fair Will Be Opened Next Sunday . . . ,* Laurent de Brunhoff, trans. Merle Haas (Random, 1954)
Crocodile Tears, André François (Universe)
I Know a Lot of Things, Ann and Paul Rand, ill. Paul Rand (Harcourt)
I Want to Paint My Bathroom Blue, Ruth Krauss, ill. Maurice Sendak (Harper)
I Will Tell You of a Town, Alastair Reid, ill. Walter Lorraine (Houghton)
Jonah the Fisherman, Reiner Zimnik, trans. Richard and Clara Winston (Pantheon)
Little Big-Feather, Joseph Longstreth, ill. Helen Borten (Abelard)
The Little Elephant, Ylla (Harper)
Really Spring, Gene Zion, ill. Margaret Bloy Graham (Harper)
Was It a Good Trade?, Beatrice Schenk de Regniers, ill. Irene Haas (Harcourt)

1957 *Big Red Bus,* Ethel Kessler, ill. Leonard Kessler (Doubleday)
The Birthday Party, Ruth Krauss, ill. Maurice Sendak (Harper)
Curious George Gets a Medal, H. A. Rey (Houghton)
Dear Garbage Man, Gene Zion, ill. Margaret Bloy Graham (Harper)
The Fisherman and His Wife, Jacob and Wilhelm Grimm, ill. Madeleine Gekiere (Pantheon)
The Friendly Beasts, Laura Baker, ill. Nicolas Sidjakov (Parnassus)
The Red Balloon, Albert Lamorisse, ill. with photos (Doubleday)
Sparkle and Spin: A Book About Words, Ann and Paul Rand, ill. Paul Rand (Harcourt)

This Is the Story of Faint George Who Wanted to Be a Knight, Robert E. Barry (Houghton)

The Unhappy Hippopotamus, Nancy Moore, ill. Edward Leight (Vanguard)

1958   *All Aboard: Poems,* Mary Britton Miller, ill. Bill Sokol (Pantheon)

Chouchou, Francoise (Scribner)

The Daddy Days, Norma Simon, ill. Abner Graboff (Abelard-Schuman)

A Friend Is Someone Who Likes You, Joan Walsh Anglund (Harcourt)

The Golden Book of Animals, Anne Terry White, ill. W. Suschitzy (Simon & Schuster)

The House That Jack Built: A Picture Book in Two Languages, Antonio Frasconi (Harcourt)

How to Hide a Hippopotamus, Volney Croswell (Dodd)

The Magic Feather Duster, William Lipkind, ill. Nicolas Mordvinoff (Harcourt)

Roland, Nelly Stephane, ill. André François (Harcourt)

What Do You Say, Dear?, Sesyle Joslin, ill. Maurice Sendak (Scott)

1959   *Animal Babies,* Arthur Gregor, ill. Arthur Gregor and Ylla (Harper)

Father Bear Comes Home, Else Holmelund Minarik, ill. Maurice Sendak (Harper)

The First Noel: The Birth of Christ from the Gospel According to St. Luke, ill. Alice and Martin Provensen (Golden)

Full of Wonder, Ann Kirn (World)

The Girl in the White Hat, Walter Thies Cummings (McGraw)

Kasimir's Journey, Monroe Stearns, ill. Marlene Reidel (Lippincott)

Little Blue and Little Yellow, Leo Lionni (Obolensky)

Pablo Paints a Picture, Warren Miller, ill. Edward Sorel (Little)

The Reason for the Pelican, John Ciardi, ill. Madeleine Gekiere (Lippincott)

This Is London, Miroslav Sasek (Macmillan)

1960   *The Adventures of Ulysses,* Jacques Lemarchand, trans. E. M. Hatt, ill. André François (Criterion)

Baboushka and the Three Kings, Ruth Robbins, ill. Nicolas Sidjakov (Parnassus)

Bruno Munari's ABC, Bruno Munari (World)

Inch by Inch, Leo Lionni (Obolensky)

Open House for Butterflies, Ruth Krauss, ill. Maurice Sendak (Harper)

Scrappy the Pup, John Ciardi, ill. Jane Miller (Lippincott)

The Shadow Book, Beatrice Schenk de Regniers and Isabel Gordon, ill. Isabel Gordon (Harcourt)

This Is New York, Miroslav Sasek (Macmillan)

Twenty-six Ways to Be Somebody, Devorah Boxer (Pantheon)

Two Little Birds and Three, Juliet Kepes (Houghton)

1961   *The Big Book of Animal Stories,* ed. Margaret Green, ill. Janusz Grabianski (Watts)
Dear Rat, Julia Cunningham, ill. Walter Lorraine (Houghton)
The Happy Hunter, Roger Duvoisin (Lothrop)
Listen—the Birds, Mary Britton Miller, ill. Evaline Ness (Pantheon)
My Time of Year, Katharine Dow, ill. Walter Erhard (Walck)
Once a Mouse, Marcia Brown (Scribner)
Sandpipers, Edith Thacher Hurd, ill. Lucienne Bloch (Crowell)
The Snow and the Sun: A South American Folk Rhyme in Two Languages, Antonio Frasconi (Harcourt)
Umbrellas, Hats and Wheels, Jerome Snyder and Ann Rand, ill. Jerome Snyder (Harcourt)
The Wing on a Flea: A Book About Shapes, Ed Emberley (Little)

1962   *Books!,* Murray McCain, ill. John Alcorn (Simon & Schuster)
The Emperor and the Drummer Boy, Ruth Robbins, ill. Nicolas Sidjakov (Parnassus)
Gennarino, Nicola Simbari (Lippincott)
The Island of Fish in the Trees, Eva-Lis Wuorio, ill. Edward Ardizzone (World)
Kay-Kay Comes Home, Nicholas Samstag, ill. Ben Shahn (Obolensky)
Little Owl, Hanne Axmann and Reiner Zimnick, ill. Hanne Axmann (Atheneum)
The Princesses: Sixteen Stories About Princesses, ed. Sally P. Johnson, ill. Beni Montresor (Harper)
The Singing Hill, Meindert DeJong, ill. Maurice Sendak (Harper)
The Tale of a Wood, Henry B. Kane (Knopf)
The Three Robbers, Tomi Ungerer (Atheneum)

1963   *The Great Picture Robbery,* Leon Harris, ill. Joseph Schindelman (Atheneum)
Gwendolyn and the Weathercock, Nancy Sherman, ill. Edward Sorel (Golden)
A Holiday for Mister Muster, Arnold Lobel (Harper)
Hurly Burly and the Knights, Milton Rugoff, ill. Emanuele Luzzati (Platt)
John J. Plenty and Fiddler Dan, John Ciardi, ill. Madeleine Gekiere (Lippincott)
Karen's Curiosity, Alice and Martin Provensen, (Golden)
Once upon a Totem, Christie Harris, ill. John Frazer Mills (Atheneum)
Plunkety Plunk, Peter J. Lippman (Farrar)
Swimmy, Leo Lionni (Pantheon)
Where the Wild Things Are, Maurice Sendak (Harper)

1964   *The Bat-Poet,* Randall Jarrell, ill. Maurice Sendak (Macmillan)
Casey at the Bat, Ernest L. Thayer, ill. Leonard Everett Fisher (Watts)

The Charge of the Light Brigade, Alfred Tennyson, ill. Alice and Martin Provensen (Golden)
Exactly Alike, Evaline Ness (Scribner)
The Giraffe of King Charles X, Miche Wynants (McGraw)
The Happy Owls, Celestino Piatti (Atheneum)
I'll Show You Cats, Crosby Newell Bonsall, ill. Ylla (Harper)
The Life of a Queen, Colette Portal, trans. Marcia Nardi (Braziller)
Rain Makes Applesauce, Julian Scheer, ill. Marvin Bileck (Holiday)
The Wave, Margaret Hodges, ill. Blair Lent (Houghton)

1965   *Alberic the Wise and Other Journeys*, Norton Juster, ill. Domenico Gnoli (Pantheon)
The Animal Family, Randall Jarrell, ill. Maurice Sendak (Pantheon)
A Double Discovery, Evaline Ness (Scribner)
Hide and Seek Fog, Alvin Tresselt, ill. Roger Duvoisin (Lothrop)
Kangaroo & Kangaroo, Kathy Braun, ill. Jim McMullan (Doubleday)
Please Share That Peanut! A Preposterous Pageant in Fourteen Acts, Sesyle Joslin and Simms Taback, ill. Simms Taback (Harcourt)
Punch and Judy: A Play for Puppets, Ed Emberley (Little)
Sven's Bridge, Anita Lobel (Harper)

1966   *Ananse the Spider: Tales from an Ashanti Village*, Peggy Appiah, ill. Peggy Wilson (Pantheon)
A Boy Went Out to Gather Pears, Felix Hoffmann (Harcourt)
Celestino Piatti's Animal ABC, Celestino Piatti (Atheneum)
The Jazz Man, Mary Hays Weik, ill. Ann Grifalconi (Atheneum)
The Magic Flute, Stephen Spender, ill. Beni Montresor (Putnam)
The Monster Den; or, Look What Happened at My House—and to It, John Ciardi, ill. Edward Gorey (Lippincott)
Nothing Ever Happens on My Block, Ellen Raskin (Atheneum)
Shaw's Fortune: The Picture Story of a Colonial Plantation, Edwin Tunis (World)
Wonderful Time, Phyllis McGinley, ill. John Alcorn (Lippincott)
Zlateh the Goat and Other Stories, Isaac Bashevis Singer, ill. Maurice Sendak (Harper)

1967   *Animals of Many Lands*, ed. Hanns Reich, ill. with photos (Hill & Wang)
Brian Wildsmith's Birds, Brian Wildsmith (Watts)
A Dog's Book of Bugs, Elizabeth Griffen, ill. Peter Parnall (Atheneum)
Fables of Aesop, Sir Roger L'Estrange, ill. Alexander Calder (Dover)
Frederick, Leo Lionni (Pantheon)
The Honeybees, Franklin Russell, ill. Colette Portal (Knopf)
Hubert, the Caterpillar Who Thought He Was a Mustache, Susan Richards and Wendy Stang, ill. Robert L. Anderson (Quist)
Knee-Deep in Thunder, Sheila Moon, ill. Peter Parnall (Atheneum)
Seashore Story, Taro Yashima (Viking)

1968 *Harriet and the Promised Land,* Jacob Lawrence (Windmill/Simon & Schuster)

A Kiss for Little Bear, Else Holmelund Minarik, ill. Maurice Sendak (Harper)

Malachi Mudge, Edward Cecil, ill. Peter Parnall (McGraw)

Mister Corbett's Ghost, Leon Garfield, ill. Alan Cober (Pantheon)

The Real Tin Flower: Poems About the World at Nine, Aliki Barnstone, ill. Paul Giovanopoulos (Crowell-Collier)

The Secret Journey of Hugo the Brat, Francois Ruy-Vidal, ill. Nicole Claveloux (Quist)

Spectacles, Ellen Raskin (Atheneum)

Story Number 1, Eugene Ionesco, ill. Etienne Delessert (Quist)

Talking Without Words, Marie Hall Ets (Viking)

The Very Obliging Flowers, Claude Roy, trans. Gerald Bertin, ill. Alain LeFoll (Grove)

1969 *Arm in Arm,* Remy Charlip (Parents)

Bang Bang You're Dead, Louise Fitzhugh and Sandra Scoppettone, ill. Louise Fitzhugh (Harper)

Birds, Juliet Kepes (Walker, 1968)

The Circus in the Mist, Bruno Munari (World)

The Dong with a Luminous Nose, Edward Lear, ill. Edward Gorey (Scott)

Free as a Frog, Elizabeth J. Hodges, ill. Paul Giovanopoulos (Addison-Wesley)

The Light Princess, George MacDonald, ill. Maurice Sendak (Farrar)

Sara's Granny and the Groodle, Joan Gill, ill. Seymour Chwast (Doubleday)

What Is It For?, Henry Humphrey (Simon & Schuster)

Winter's Eve, Natalia M. Belting, ill. Alan E. Cober (Holt)

1970 *Alala,* Guy Monreal, ill. Nicole Claveloux (Quist)

Finding a Poem, Eve Merriam, ill. Seymour Chwast (Atheneum)

The Gnu and the Guru Go Behind the Beyond, Peggy Clifford, ill. Eric von Schmidt (Houghton)

Help, Help, the Globolinks!, Gian-Carlo Menotti, adapt. Leigh Dean, ill. Milton Glaser (McGraw)

In the Night Kitchen, Maurice Sendak (Harper)

Lift Every Voice and Sing: Words and Music, J. Rosamund and James Weldon Johnson, ill. Mozelle Thompson (Hawthorn)

Matilda Who Told Lies and Was Burned to Death, Hilaire Belloc, ill. Steven Kellogg (Dial)

Timothy's Horse, Vladimir Mayakovsky, adapt. Guy Daniels, ill. Flavio Constantini (Pantheon)

Topsy Turvies: Pictures to Stretch the Imagination, Mitsumasa Anno (Walker/Weatherhill)

You Are Ri-di-cu-lous, André François (Pantheon)

1971   *Amos and Boris*, William Steig (Farrar)
        Bear Circus, William Pène du Bois (Viking)
        The Beast of Monsieur Racine, Tomi Ungerer (Farrar)
        Changes, Changes, Pat Hutchins (Macmillan)
        Look Again!, Tana Hoban (Macmillan)
        Look What I Can Do, Jose Aruego (Scribner)
        The Magic Tears, Jack Sendak, ill. Mitchell Miller (Harper)
        Mr. Gumpy's Outing, John Burningham (Holt)
        One Dancing Drum, Gail Kredenser and Stanley Mack, ill. Stanley Mack (Phillips)
        The Shrinking of Treehorn, Florence Parry Heide, ill. Edward Gorey (Holiday)

1972   *Behind the Wheel*, Edward Koren (Holt)
        Count and See, Tana Hoban (Macmillan)
        George and Martha, James Marshall (Houghton)
        Hosie's Alphabet, Hosea, Tobias, and Lisa Baskin, ill. Leonard Baskin (Viking)
        Just So Stories, Rudyard Kipling, ill. Etienne Delessert (Doubleday)
        A Little Schubert, M. B. Goffstein (Harper)
        Miss Jaster's Garden, N. M. Bodecker (Golden)
        Mouse Cafe, Patricia Coombs (Lothrop)
        Simon Boom Gives a Wedding, Yuri Suhl, ill. Margot Zemach (Four Winds)
        Where's Al?, Byron Barton (Seabury)

1973   *Cathedral: The Story of Its Construction*, David Macaulay (Houghton)
        The Emperor's New Clothes: A Fairy Tale, Hans Christian Andersen, ill. Monica Laimgruber (Addison)
        Hector Penguin, Louise Fatio, ill. Roger Duvoisin (McGraw)
        The Juniper Tree and Other Tales from Grimm, trans. Lore Segal and Randall Jarrell, ill. Maurice Sendak (Farrar)
        King Grisly-Beard: A Tale from the Brothers Grimm, trans. Edgar Taylor, ill. Maurice Sendak (Farrar)
        The Number 24, Guy Billout (Quist)
        A Prairie Boy's Winter, William Kurelek (Houghton)
        The Silver Pony, Lynd Ward (Houghton)
        Tim's Last Voyage, Edward Ardizzone (Walck)

1974   *The Girl Who Cried Flowers*, Jane Yolen, ill. David Palladini (Crowell)
        A Home, Lennart Rudstrom, ill. Carl Larsson (Putnam)
        Lumberjack, William Kurelek (Houghton)
        The Man Who Took the Indoors Out, Arnold Lobel (Harper)
        Miss Suzy's Birthday, Miriam Young, ill. Arnold Lobel (Parents)
        A Storybook, ed. and ill. Tomi Ungerer (Watts)
        There Was an Old Woman, Steven Kellogg (Parents)

1975 *Anno's Alphabet: An Adventure in Imagination,* Mitsumasa Anno (Crowell)

A Book of A-maze-ments, Jean Seisser (Quist, 1974)

Mr. Michael Mouse Unfolds His Tale, Walter Crane (Merrimack)

The Pig-Tale, Lewis Carroll, ill. Leonard B. Lubin (Little)

There's a Sound in the Sea: A Child's Eye View of the Whale, comp. Tamar Griggs, ill. with paintings by schoolchildren (Scrimshaw)

Thirteen, Jerry Joyner and Remy Charlip (Parents)

The Tutti-Frutti Case: Starring the Four Doctors of Goodge, Harry Allard, ill. James Marshall (Prentice)

1976 *Ashanti to Zulu: African Traditions,* Margaret Musgrove, ill. Leo and Diane Dillon (Dial)

As Right as Right Can Be, Anne Rose, ill. Arnold Lobel (Dial)

The Bear and the Fly, Paula Winter (Crown)

Everyone Knows What a Dragon Looks Like, Jay Williams, ill. Mercer Mayer (Four Winds)

Fly by Night, Randall Jarrell, ill. Maurice Sendak (Farrar)

Little Though I Be, Joseph Low (McGraw)

Merry Ever After: The Story of Two Medieval Weddings, Joe Lasker (Viking)

The Mother Goose Book, Alice and Martin Provensen (Random)

A Near Thing for Captain Najork, Russell Hoban, ill. Quentin Blake (Atheneum)

1977 *The Church Mice Adrift,* Lore Segal, ill. Graham Oakley (Atheneum)

Come Away from the Water, Shirley, John Burningham (Crowell)

It Could Always Be Worse: A Yiddish Folk Tale, retold and ill. Margot Zemach (Farrar)

Jack and the Wonder Beans, James Still, ill. Margot Tomes (Putnam)

Merry, Merry FIBruary, Doris Orgel, ill. Arnold Lobel (Parents)

My Village, Sturbridge, Gary Bowen, ill. Gary Bowen and Randy Miller (Farrar)

Noah's Ark, Peter Spier (Doubleday)

The Surprise Picnic, John S. Goodall (Atheneum/McElderry)

When the Wind Blew, Margaret Wise Brown, ill. Geoffrey Hayes (Harper)

1978 *Cloudy with a Chance of Meatballs,* Judi Barrett, ill. Ron Barrett (Atheneum)

The Forbidden Forest, William Pène du Bois (Harper)

The Great Song Book, ed. Timothy John, music ed. Peter Hankey, ill. Tomi Ungerer (Doubleday)

Hanukah Money, Sholem Aleichem, adapt. and ill. Uri Shulevitz (Greenwillow)

The Legend of Scarface: A Blackfoot Indian Tale, Robert San Souci, ill. Daniel San Souci (Doubleday)

The Nutcrackers and the Sugar-Tongs, Edward Lear, ill. Marcia Sewall (Atlantic-Little)

Odette: A Bird in Paris, Kay Fender, ill. Phillipe Dumas (Prentice)

A Peaceable Kingdom: The Shaker Abecedarius, ill. Alice and Martin Provensen (Viking)

There Once Was a Woman Who Married a Man, Norma Farber, ill. Lydia Dabcovich (Addison)

This Little Pig-a-Wig and Other Rhymes About Pigs, Lenore Blegvad, ill. Erik Blegvad (Atheneum/McElderry)

1979   *By Camel or by Car: A Look at Transportation*, Guy Billout (Prentice)

The Garden of Abdul Gasazi, Chris Van Allsburg (Houghton)

Happy Birthday, Oliver!, Pierre Le-Tan (Random)

King Krakus and the Dragon, Janina Domanska (Greenwillow)

The Long Dive, Catriona and Ray Smith (Atheneum/Jonathan Cape)

Natural History, M. B. Goffstein (Farrar)

Ox-Cart Man, Donald Hall, ill. Barbara Cooney (Viking)

The Tale of Fancy Nancy: A Spanish Folk Tale, adapt. Marion Koenig, ill. Klaus Ensikat (Chatto, 1978)

Tilly's House, Faith Jacques (Atheneum/McElderry)

The Treasure, Uri Shulevitz (Farrar)

1980   *An Artist*, M. B. Goffstein (Harper)

A Child's Christmas in Wales, Dylan Thomas, ill. Edward Ardizzone (Godine)

Gorky Rises, William Steig (Farrar)

The Headless Horseman Rides Tonight: More Poems to Trouble Your Sleep, Jack Prelutsky, ill. Arnold Lobel (Greenwillow)

Howard, James Stevenson (Greenwillow)

The Lucky Yak, Annetta Lawson, ill. Allen Say (Parnassus/Houghton)

Mr. Miller the Dog, Helme Heine (Atheneum/McElderry)

Stone and Steel: A Look at Engineering, Guy Billout (Prentice)

Unbuilding, David Macaulay (Houghton)

The Wonderful Travels and Adventures of Baron Munchhausen, Peter Nickl, trans. Elizabeth Buchanan Taylor, ill. Binette Schroeder (Chatto & Windus, 1979)

1981   *The Crane Wife*, retold by Sumiko Yagawa, trans. Katherine Paterson, ill. Suekichi Akaba (Morrow)

Flight: A Panorama of Aviation, Melvin B. Zisfein, ill. Robert Andrew Parker (Pantheon, 1979)

Jumanji, Chris Van Allsburg (Houghton Mifflin)

The Maid and the Mouse and the Odd-Shaped House: A Story in Rhyme, adapt. and ill. Paul O. Zelinsky (Dodd)

My Mom Travels a Lot, Caroline Feller Bauer, ill. Nancy Winslow Parker (Warne)

The Nose Tree, adapt. and ill. Warwick Hutton (Atheneum/McElderry, 1980; Julia MacRae, 1981)

On Market Street, Arnold Lobel, ill. Anita Lobel (Greenwillow)

Outside Over There, Maurice Sendak (Harper)

The Story of Old Mrs. Brubeck, and How She Looked for Trouble and Where She Found Him, Lore Segal, ill. Marcia Sewall (Pantheon, 1979)

Where the Buffaloes Begin, Olaf Baker, ill. Stephen Gammell (Warne)

1982   *Anno's Britain,* Mitsumasa Anno (Philomel)

Ben's Dream, Chris Van Allsburg (Houghton)

The Gift of the Magi, O. Henry, ill. Lisbeth Zwerger, lettering Michael Neugebauer (Neugebauer Press)

My Uncle, Jenny Thorne (Atheneum/McElderry)

Paddy Goes Traveling, John S. Goodall (Atheneum/McElderry)

Rainbows Are Made: Poems by Carl Sandburg, ed. Lee Bennett Hopkins, ill. Fritz Eichenberg (Harcourt)

Smile, Ernest and Celestine, Gabrielle Vincent (Greenwillow)

Squid and Spider: A Look at the Animal Kingdom, Guy Billout (Prentice-Hall)

The Strange Appearance of Howard Cranebill, Jr., Henrik Drescher (Lothrop)

The Tiny Visitor, Oscar de Mejo (Pantheon)

1983   *The Favershams,* Roy Gerrard (Farrar)

Leonard Baskin's Miniature Natural History: First Series, Leonard Baskin (Pantheon)

Little Red Cap, Jacob and Wilhelm Grimm, trans. Elizabeth D. Crawford, ill. Lisbeth Zwerger (Morrow)

Round Trip, Ann Jonas (Greenwillow)

Simon's Book, Henrik Drescher (Lothrop)

Tools, Ken Robbins (Four Winds)

Twelve Cats for Christmas, Jill Leman, ill. Martin Leman (Pelham/Merrimack)

Up a Tree, Ed Young (Harper)

The Wreck of the Zephyr, Chris Van Allsburg (Houghton)

1984   *Animal Alphabet,* Bert Kitchen (Dial)

Babushka, Charles Mikolaycak (Holiday)

If There Were Dreams to Sell, Barbara Lalicki, ill. Margot Tomes (Lothrop)

Jonah and the Great Fish, Warwick Hutton (Atheneum/McElderry)

The Mysteries of Harris Burdick, Chris Van Allsburg (Houghton)

The Napping House, Audrey Wood, ill. Don Wood (Harcourt)

Nutcracker, E. T. A. Hoffman, ill. Maurice Sendak (Crown)
Saint George and the Dragon, Margaret Hodges, ill. Trina Schart Hyman
    (Little)
Sir Cedric, Roy Gerrard (Farrar)
Where the River Begins, Thomas Locker (Dial)

1985   *Gorilla,* Anthony Browne (Knopf)
    Granpa, John Burningham (Crown)
    Hazel's Amazing Mother, Rosemary Wells (Dial)
    The Inside-Outside Book of New York City, Roxie Munro (Dodd)
    The Legend of Rosepetal, Clemens Brentano, ill. Lisbeth Zwerger (Picture
       Book Studio)
    The Nightingale, Hans Christian Andersen, ill. Demi (Harcourt)
    The People Could Fly: American Black Folktales, Virginia Hamilton, ill.
       Leo and Diane Dillon (Knopf)
    The Polar Express, Chris Van Allsburg (Houghton)
    The Relatives Came, Cynthia Rylant, ill. Stephen Gammell (Bradbury)
    The Story of Mrs. Lovewright and Purrless Her Cat, Lore Segal, ill. Paul
       O. Zelinsky (Knopf)

CORETTA SCOTT KING AWARD

Presented annually at the American Library Association convention since 1970,
this award was established in memory of Dr. Martin Luther King, Jr., and in
honor of his wife, Coretta Scott King. It is intended to promote world peace
and brotherhood by encouraging creative artists and young people to devote
their energies to these goals. An award for illustration was added in 1979. The
winning titles were published during the year preceding the award.

1970   *Martin Luther King, Jr.: Man of Peace,* Lillie Patterson, ill. Victor Mays
    (Garrard)

1971   *Black Troubadour: Langston Hughes,* Charlemae Rollins, ill. with photos
    (Rand)

1972   *Seventeen Black Artists,* Elton Clay Fax, ill. with photos (Dodd)

1973   *I Never Had It Made,* Jackie Robinson as told to Alfred Duckett, ill.
    with photos (Putnam)

1974   *Ray Charles*, Sharon Bell Mathis, ill. George Ford (Crowell)

1975   The Legend of Africania, Dorothy Robinson, ill. Herbert Temple (Johnson)

1976   *Duey's Tale*, Pearl Bailey, photos Arnold Skolnick and Gary Azon (Harcourt)

1977   *The Story of Stevie Wonder*, James Haskins, ill. with photos (Lothrop)

1978   *African Dream*, Eloise Greenfield, ill. Carole Byard (Day)

1979   Text: *Escape to Freedom: A Play About Young Frederick Douglass*, Ossie Davis (Viking)
        Illustration: *Something on My Mind*, Nikki Grimes, ill. Tom Feelings (Dial)

1980   Text: *The Young Landlords*, Walter Dean Myers (Viking)
        Illustration: *Corn Rows*, Camile Yarbrough, ill. Carole Byard (Coward)

1981   Text: *This Life*, Sidney Poitier (Knopf)
        Illustration: *Beat the Story-Drum, Pum-Pum*, Ashley Bryan (Atheneum)

1982   Text: *Let the Circle Be Unbroken*, Mildred D. Taylor (Dial)
        Illustration: *Mother Crocodile = Maman-Caiman*, Birago Diop, trans. and adapt. Rosa Guy, ill. John Steptoe (Delacorte)

1983   Text: *Sweet Whispers, Brother Rush*, Virginia Hamilton (Philomel)
        Illustration: *Black Child*, Peter Magubane (Knopf)

1984   Text: *Everett Anderson's Goodbye*, Lucille Clifton, ill. Ann Grifalconi (Holt)
        Illustration: *My Mama Needs Me*, Mildred Pitts Walter, ill. Pat Cummings (Lothrop, Lee & Shepard)

1985   Text: *Motown and Didi*, Walter Dean Myers, ill. (Viking)
        Illustration: No award

1986   Text: *The People Could Fly: American Black Folktales*, Virginia Hamilton ill. Leo 'and Diane Dillon (Knopf)
        Illustration: *The Patchwork Quilt*, Valerie Flournoy, ill. Jerry Pinkney (Dial)

INTERNATIONAL READING ASSOCIATION CHILDREN'S BOOK AWARD

Established in 1975, this annual award encourages newer writers in the field of children's literature. The International Reading Association Children's Book Award subcommittee considers only an author's first or second books intended for a young readers and published during the preceding year.

1975 *Transport 7-41-R*, T. Degens (Viking)

1976 *Dragonwings*, Laurence Yep (Harper)

1977 *A String in the Harp*, Nancy Bond, ill. Allen Davis (Atheneum/Mc-Elderry)

1978 *A Summer to Die*, Lois Lowry, ill. Jenni Oliver (Houghton)

1979 *Reserved for Mark Anthony Crowder*, Alison Smith (Dutton)

1980 *Words by Heart*, Ouida Sebestyen (Atlantic-Little)

1981 *My Own Private Sky*, Delores Beckman (Dutton)

1982 *Good Night, Mr. Tom*, Michelle Magorian (Kestrel)

1983 *The Darkangel*, Meredith Ann Pierce (Little)

1984 *Ratha's Creature*, Clare Bell (Atheneum/McElderry)

1985 *Badger on the Barge and Other Stories*, Janni Howker (Greenwillow)

1986 *Prairie Songs*, Pam Conrad, ill. Darryl S. Zudeck (Harper)

ANDREW CARNEGIE MEDAL

This medal, established in 1937 on the centenary of Andrew Carnegie's birth, is awarded annually by the British Library Association to the author of the outstanding children's book written in English and published in the United Kingdom during the preceding year.

1937   *Pigeon Post,* Arthur Ransome, ill. (Cape)

1938   *The Family from One End Street,* Eve Garnett, ill. (Muller)

1939   *The Circus Is Coming,* Noel Streatfeild, ill. Steven Spurrier (Dent); published in the U.S. as *Circus Shoes*

1940   *The Radium Woman: A Youth Edition of the Life of Madame Curie,* Eleanor Doorly, ill. Robert Gibbings (Heinemann)

1941   *Visitors from London,* Kitty Barne, ill. Ruth Gervis (Dent)

1942   *We Couldn't Leave Dinah,* Mary Treadgold, ill. Stuart Tresilian (Cape); published in the U.S. as *Left Till Called For*

1943   *The Little Grey Men: A Story for the Young in Heart,* Denys James Watkins-Pitchford, ill. (Eyre & Spottiswoode)

1944   No award

1945   *The Wind on the Moon: A Story for Children,* Eric Linklater, ill. Nicolas Bentley (Macmillan)

1946   No award

1947   *The Little White Horse,* Elizabeth Goudge, ill. C. Walter Hodges (University of London)

1948   *Collected Stories for Children,* Walter John de la Mare, ill. Irene Hawkins (Faber)

1949   *Sea Change,* Richard Armstrong, ill. Michael Leszczynski (Dent)

1950   *The Story of Your Home,* Agnes Allen, ill. Agnes and Jack Allen (Faber)

1951   *The Lark on the Wing,* Elfrida Vipont Foulds, ill. Terence Reginald Freeman (Oxford)

1952   *The Wool-Pack,* Cynthia Harnett, ill. (Methuen)

1953   *The Borrowers,* Mary Norton, ill. Diana Stanley (Dent)

1954   *A Valley Grows Up,* Edward Osmond, ill. (Oxford)

1955   *Knight Crusader,* Ronald Welch, ill. William Stobbs (Oxford)

1956   *The Little Bookroom: Eleanor Farjeon's Short Stories for Children Chosen by Herself,* Eleanor Farjeon, ill. Edward Ardizzone (Oxford)

1957   *The Last Battle: A Story for Children,* C. S. Lewis, ill. Pauline Baynes (Bodley Head)

1958   *A Grass Rope,* William Mayne, ill. Lynton Lamb (Oxford)

1959   *Tom's Midnight Garden,* A. Philippa Pearce, ill. Susan Einzig (Oxford)

1960   *The Lantern Bearers,* Rosemary Sutcliff, ill. Charles Keeping (Oxford)

1961   *The Making of Man,* Ian Wolfram Cornwall, ill. M. Maitland Howard (Phoenix)

1962   *A Stranger at Green Knowe,* Lucy M. Boston, ill. Peter Boston (Faber)

1963   *The Twelve and the Genii,* Pauline Clarke, ill. Cecil Leslie (Faber); published in the U.S. as *The Return of the Twelves*

1964   *Time of Trial,* Hester Burton, ill. Victor Ambrus (Oxford)

1965   *Nordy Bank,* Sheena Porter, ill. Annette Macarthur-Onslow (Oxford)

1966   *The Grange at High Force,* Philip Turner, ill. William Papas (Oxford)

1967   No award

1968   *The Owl Service,* Alan Garner (Collins)

1969   *The Moon in the Cloud,* Rosemary Harris (Faber)

1970   *The Edge of the Cloud,* K. M. Peyton, ill. Victor Ambrus (Oxford)

1971   *The God Beneath the Sea,* Leon Garfield and Edward Blishen, ill. Charles Keeping (Longmans)

1972   *Josh,* Ivan Southall (Angus & Robertson)

1973   *Watership Down,* Richard Adams (Rex Collings; Macmillan)

1974   *The Ghost of Thomas Kempe,* Penelope Lively, ill. Antony Maitland (Hei-
        nemann)

1975   *The Stronghold,* Mollie Hunter (Hamilton)

1976   *The Machine Gunners,* Robert Westall (Macmillan)

1977   *Thunder and Lightnings,* Jan Mark, ill. Jim Russell (Kestrel)

1978   *The Turbulent Term of Tyke Tiler,* Gene Kemp, ill. Carolyn Dinan (Faber)

1979   *Exeter Blitz,* David Rees (Hamilton)

1980   *Tulku,* Peter Dickinson (Unicorn/Dutton)

1981   *City of Gold and Other Stories from the Old Testament,* Peter Dickinson,
        ill. Michael Foreman (Gollancz)

1982   *The Scarecrows,* Robert Westall (Chatto & Windus)

1983   *The Haunting,* Margaret Mahy (Dent)

1984   *Handles,* Jan Mark (Kestrel)

1985   *The Changeover,* Margaret Mahy (Dent)

KATE GREENAWAY MEDAL

Named for nineteenth-century British illustrator Kate Greenaway, this annual
award was established in 1955 to honor the most distinguished work of illustration for children published in the United Kingdom during the preceding
year. It is administered by the British Library Association, and the winner is
chosen by the same committee that selects the Carnegie Medal winner.

1956   No award

1957   *Tim All Alone,* Edward Ardizzone (Oxford)

1958   *Mrs. Easter and the Storks,* Violet Hilda Drummond (Faber)

1959   No award

1960   *A Bundle of Ballads,* comp. Ruth Manning-Sanders, ill. William Stobbs
        (Oxford)
        Kashtanka, Anton Chekhov, trans. Charles Dowsett, ill. William Stobbs
        (Oxford)

1961   *Old Winkle and the Seagulls*, Elizabeth Rose, ill. Gerald Rose (Faber)

1962   *Mrs. Cockle's Cat*, A. Philippa Pearce, ill. Antony Maitland (Kestrel) 1961.

1963   *Brian Wildsmith's ABC*, Brian Wildsmith (Oxford)

1964   *Borka: The Adventures of a Goose with No Feathers*, John Burningham (Cape)

1965   *Shakespeare's Theatre*, C. Walter Hodges (Oxford)

1966   *Three Poor Tailors*, Victor G. Ambrus (Hamilton)

1967   *Mother Goose Treasury*, Raymond Briggs (Hamilton)

1968   *Charley, Charlotte and the Golden Canary*, Charles Keeping (Oxford)

1969   *Dictionary of Chivalry*, Grant Uden, ill. Pauline Baynes (Kestrel)

1970   *Dragon of an Ordinary Family*, Margaret May Mahy, ill. Helen Oxenbury (Heinemann)

1971   *Mr. Gumpy's Outing*, John Burningham (Cape)

1972   *The Kingdom Under the Sea*, Jan Pienkowski (Cape)

1973   *The Woodcutter's Duck*, Krystyna Turska (Hamilton)

1974   *Father Christmas*, Raymond Briggs (Hamilton)

1975   *The Wind Blew*, Pat Hutchins (Bodley Head)

1976   *Horses in Battle*, Victor G. Ambrus (Oxford)
        Mishka, Victor G. Ambrus (Oxford)

1977   *The Post Office Cat*, Gail E. Haley (Bodley Head)

1978   *Dogger*, Shirley Hughes (Bodley Head)

1979   *Each Peach, Pear, Plum*, Allan and Janet Ahlberg (Kestrel)

1980   *Haunted House*, Jan Pienkowski (Dutton)

1981   *Mr. Magnolia*, Quentin Blake (Cape)

1982   *The Highwayman,* Alfred Noyes, ill. Charles Keeping (Oxford)

1983   *Long Neck and Thunder Foot,* Helen Piers, ill. Michael Foreman (Kestrel)
         Sleeping Beauty and Other Favourite Fairy Tales, sel. and trans. Angela
           Carter, ill. Michael Foreman (Gollancz)

1984   *Gorilla,* Anthony Browne (McCrae)

1985   *Hiawatha's Childhood,* Errol Le Cain (Faber)

GUARDIAN AWARD FOR CHILDREN'S FICTION

Since 1967, the *Guardian* newspaper has presented an annual award for the
preceding year's "outstanding work of fiction for children by a British or Com-
monwealth author."

1967   *Devil-in-the-Fog,* Leon Garfield, ill. Antony Maitland (Kestrel)

1968   *The Owl Service,* Alan Garner (Collins)

1969   *The Whispering Mountain,* Joan Aiken, ill. Frank Bozzo (Cape)

1970   *Flambards* (trilogy), K. M. Peyton, ill. Victor G. Ambrus (Oxford, 1967;
           World, 1968)

1971   *The Guardians,* John Christopher (Macmillan)

1972   *A Likely Lad,* Gillian E. Avery, ill. Faith Jacques (Collins)

1973   *Watership Down,* Richard Adams (Rex Collings; Macmillan)

1974   *The Iron Lily,* Barbara Willard (Longmans)

1975   *Gran at Coalgate,* Winifred Cawley, ill. F. Rocker (Oxford)

1976   *The Peppermint Pig,* Nina Bawden, ill. Charles Lilly (Gollancz)

1977   *The Blue Hawk,* Peter Dickinson, ill. David Smee (Gollancz)

1978   *A Charmed Life,* Diana Wynne Jones (Macmillan)

1979   *Conrad's War,* Andrew Davies (Blackie)

1980   *The Vandal,* Ann Schlee (Macmillan)

1981   *The Sentinels,* Peter Carter (Oxford)

1982   *Goodnight, Mister Tom,* Michelle Magorian (Kestrel)

1983   *The Village by the Sea,* Anita Desai (Heinemann)

1984   *The Sheep-Pin,* Dick King-Smith (Gollancz)

1985   *What Is the Truth?,* Ted Hughes (Faber)

CANADIAN LIBRARY ASSOCIATION
BOOK OF THE YEAR FOR CHILDREN AWARD

This award was established in 1946 to promote the writing of children's books in Canada. Each year the Canadian Association of Children's Librarians selects the preceding year's outstanding book by a Canadian citizen or resident, who is honored at the Canadian Library Association convention. From 1954 to 1973 the award was also given to a French-language children's book (listing omitted).

1947   *Starbuck Winter Valley,* Roderick Haig-Brown, ill. Charles DeFeo (Morrow, 1943; Collins, 1944)

1948   No award

1949   *Kristli's Trees,* Mabel Dunham, ill. Selwyn Dewdney (McClelland & Stewart)

1950   *Franklin of the Arctic: A Life of Adventure,* Richard S. Lambert, ill. with maps by Julius Griffith (McClelland & Stewart)

1951   No award

1952   *The Sun Horse,* Catherine Anthony Clark. ill. Clare Bice (Macmillan)

1953   No award

1954   No award

1955   No award

1956   *Train for Tiger Lily*, Louise Riley, ill. Christine Price (Macmillan, 1954)

1957   *Glooskap's Country and Other Indian Tales*, Cyrus Macmillan, ill. John A. Hall (Oxford)

1958   *Lost in the Barrens*, Farley Mowat, ill. Charles Geer (Little, 1956)

1959   *The Dangerous Cove: A Story of Early Days in Newfoundland*, John F. Hayes, ill. Fred J. Finley (Copp Clark, 1957)

1960   *The Golden Phoenix and Other French Canadian Fairy Tales*, Charles Marius Barbeau, retold Michael Hornyansky, ill. Arthur Price (Oxford, 1958)

1961   *The St. Lawrence*, William Toye, ill. Leo Rampen (Oxford, 1959)

1962   No award

1963   *The Incredible Journey: A Tale of Three Animals*, Shelia Every Burnford, ill. Carl Burger (Little, 1961)

1964   *The Whale People*, Roderick Haig-Brown, ill. Mary Weiler (Collins, 1962)

1965   *Tales of Nanabozho*, Dorothy Reid, ill. Donald Grant (Oxford)

1966   *Tikta'liktak: An Eskimo Legend*, James Houston, ill. (Longmans)
        The Double Knights: More Tales from Round the World, James McNeill, ill. Theo Dimson (Oxford)

1967   *Raven's Cry*, Christie Harris, ill. Bill Reid (McClelland & Stewart)

1968   *The White Archer: An Eskimo Legend*, James Houston, ill. (Longmans)

1969   *And Tomorrow the Stars: The Story of John Cabot*, Kay Hill, ill. Laszlo Kubinyi (Dodd)

1970   *Sally Go Round the Sun*, Edith Fowke, ill. Carlos Marchiori (McClelland & Stewart)

1971   *Cartier Discovers the St. Lawrence*, William Toye, ill. Laszlo Gal (Oxford)

1972   *Mary of Mile 18*, Ann Blades, ill. (Tundra)

1973   *The Marrow of the World*, Ruth Nichols, ill. Trina Schart Hyman (Macmillan)

1974   *The Miraculous Hind*, Elizabeth Cleaver, ill. (Holt)

1975   *Alligator Pie*, Dennis Lee, ill. Frank Newfeld (Macmillan)

1976   *Jacob Two-Two Meets the Hooded Fang*, Mordecai Richler, ill. Fritz Wegner (McClelland & Stewart)

1977   *Mousewoman and the Vanished Princesses*, Christie Harris, ill. Douglas Tait (McClelland & Stewart)

1978   *Garbage Delight*, Dennis Lee, ill. Frank Newfeld (Macmillan)

1979   *Hold Fast*, Kevin Major (Clarke, Irwin)

1980   *River Runners: A Tale of Hardship and Bravery*, James Houston, ill. (McClelland & Stewart)

1981   *The Violin Maker's Gift*, Donn Kushner (Macmillan, 1980?)

1982   *The Root Cellar*, Janet Lunn, ill. with maps (Dennys)

1983   *Up to Low*, Brian Doyle (Douglas & McIntyre)

1984   *Sweetgrass*, Jan Hudson (Tree Frog)

1985   *Mama's Going to Buy You a Mockingbird*, Jean Little (Penguin)

AMELIA FRANCES HOWARD-GIBBON ILLUSTRATOR'S AWARD

Established in 1969 by the Canadian Association of Children's Literature, this annual award recognizes the preceding year's "outstanding illustrations by a Canadian for a work published in Canada, whether picture book, fiction, or nonfiction." It is named for the illustrator of *An Illustrated Comic Alphabet*.

1971   *The Wind Has Wings: Poems from Canada,* comp. Mary Alice Downie and Barbara Robertson, ill. Elizabeth Cleaver (Oxford, 1968)

1972   *A Child in Prison Camp,* Shizuye Takashima (Tundra)

1973   *Beyond the Sun/Au dela du soleil,* Jacques de Roussan (Tundra)

1974   *A Prairie Boy's Winter,* William Kurelek (Tundra)

1975   *The Sleighs of My Childhood/Les traineaux de mon enfance* (bilingual text), Carlo Italiano (Tundra)

1976   *A Prairie Boy's Summer,* William Kurelek (Tundra)

1977   *Down by Jim Long's Stage: Rhymes for Children and Young Fish,* Al Pittman, ill. Pam Hall (Breakwater)

1978   *Loon's Necklace,* William Toye, ill. Elizabeth Cleaver (Oxford)

1979   *A Salmon for Simon,* Betty Waterton, ill. Ann Blades (Douglas & McIntyre)

1980   *Twelve Dancing Princesses: A Fairy Story,* retold Janet Lunn, ill. Laszlo Gal (Methuen)

1981   *The Trouble with Princesses,* Christie Harris, ill. Douglas Tait (McClelland & Stewart)

1982   *Ytek and the Arctic Orchid: An Inuit Legend,* Garnet Hewitt, ill. Heather Woodall (Douglas & McIntyre)

1983   *Chester's Barn,* Lindee Climo (Tundra)

1984   *Zoom at Sea,* Tim Wynne-Jones, ill. Ken Nutt (Douglas & McIntyre)

1985   *Chin Chiang and the Dragon's Dance,* Ian Wallace (Groundwood)

AUSTRALIAN CHILDREN'S BOOK AWARDS

Established in 1946, this annual award is administered by the Australian Children's Book Council. Originally only one book was recognized, but the council added a picturebook category in 1956, and a junior book category in 1983. Awards are not always given in every category.

1946   *Story of Karrawinga, the Emu,* Leslie Rees, ill. Walter Cunningham (Sands, 1946)

1947   No award

1948   *Shackleton's Argonauts: A Saga of the Antarctic Ice-Packs,* Frank Hurley, ill. (Angus & Robertson, 1948)

1949   *Whalers of the Midnight Sun: A Story of Modern Whaling in the Antarctic,* Alan John Villiers, ill. Charles Pont (Angus & Robertson, 1949)

1950   No award

1951   *Verity of Sydney Town,* Ruth Williams, ill. Rhys Williams (Angus & Robertson, 1950)

1952   *The Australian Book,* Eve Pownall, ill. Margaret Senior (Sands, 1952)

1953   *Aircraft of Today and Tomorrow,* James Henry and William Donald Martin, ill. with photos (Angus & Robertson, 1953)
        Good Luck to the Rider, Joan Phipson, ill. Margaret Horder (Angus & Robertson, 1953)

1954   *Australian Legendary Tales,* K. Langloh Parker, ill. Elizabeth Durack (Angus & Robertson, 1953)

1955   *The First Walkabout,* Harold Arthur Lindsay and Norman Barnett Tindale, ill. Madeleine Boyce (Longmans, 1954)

1956   Text: *The Crooked Snake,* Patricia Wrightson, ill. Margaret Horder (Angus & Robertson, 1955)
        Picturebook: *Wish and the Magic Nut,* Peggy Barnard, ill. Sheila Hawkins (Sands, 1956)

1957   Text: *The Boomerang Book of Legendary Tales,* Enid Moodie-Heddle, ill. Nancy Parker (Longmans, 1957)

1958   Text: *Tiger in the Bush,* Nan Chauncy, ill. Margaret Horder (Oxford, 1957)
        Picturebook: *Piccaninny Walkabout: A Story of Two Aboriginal Children,* Axel Poignant, ill. with photos (Angus & Robertson, 1957)

1959   Text: *Devil's Hill,* Nan Chauncy, ill. Geraldine Spence (Oxford, 1958)
Text: *Sea Menace,* John Gunn, ill. Brian Keogh (Constable, 1958)

1960   Text: *All the Proud Tribesmen,* Kylie Tennant, ill. Clem Seale (Macmillan/London, 1959)

1961   *Tangara; Let Us Set Off Again,* Nan Chauncy, ill. Brian Wildsmith (Oxford, 1960); published in the U.S. as *The Secret Friends*

1962   Text: *The Racketty Street Gang,* Leonard Herbert Evers (Hodder & Stoughton, 1961)
Text: *Rafferty Rides a Winner,* Joan Woodberry, ill. (Parrish, 1961)

1963   Text: *The Family Conspiracy,* Joan M. Phipson, ill. Margaret Horder (Angus & Robertson, 1962)

1964   Text: *The Green Laurel,* Eleanor Spence, ill. Geraldine Spence (Oxford, 1963)

1965   Text: *Pastures of the Blue Crane,* Hesba Fay Brinsmead, ill. Annette Macarthur-Onslow (Oxford, 1964)
Picturebook: *Hugo's Zoo,* Elisabeth MacIntyre (Angus & Robertson, 1964)

1966   Text: *Ash Road,* Ivan Southall, ill. Clem Seale (Angus & Robertson, 1965)

1967   Text: *The Min-Min,* Mavis Thorpe Clark, ill. Genevieve Melrose (Angus & Robertson, 1967)

1968   Text: *To the Wild Sky,* Ivan Southall, ill. Jennifer Tuckwell (Angus & Robertson, 1967)

1969   Text: *When Jays Fly to Barbmo,* Margaret Balderson, ill. Victor G. Ambrus (Oxford, 1968)
Picturebook: *Sly Old Wardrobe,* Ivan Southall, ill. Ted Greenwood (Cheshire, 1968)

1970   Text: *Uhu,* Annette Macarthur-Onslow, ill. (Ure Smith, 1969)

1971   Text: *Bread and Honey,* Ivan Southall (Angus & Robertson, 1970); published in the U.S. as *Walk a Mile and Get Nowhere*
Picturebook: *Waltzing Matilda,* Andrew Barton Paterson, ill. Desmond Digby (Collins, 1970)

1972   Text: *Longtime Passing*, Hesba Fay Brinsmead (Angus & Robertson, 1971)

1973   Text: *Family at the Lookout*, Noreen Shelley, ill. R. Micklewright (Oxford, 1972)

1974   Text: *The Nargun and the Stars*, Patricia Wrightson (Hutchinson, 1973)
Picturebook: *The Bunyip of Berkeley's Creek*, Jenny Wagner, ill. Ron Brooks (Longmans, 1974)
Visual Arts: *Mulga Bill's Bycycle*, A. B. Paterson, ill. Deborah and Kilmeny Niland (Collins, 1973)

1975   Picturebook: *The Man from Ironbark*, Andrew Barton Paterson, ill. Quentin Hole (Collins, 1974)
Visual Arts: *The Magpie Island*, Colin Thiele, ill. Roger Haldane (Rigby, 1975)
Visual Arts: *Storm Boy*, Colin Thiele, ill. Robert Ingpen (Rigby, 1963)

1976   *Fly West*, Ivan Southall (Angus & Robertson, 1974)
Picturebook: *The Rainbow Serpent*, Dick Roughsey (Collins, 1975)
Visual Arts: *Terry's Brrrmmm GT*, Ted Greenwood (Angus & Robertson, 1976)

1977   Text: *The October Child*, Eleanor Spence, ill. Malcolm Green (Oxford, 1976)
Picturebook: *ABC of Monsters*, Deborah and Kilmeny Niland (Hodder & Stoughton, 1977)

1978   Text: *The Ice Is Coming*, Patricia Wrightson, ill. with maps (Hutchinson, 1977)
Picturebook: *John Brown, Rose and the Midnight Cat*, Jenny Wagner, ill. Ron Brooks (Kestrel, 1977)

1979   Text: *The Plum-Rain Scroll*, Ruth Manley, ill. Marianne Yamaguchi (Hodder & Stoughton, 1978)
Picturebook: *The Quinkins*, Percy J. Trezise and Dick Roughsey (Collins, 1978)

1980   Text: *Displaced Person*, Lee Harding (Hyland House, 1979); published in the U.S. as *Misplaced Persons*
Picturebook: *One Dragon's Dream*, Peter Pavey (Nelson, 1979)

1981   Text: *Playing Beatie Bow*, Ruth Park (Kestrel, 1981)

1982   Text: *The Valley Between*, Colin Thiele (Rigby, 1981)
Picturebook: *Sunshine*, Jan Ormerod (Kestrel, 1981; Penguin, 1981)

1983   Text: *Master of the Grove,* Victor Kelleher (Penguin, 1982)
        Picturebook: *Who Sank the Boat?,* Pamela Allen (Nelson, 1982)
        Junior book: *Thing,* Robin Klein, ill. Alison Lester (Oxford, 1982)

1984   Text: *A Little Fear,* Patricia Wrightson (Hutchinson, 1983)
        Picturebook: *Bertie and the Bear,* Pamela Allen (Nelson, 1983)
        Junior book: *Bernice Knows Best,* Max Dann (Oxford, 1983)

1985   Text: *The True Story of Lily Stubeck,* James Aldridge (Highland, 1984)
        Junior book: *Something Special,* Emily Rodda (Angus & Robertson, 1984)

HANS CHRISTIAN ANDERSEN MEDAL

This biennial award was established in 1956 by the International Board on Books for Young People. It was originally given to individual books, but since 1962 an author's entire body of work has been considered. In 1966 a separate illustrator's medal was added. The candidates are nominated by the board's national sections, and the winners are chosen by an international jury for their lasting contribution to children's literature.

1956   *The Little Bookroom,* Eleanor Farjeon, ill. Edward Ardizzone (Oxford, 1955)
        Julia Lepman for her service to international children's literature

1958   *Rasmus pa luffen,* Astrid Lindgren, ill. Eric Palmquist (Raben & Sjogren, 1956)

1960   *Als Ich ein kleiner Junge war,* Erich Kästner, ill. Horst Lemke (Dressler, 1957)

1962   Meindert DeJong, United States

1964   René Guillot, France

1966   Author: Tove Jansson, Finland
        Illustrator: Alois Carigiet, Switzerland

1968   Author: Jose Maria Sanchez-Silva, Spain
        Author: James Krüss, German Federal Republic
        Illustrator: Jiri Trnka, USSR

1970   Author: Gianni Rodari, Italy
        Illustrator: Maurice Sendak, United States

1972   Author: Scott O'Dell, United States
        Illustrator: Ib Spang Ohlsson, Denmark

1974   Author: Maria Gripe, Sweden
        Illustrator: Farshid Mesghali, Iran

1976   Author: Cecil Bødker, Denmark
        Illustrator: Tatjana Mawrina, USSR

1978   Author: Paula Fox, United States
        Illustrator: Otto S. Svend, Denmark

1980   Author: Bohumil Riha, USSR
        Illustrator: Suekichi Akaba, Japan

1982   Author: Lygia Bojunga Nunes, Brazil
        Illustrator: Zbigniew Rychlicki, Poland

1984   Author: Christine Nöstlinger, Austria
        Illustrator: Mitsumasa Anno, Japan

1986   Author: Patricia Wrightson, Australia
        Illustrator: Robert Ingpen, Australia

INTERNATIONAL BOARD ON BOOKS FOR YOUNG PEOPLE HONOR LIST

Presented every two years in conjunction with the Hans Christian Andersen Medal, this award recognizes outstanding children's books from each member country with the goal of promoting world understanding through children's literature. Originally chosen by the Hans Christian Andersen Jury, the winners are now selected with the participation of the national sections. There are three categories of excellence: writing, illustration (since 1974), and translation (since 1978). This listing omits winners from non-English-speaking countries.

1956   GREAT BRITAIN
        Lavender's Blue, Kathleen Lines, ill. Harold Jones (Watts, 1954)
        Minnow on the Say, A. Philippa Pearce, ill. Edward Ardizzone (Oxford, 1955)

UNITED STATES
Carry On, Mr. Bowditch, Jean Lee Latham, ill. J. O. Cosgrove (Houghton, 1955)
Men, Microscopes and Living Things, Katherine B. Shippen, ill. Anthony Ravielli (Viking, 1955)
Play with Me, Marie Hall Ets, ill. (Viking, 1955)

1958 CANADA
Lost in the Barrens, Farley Mowat, ill. Charles Geer (Little, 1956)

GREAT BRITAIN
The Fairy Doll, Rumer Godden, ill. Adrienne Adams (Macmillan, 1956)

UNITED STATES
The House of Sixty Fathers, Meindert DeJong, ill. Maurice Sendak (Harper, 1956)

1960 CANADA
Nkwala, Edith Lambert Sharp, ill. William Winter (Little, 1958)

GREAT BRITAIN
Tom's Midnight Garden, A. Philippa Pearce, ill. Susan Einzig (Oxford, 1958)
Warrior Scarlet, Rosemary Sutcliff, ill. Charles Keeping (Oxford, 1958)

UNITED STATES
Along Came a Dog, Meindert DeJong, ill. Maurice Sendak (Harper, 1958)
The Witch of Blackbird Pond, Elizabeth George Speare (Houghton, 1958)

1962 CANADA
The Sunken City, James McNeill, ill. Theo Dimson (Oxford, 1959)

GREAT BRITAIN
Tangara: Let Us Set Off Again, Nan Chauncy, ill. Brian Wildsmith (Oxford, 1960); published in the U.S. as *The Secret Friends*
The Borrowers Afloat, Mary Norton, ill. Diana Stanley (Dent, 1959)

UNITED STATES
Island of the Blue Dolphins, Scott O'Dell, ill. Evaline Ness (Houghton, 1960)

1964 CANADA
The Incredible Journey: A Tale of Three Animals, Shelia Every Burnford, ill. Carl Burger (Little, 1961)

GREAT BRITAIN
The Twelve and the Genii, Pauline Clarke, ill. Cecil Leslie (Faber, 1962); published in the U.S. as *The Return of the Twelves*

UNITED STATES
The Bronze Bow, Elizabeth George Speare (Houghton, 1961)

1966   GREAT BRITAIN
The Namesake: A Story of King Alfred, C. Walter Hodges, ill. (Bell, 1964)

UNITED STATES
Where the Wild Things Are, Maurice Sendak, ill. (Harper, 1963)

1968   GREAT BRITAIN
Louie's Lot, E. W. Hildick, ill. Iris Schweitzer (Faber, 1965)

UNITED STATES
Valley of the Smallest: The Life Story of a Shrew, Aileen Fisher, ill. Jean Zallinger (Crowell, 1966)

1970   AUSTRALIA
I Own the Racecourse, Patricia Wrightson, ill. Margaret Horder (Hutchinson, 1969)

UNITED STATES
Up a Road Slowly, Irene Hunt (Follet, 1966)

1972   AUSTRALIA
Blue Fin, Colin Thiele, ill. Roger Haldane (Rigby, 1969)

UNITED STATES
The Trumpet of the Swan, E. B. White, ill. Edward Frascino (Harper, 1970)

1974   AUSTRALIA
Text: *Josh,* Ivan Southall (Angus & Robertson, 1971)
Illustration: *Joseph and Lulu and the Prindiville House Pigeons,* Ted Greenwood (Angus & Robertson, 1972)

GREAT BRITAIN
Text: *What the Neighbours Did and Other Stories,* A. Philippa Pearce, ill. Faith Jacques (Longmans, 1972)
Illustration: *Titch,* Pat Hutchins (Bodley Head, 1972)

UNITED STATES
Text: *The Headless Cupid,* Zilpha Keatley Snyder, ill. Alton Raible (Atheneum, 1971)
Illustration: *The Funny Little Woman,* Arlene Mosel, ill. Blair Lent (Dutton, 1972)

1976   AUSTRALIA
       Text: *The Nargun and the Stars,* Patricia Wrightson (Hutchinson, 1973)
       Illustration: *Mulga Bill's Bycycle,* A. B. Paterson, ill. Deborah and Kil-
       meny Niland (Collins, 1973)

       CANADA
       Text: *Alligator Pie,* Dennis Lee, ill. Frank Newfeld (Macmillan, 1974)
       Illustration: *The Sleighs of My Childhood/Les traineaux de mon enfance*
       (bilingual text), Carlo Italiano, (Tundra, 1974)

       GREAT BRITAIN
       Text: *The Ghost of Thomas Kempe,* Penelope Lively, ill. Antony Maitland
       (Heinemann, 1973)
       Illustration: *How Tom Beat Captain Najork and His Hired Sportsmen,*
       Russell Hoban, ill. Quentin Blake (Cape, 1974)

       UNITED STATES
       Text: *M. C. Higgins, the Great,* Virginia Hamilton (Macmillan, 1974)
       Illustration: *Dawn,* Uri Shulevitz (Farrar, 1974)

1978   AUSTRALIA
       Text: *The October Child,* Eleanor Spence, ill. Malcolm Green (Oxford,
       1976)
       Illustration: *The Runaway Punt,* Michael F. Page, ill. Robert R. Ingpen
       (Rigby, 1976)

       CANADA
       Text: *Garbage Delight,* Dennis Lee, ill. Frank Newfeld (Macmillan,
       1977)
       Text: *Mousewoman and the Vanished Princesses,* Christie Harris, ill.
       Douglas Tait (McClelland & Stewart, 1976)
       Illustration: *La cachette,* Ginette Anfousse (La Tamanoir, 1976)

       GREAT BRITAIN
       Text: *A Year and a Day,* William Mayne, ill. Krystyna Turska (Hamilton,
       1976)
       Illustration: *Thorn Rose,* Jacob and Wilhelm Grimm, ill. Errol LeCain
       (Faber, 1975)
       Translation: *The Cucumber King: A Story with a Beginning, a Middle,
       and an End . . . ,* Christine Nöstlinger, trans. Anthea Bell, ill. Werner
       Maurer (Abelard Schuman, 1975)

       UNITED STATES
       Text: *Tuck Everlasting,* Natalie Babbitt (Farrar, 1975)
       Illustration: *Hush, Little Baby,* Margot Zemach (Dutton, 1976)
       Translation: *Glassblower's Children,* Maria Gripe, trans. Sheila La Farge,
       ill. Harald Gripe (Delacorte/Lawrence, 1973)

1980   AUSTRALIA
Text: *A Dream of Seas,* Lilith Norman, ill. Edwina Bell (Collins, 1978)
Illustration: *The Quinkins,* Percy J. Trezise and Dick Roughsey (Collins, 1978)

CANADA
Text: *Hold Fast,* Kevin Major (Clark, Irwin, 1978)
Illustration: *La Chicane (The Wrangle),* Ginette Anfousse (La Courte Echelle, 1978)
Translation: *Les Chemins secrets de la liberté,* Barbara Smucker, trans. Paule Daveluy, ill. Tom McNeeley (Pierre Tisseyire, 1978)

GREAT BRITAIN
Text: *The Gods in Winter,* Patricia Miles (Hamilton, 1978)
Illustration: *Each Peach, Pear, Plum,* Janet and Allan Ahlberg (Kestrel, 1978)
Translation: *The Sea Lord,* Alet Schouten, trans. Patricia Crampton, ill. Rien Poortvliet (Methuen, 1977)

UNITED STATES
Text: *Ramona and Her Father,* Beverly Cleary, ill. Alan Tiegreen (Morrow, 1977)
Illustration: *Noah's Ark,* Peter Spier (Doubleday, 1977)
Translation: *The Magic Stone,* Leonie Kooiker, trans. Clara and Richard Winston, ill. Carl Hollander (Morrow, 1978)

1982   AUSTRALIA
Text: *Playing Beatie Bow,* Ruth Park (Kestrel, 1981)
Illustration: *The Rainforest Children,* Margaret Pittaway, ill. Heather Philpott (Oxford, 1980)

CANADA
Text: *The Keeper of the Isis Light,* Monica Hughes (Hamish Hamilton, 1980)
Illustration: *Petrouchka,* adapt. and ill. Elizabeth Cleaver, based on the works of Igor Stravinsky and Alexandre Benois (Macmillan, 1980)
Translation: *The King's Daughter,* Suzanne Martel, trans. David Toby Homel and Margaret Rose (Douglas & McIntyre, 1980)

GREAT BRITAIN
Text: *Tulku,* Peter Dickinson (Gollancz, 1979)
Illustration: *Mister Magnolia,* Quentin Blake (Cape, 1980)
Translation: *The Big Janosch Book of Fun and Verse,* Janosch, trans. Anthea Bell (Andersen, 1980)

UNITED STATES
Text: *Autumn Street,* Lois Lowry (Houghton, 1980)
Illustration: *The Garden of Abdul Gasazi,* Chris Van Allsburg (Houghton, 1979)

Translation: *Zlateh the Goat and Other Stories,* Isaac Bashevis Singer, trans. Elizabeth Shub, ill. Maurice Sendak (Harper, 1966)

1984   UNITED STATES
Text: *Sweet Whispers, Brother Rush,* Virginia Hamilton (Philomel, 1982)
Illustration: *Doctor De Soto,* William Steig (Farrar, 1984)
Translation: *The Battle Horse,* Harry Kullman, trans. George Blecher and Lone Thygesen-Blecher (Bradbury, 1981)

1986   UNITED STATES
Text: *One-Eyed Cat,* Paula Fox (Bradbury, 1984)
Illustration: *The People Could Fly: American Black Folktales,* Virginia Hamilton, ill. Leo and Diane Dillon (Knopf, 1985)
Translation: Edward Fenton for his translations from Greek of books by Alki Zei

Notes on Contributors

WILLIAM T. MOYNIHAN, head of the English Department at the University of Connecticut (Storrs), is a founding member of the advisory board of the journal *Children's Literature*. He has written widely on modern poetry and is the author of *The Craft and Art of Dylan Thomas* (Cornell University Press, 1968).

MARY E. SHANER is Professor of English at the University of Massachusetts (Boston). A specialist in medieval literature and children's literature, she has written numerous articles and reviews and co-edited (with A. S. G. Edwards) *The Legend of Good Women* (Houghton Mifflin, forthcoming).

ROSANNE DONAHUE is currently finishing her first novel in the New Realistic genre, in addition to writing about the New Realism in children's fiction. She is a member of the Children's Literature Association and the Professional Bowlers Association of America.

JAMES A. MILLER is Associate Professor of English and Intercultural Studies at Trinity College in Hartford. A specialist in Afro-American literature and culture, he has written on Amiri Baraka, Zora Neale Hurston, David Bradley, and Chinua Achebe ("The Novelist as Teacher: Chinua Achebe's Literature for Children," *Children's Literature* 9, 1981).

THOMAS J. WEBER is a freelance writer who divides his time between Seattle and New York. He has published music criticism and commentary about science fiction in a variety of little magazines, and co-edits the journal *Vertigo*. An expert on British SF, he discussed its relationship to the American field on the program of the 1985 British National SF Convention in Leeds. He is currently editing a collection of SF criticism for Serconia Press.

ANNE DEVEREAUX JORDAN founded the Children's Literature Association and has reviewed children's books for the *New York Times Book Review*. She teaches at the University of Hartford and is managing editor of the *Magazine of Fantasy and Science Fiction*.

Acknowledgments

A & C Black. Illustration appearing on page 20. From *Five Children and It* by Edith Nesbit, illustrations by J. S. Goodall. Copyright © 1959 by Ernest Benn Publishers. Reprinted by permission of A & C Black.

Atheneum Publishers, Inc. Illustration appearing on page 121. Illustration by Gail Garraty from *The Farthest Shore* by Ursula Le Guin is used by permission of Atheneum Publishers, Inc. Copyright © 1972 by Ursula K. Le Guin. Illustration appearing on page 83. Jacket illustration by Ted Lewin in *Homecoming* by Cynthia Voight. Copyright © 1981 by Cynthia Voight. Reprinted by permission of Ted Lewin.

The Atlantic Monthly Press. Illustration appearing on page 28. From *On Fire* by Ouida Sebestyen. Jacket illustration by Richard Williams. Reproduced by permission of The Atlantic Monthly Press.

Avon Books. Illustration appearing on page 78. Taken from an illustration from the Avon paperback edition of *Mom, the Wolfman, and Me* by Norma Klein. Copyright © 1980 by Norma Klein. Reprinted with permission of Avon Books.

The Berkley Publishing Group. Illustration appearing on page 174. From *Rite of Passage* by Alexei Panshin. Jacket illustration by Leo and Diane Dillon. Reproduced by permission of The Berkley Publishing Group.

William Collins Sons & Company Ltd. Illustration appearing on page 141. Black and white illustration from *Paddington Takes the Air* by Michael Bond. Copyright © illustrations Peggy Fortnum 1970, published by Collins. Reprinted by permission of William Collins Sons & Company Ltd.

Coward-McCann, Inc. Illustration appearing on page 200. Illustration by Wanda Gág reprinted by permission of Coward-McCann from *Millions of Cats* by Wanda Gág. Copyright © 1928 by Coward-McCann, Inc., renewed © 1956 by Robert Janssen.

Del Ray Books. Illustration appearing on page 165. Jacket art by Darrell Sweet in *Have Space Suit — Will Travel* by Robert Heinlein. Copyright © 1958 by Robert Heinlein. Reprinted with permission of Del Ray Books.

Dell Publishing Co., Inc. Illustration appearing on page 12. From *The Chocolate War* by Robert Cormier. Copywright © 1974 by Robert Cormier. Reprinted by permission of Dell Publishing Co., Inc. Illustration appearing on page 78. From *Happy Endings are All Alike* by Sandra Scoppettone. Copyright © 1978 by Sandra Scoppettone. Reprinted by permission of Dell Publishing Co., Inc.

Houghton Mifflin Company. Illustration appearing on page 200. From *Mike Mulligan and His Steam Shovel* by Virginia Lee Burton. Copyright © 1939 and © 1967 by Virginia Lee Demetrios. Reprinted by permission of Houghton Mifflin Company. Illustration appearing on page 62. Illustration by Lynd Ward from *Johnny Tremain* by Esther Forbes. Copyright © 1943 by Esther Forbes Hoskins. Copyright © renewed 1971 by Linwood M. Erskine, Jr., Executor of the Estate. Reprinted by permission of Houghton Mifflin Company. Illustration appearing on page 39. Jacket illustration © 1986 by Diane de Groat from *Anastasia on Her Own* by Lois Lowry. Copyright © 1985 by Lois Lowry. Reprinted by permission of Houghton Mifflin Company. Illustration appearing on page 150. Illustration by J. R. R. Tolkien from *The Hobbit* by J. R. R. Tolkien. Copyright © 1966 by J. R. R. Tolkien. Reprinted by permission of Houghton Mifflin Company.

Trina Schart Hyman. Illustration appearing on page 11. Illustration copyright © 1986. Used by permission of Trina Schart Hyman.

Macmillan Publishing Company. Illustration appearing on page 173. Reprinted with permission of Macmillan Publishing Company from *The White Mountains* by John Christopher, illustrated by Elaine Sorel. Illustration copyright © 1967 by Macmillan Publishing Company. Illustration appearing on page 115. From *Zeely* by Virginia Hamilton, illustrated by Symeon Shimin. Illustration copyright © 1967 by Macmillan Publishing Company. Reprinted by permission of Macmillan Publishing Company. Illustration appearing on page 149. From *The Lion, the Witch and the Wardrobe* by C. S. Lewis, illustrated by Michael Hague. Illustration copyright © 1981 by Macmillan Publishing Company. Reprinted by permission of Macmillan Publishing Company.

Oxford University Press. Illustration appearing on page 205. From *Kaleidoscope* by Eleanor Farjeon, illustrated by Edward Ardizzone. Copyright © 1963 by Henry Z. Walck, Inc. Reprinted by permission of Oxford University Press.

Penguin Books Ltd. Illustration appearing on page 19. From *The Tale of Peter Rabbit* by Beatrix Potter (Frederick Warne, 1902) page 12, copyright © 1902 by Frederick Warne & Co. Reproduced by permission of Penguin Books Ltd.

S. G. Phillips. Illustration appearing on page 53. From *Viking's Dawn* by Henry Treece, illustrated by Christine Price. Published by S. G. Phillips.

Random House. Illustration appearing on page 181. From *Charlie and the Chocolate Factory* by Roald Dahl, illustrated by Joseph Schindelman. Copyright © 1964 by Roald Dahl. Reprinted by permission of Random House. Illustration appearing on page 54. From *Smith* by Leon Garfield, illustrated by Anthony Maitland. Copyright © 1967 by Leon Garfield. Reprinted by permission of Random House. Illustration appearing on page 212. From *The Cat in the Hat* written and illustrated by Dr. Seuss. Copyright © 1957 by Dr. Seuss. Reprinted by permission of Random House.

Seabury Press. Illustration appearing on page 116. From *Zamani Goes to Market* by Tom Feelings. Copyright © 1970 by Tom Feelings. Reprinted by permission of Tom Feelings.

Scholastic Books, Inc. Illustration appearing on page 91. From *The Pinballs* by Betsy Byars. Jacket illustration by Tom Newsom. Copyright © 1977 by Betsy Byars. Reprinted by permission of Scholastic Books, Inc.

Charles Scribner's Sons. Illustration appearing on page 199. *Otto of the Silver Hand* by Howard Pyle. Published by Charles Scribner's Sons. Illustration appearing on page 218.

Index

Numbers preceding colons refer to the volume of MASTERWORKS OF CHILDREN'S LITERATURE: vols. 1 & 2, *The Early Years* (1550–1739); vols. 3 & 4, *Middle Period* (1740–1836); vols. 5 (parts 1 & 2) & 6, *The Victorian Age* (1837–1900); vol. 7, *Victorian Color Picture Books;* and vol. 8, *The Twentieth Century.* Italicized numbers indicate pages where a text or illustration is reproduced.